LILIES

CARL FELDMAIER

LILIES

Translated by MATT TEMPLETON FLS

B. T. BATSFORD LTD London

Originally published under the title *Die neuen Lilien* by
Verlag Eugen Ulmer, Stuttgart

First published in English edition 1970
© Carl Feldmaier 1970
7134 0401 9

Plates printed by Ungeheuer & Ulmer, Ludwigsburg, Germany. Text printed
and bound in Great Britain by William Clowes and Sons Ltd, London and
Beccles, for the publishers

B. T. Batsford Ltd, 4 Fitzhardinge Street, London W1

Contents

Well-known lilies; geographical distribution of wild lilies; soil and environment of wild lilies; the difficulties of planting wild lilies; breeding overcomes cultural difficulties; the advantages of hybrids

Lilies for borders and edging; lilies for colour; lilies as companion plants; companion plants for lilies; tall lilies as dot plants; background for lilies; lilies and rhododendrons; lilies for the rock-garden; lilies for potting; lily-forcing; lilies for cutting; lilies for decoration

The structure of the lily bulb; bulb-planting; the transplanting of lilies

What is a lily?; bulbs and roots; stems and leaves; flowers; seed and seed capsules

Illustrations

* indicates colour illustration

Drawings

Acknowledgment

Grateful thanks are due to Dr R. W. Lighty and the RHS for allowing the diagram on page 88 to be reproduced from the Lily Year Book for 1968. Illustrations appear by courtesy of the following:

W. Schacht, 1, 4, 5, 26–28, 32, 36, 42, 43, 47; F. Köhlein, 2, 11; H. v. Wall, 3, 6, 7, 9, 18, 19, 30, 35, 45, 53, 56, 57, 64–66, 68, 71; J. E. Downward, 39–41, 55, 61–63, 67; Photo-Art Commercial Studios, Portland, 13; E. Hahn, 14, 33, 38, 49, 50; Dr H. Steiner, 22; A. Gutschow, 25; G. Brünner, 29, 31, 34, 46; L. Steffen, 37; Moto'o Shimizu, 44; Bildarchiv der Madonnenkapellenpflege, Stuppach, 72; C. Weber, 73.

All drawings and all other illustrations are by the Author.

Foreword

Over the past 30 years, about 1,000 new hybrid lilies have been bred and registered in Australia, New Zealand, Russia, Germany, Canada, the United States and Britain. This tremendous increase in enthusiasm and output is the reason I lay such emphasis on hybrids and their cultivation in this book. I have tried to give gardeners not merely the basic information about lilies but also a knowledge of biological and genetic factors and hybridization procedures which will enable them to join in the exciting process of creating new variants.

It must not be imagined that this process is the exclusive preserve of the dedicated professional gardener. The reproductive organs of the lily are of a size that anyone following basic rules and techniques can successfully carry out crosses and produce his own lilies. It is my hope that this book will interest a wide gardening public in lily-breeding, and add a new dimension to their favourite hobby.

I should like to thank my publishers Batsfords and Arco, and also Verlag Eugen Ulmer, who published this work in its original German edition. The Lily Year Books of the Royal Horticultural Society and the North American Lily Society have been extremely valuable, and I have relied for much of my technical data on Woodcock and Stearn's indispensable *Lilies of the World*.

I wish to remember the lily enthusiasts and breeders all over the world, but particularly in the United States and Canada, who have helped me so generously with gifts of material and literature and unselfishly given me the benefit of their experience. I am especially grateful to my friend Sam L. Emsweller, who not only secured my admission to the North American Lily Society but has provided a rich fund of plants, literature, information and ideas. Finally I wish to thank my mother, who first gave me my love for gardening and introduced me to lilies. This book is the fruit of her teaching.

I hope that this book will increase interest in lilies and their breeding and bring many more gardeners to enjoy this most beautiful of flowers.

C. F.

1. From wild to cultivated lilies

Well-known lilies

Many have sung the praise of roses and lilies. Both flowers arouse people's emotion and touch their soul. While the rose – whether white, red, or pink – is considered as the flower of love and affection, the lily, particularly the white lily, is the flower of innocence, purity, and chastity. Since the early Middle Ages the lily has been the attribute of many saints, but particularly of the Virgin Mary. Many artists have also depicted the lily when painting the Virgin Mary.

There are five lilies commonly grown in our gardens.

The first is the white Madonna Lily, *Lilium candidum*. It grows in many a garden corner, neglected for years, and yet every time June turns into July it regularly produces immaculate white blooms. It is often found in old-fashioned gardens, planted in rows along the paths, and during the flowering period its scent pervades the whole garden.

The Fire Lily, *Lilium bulbiferum*, usually has also to be satisfied with a corner of the garden. In June the flower buds develop into clusters of saucer-shaped blooms of mandarin-red. No rose, no carnation can compete with these gaily coloured flowers. This prolific lily produces ever bigger and thicker patches of glorious colour each year.

The native Turk's Cap, *Lilium martagon*, is by comparison a rather modest bloom, well known only to the initiated. Pharmacists, naturalists, and mountain-climbers value the beauty and individuality of this lily, which is usually concealed beneath hedges and undergrowth and which flourishes in mountainous country at heights varying from low wooded slopes up to the middle ranges. It prefers calcareous soil, or at least calcareous subsoil. To stumble upon it growing wild, with its dull, rose, panicled blooms, under beech trees or among viburnum or buck-thorn, is a rare pleasure: one plant may be densely spotted, the next a little less so, and finally one will find a completely clear pink flower. This lily was already well known during the Middle Ages, principally on account of its yellow bulb, and was much sought after for its medicinal properties.

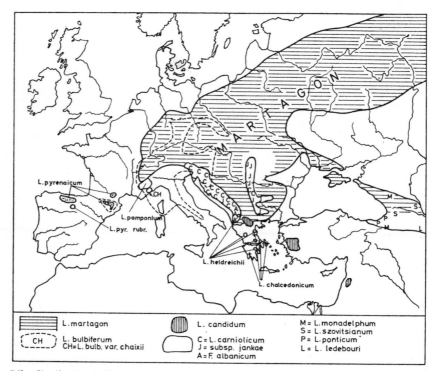

Lily distribution in Europe

The Tiger Lily, *Lilium tigrinum*, originally came from China and Japan. It is a robust, strong, and healthy plant, full of vigour, which, during August, produces a great number of salmon-orange-coloured, strongly recurved, nodding flowers, marked with large, chocolate-brown spots. The black, spherical objects in its leaf axils are intriguing. They are bulbils, which eventually fall to the ground and in turn produce roots and leaves – a marvellous method of reproduction. Were it not for these axil bulbils, the Tiger Lily would eventually cease to exist, as it does not set seed.

The fifth lily also originated in China: *Lilium regale*, the Regal Lily. First discovered in 1903, its beauty helped it to achieve rapid popularity. It bears white, funnel-shaped flowers with a yellow throat, on elegant, long stems, with fine, grass-like leaves. Its heavy fragrance pervades the air on a still evening.

Geographical distribution of wild lilies

In these five lilies alone, there is considerable variation, not only in shape, growing habit, and colour, but also in soil and climatic preferences.

Only when we realize that the genus has approximately 100 species (this is not to mention the many colour variations), and that it flourishes in climates ranging from the temperate zone of the Northern Hemisphere to the subtropical regions, however, do we begin to appreciate what a tremendous variety of shape, colour, and condition the lily offers. It grows equally well in Europe, Asia, Japan, North America, and Canada.

The Turk's Cap, *L. martagon*, has the widest distribution in Europe, which has only few lilies. It is found in central Europe – stretching as far as Italy and Greece to the south and south-east, but just missing the North Sea coast – north-western France, the Iberian peninsula, and England. It spreads eastwards through the whole of Russia to Mongolia and up to the Amur.

The Fire Lily, *L. bulbiferum*, extends from mid-Europe to the south of Italy, where at one time it was a common weed on farmland.

The bright-red *L. pomponium* is confined to a small area of the Maritime Alps, while *L. pyrenaicum* has been driven back to a tiny section of the French Pyrenees.

L. carniolicum is found in the Balkan countries, and the similar *L. chalcedonicum* and *L. heldreichii* are confined to Greece.

The home of *L. candidum*, the white Madonna Lily, seems to have been in Asia, the Lebanon, and northern Greece. Its original location is now difficult to establish, as this lily was for long cultivated for its medicinal value throughout the Middle East. Its subsequent spread into northern Europe was undoubtedly assisted by the Romans and later the Crusaders.

Of approximately 62 lily species found growing in Asia, some reach as far north as the 60th Parallel, while the most southerly is *L. neilgherrense*

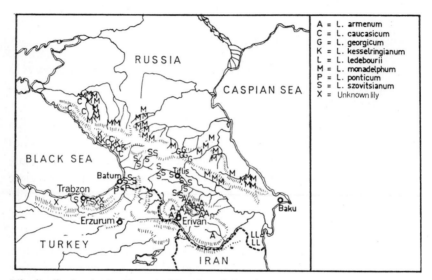

Lily distribution in the Caucasus (Eremin and Furse)

along the 10th Parallel in India. Many Japanese lilies grow on the coast. In the Himalayas lilies can be seen at elevations of up to 13,000 feet.

The yellow-flowering *L. monadelphum* and *L. szovitsianum* grow in the Caucasus, in addition to other species within a limited range. A much wider distribution is enjoyed by the orange-yellow saucer lily, *L. dauricum*, found throughout Russia from Altai to Siberia and reaching as far as the Japanese islands. The fine and delicate *L. pumilum*, with its sealingwax-red Turk's Cap flowers, ranges from Lake Baykal through Manchuria to China. By far the greatest number of lily species occur in

1. *Enchantment*, one of Jan de Graaff's most colourful hybrids

2. *L. candidum*, the Madonna Lily, cultivated in the Middle East since the earliest times. Its pure-white flowers show up most effectively against a dark background. Does not like being transplanted and does best in full sunlight and in rich soil

3. *Destiny*, an erect, lemon-yellow, saucer-shaped lily which always catches the eye. *Croesus* is of similar type, with erect, saucer-shaped, cadmium-orange flowers, and so is *Prosperity*, with pale-gold-yellow, outward-facing blooms

4. *L. bulbiferum*, the Fire Lily, brilliant red-orange

5. *Fire King*, an English hybrid with glowing, orange-red blooms

6. *Shuksan*. This Bellingham hybrid, like most hybrid lilies from America, combines grace, charm and elegance. It prefers damp, lime-free soils and is therefore an ideal companion plant for rhododendrons

7. Sentinel strain, elegant white trumpets enhanced by long pedicels
8. Harmony hybrids multiply well and quickly and produce bright, orange flowers towards the end of June

9. Harlequin hybrids have made it possible to grow strongly recurved, delicate pastel-coloured, Martagon-flowered lilies

the Himalayas and in the monsoon-swept mountain ranges of Burma and west China, including the provinces of Yunnan and Szechwan. Fortunately, still more lily species have been discovered in these regions

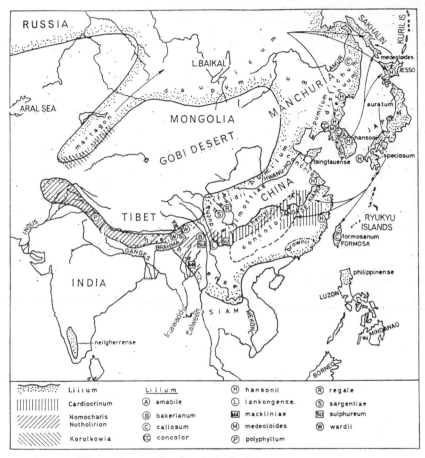

Distribution of lilies and near-related varieties in Asia

during the last few decades, and so have provided fresh material for lily hybridization.

The Turk's Cap *L. polyphyllum*, with its greenish, creamy-white blooms, and also *L. wallichianum*, with slender but wide, open trumpets, grow in the west Himalayas. The pea-green-flowered *L. nepalense* and the delicate *L. oxypetalum* are found at heights from 10,000 to 13,000 feet in the central Himalayas. In a small area where the River Brahmaputra

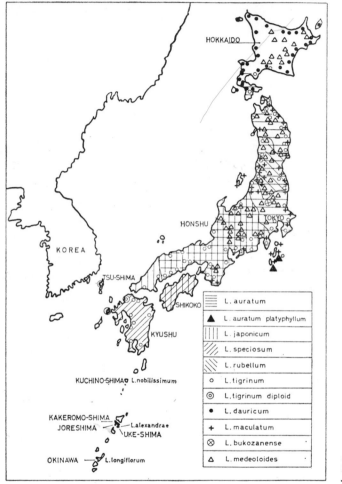

Lily distribution in Japan

breaks through the Himalayas flourishes the deep-pink, Martagon-flowered *L. wardii*. Frank KingdonWard first discovered this lily, as he also discovered *L. mackliniae*, which only grows on one particular mountain, in Burma, during 1946. His most outstanding find, again in Burma, was the apple-green *L. arboricola*, a small lily which grows on trees.

A veritable El Dorado for lilies are the deep, north-to-south running valleys of the Irrawaddy, Salween, Mekong and Yangtze Rivers, flanked by mountains which in the Yunnan and Szechwan provinces of China are regularly swept by southerly monsoons. Many lilies grow in this area: *L. amoenum*, the variable *L. bakerianum*, the tall *L. davidii* with the graceful *L. willmottiae*, *L. duchartrei* with its marble-white Turk's Cap trumpets, *L. fargesii*, the dainty *L. henrici*, *L. lankongense* with its delicate, pink, Turk's Cap flowers, the rare black-purple *L. papilliferum* at heights of 10,000 feet, the single-flowered *L. paradoxum*, the very variable, greenish-yellow *L. primulinum*, the almost unknown *L. sempervivoideum*, the magnificent sulphur-yellow trumpet lily *L. sulphureum*, the small and scarce *L. stewartianum*, and the scented, white-flowered, purple-speckled *L. taliense*. In the dry regions of two of the Szechwan valleys grow *L. regale* and *L. sargentiae*, both first discovered by E. H. Wilson in 1903. Along the Yangtze in central China grow the majestic *L. henryi*, and *L. concolor* with its star-shaped flowers.

L. brownii is found round Hong Kong, and *L. tsingtauense* was named after the place of its first discovery – Tsingtao. The lilac-flowered *L. cernuum* is native to Korea and Manchuria, as are the brilliant red *L. amabile*, the small-flowered, brick-red *L. callosum*, and *L. hansonii*, sister to *L. martagon*, and the Korean yellow Turk's Cap and small-flowered *L. distichum*.

L. philippinense grows on the steep mountain ranges of Luzon, one of the Philippine Islands. The similar *L. formosanum* is found at heights of up to 12,000 feet in Formosa in a variety of different forms.

The Japanese islands are the home of several of the most beautiful lilies. *L. longiflorum*, the Easter Lily, comes from the Ryukyu Islands, where two other scarce lilies are also found – *L. alexandrae* and *L. nobilissimum*.

Japan is the home of some of the finest lilies of all, such as *L. auratum*, the Golden-Rayed Lily of Japan, and the equally marvellous *L. speciosum* with its many varieties. Two other Japanese lilies are the pink-flowered

L. rubellum and *L. japonicum*. *L. tigrinum* and *L. leichtlinii* also come from Japan; *L. tigrinum* bulbs are specially grown, cultivated, and eaten by the Japanese as a delicacy. The northern main island of Honshu is the home of *L. dauricum* and *L. maculatum*, both cup-shaped types. A new discovery, *L. bukozanense*, has only been found on one particular mountain north of

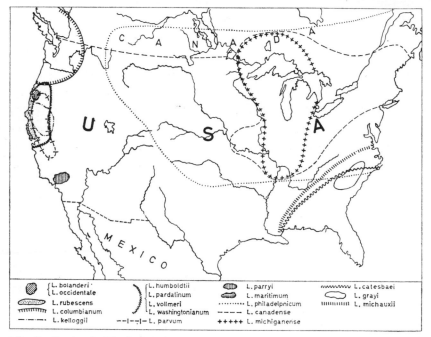

Lily distribution in North America

Tokyo. The Martagon type *L. medeoloides*, known as the Wheel Lily, grows in almost every part of Japan.

On the other side of the Pacific, the lily has the following main areas of distribution in North America: the Pacific coast of Canada, and the states of Washington, Oregon, and California in the United States. *L. columbianum* is widespread in the north. Both bog and dry-land lilies are distributed in Oregon and California. The bog types grow near the coast, where there is a high frequency of precipitation. They are easily recognized by their rhizomatous bulbs, which often take the form of a simple longish rhizome, and grow chiefly in very damp situations along streams and rivers. To this group belong: *L. pardalinum, L. harrisianum, L. kelleyanum, L. maritimum, L. nevadense, L. occidentale, L. parvum, L. pitkinense, L. shastense, L. vollmeri,* and *L. wigginsii.* The dry-land type grow from the conventional lily bulb and prefer the dry, stony soils of the landward side of the mountains, where precipitation is less frequent. The dry-land varieties are: *L. bolanderi, L. humboldtii, L. kelloggii, L. ocellatum, L. parryi, L. rubescens,* and *L. washingtonianum.*

The American cup lily, *L. philadelphicum,* grows throughout the vast North American region from the Rocky Mountains to the Atlantic and from the lakes at the Canadian frontier southwards to a point where the Mississippi and the Missouri join. This is the second distribution area in North America. It is also in this last area that *L. canadense* and the related *L. michiganense* grow.

L. grayi, L. michauxii, L. catesbaei, and *L. iridollae* are found in a third distribution area stretching from the south-east of the United States to Florida.

Soil and environment of wild lilies

Lilies like *L. martagon* and *L. carniolicum* grow on calcareous soils, while *L. longiflorum* even grows on the coral reefs of the Japanese islands; by contrast, the Golden-Rayed Lily of Japan flourishes best in very poor volcanic ash and lava. *L. dauricum, L. pumilum, L. concolor* are found on the Russian–Manchurian steppes, while *L. rubellum* and *L. japonicum* love to grow among the roots of bamboo and rhododendron, as their shelter keeps the soil damp. *L. sulphureum, L. primulinum, L. bakerianum,* and *L. nepalense* flourish on the monsoon mountain ranges of Burma and on the southern side of the Himalayas, where they are subjected to almost daily cloudbursts during June and July and buried by deep snow from around Christmas until March or April.

The bog-type lilies of the American Pacific coast prefer to have their rhizomes in acid, damp ground, even in sphagnum bogs, as opposed to the dry-land type, which favour hard, dry and stony soils.

There are many lilies which grow at sea level – *L. longiflorum, L. nobilissimum,* and *L. alexandrae,* for instance – and lilies such as *L. papilliferum* and *L. stewartianum* grow under Alpine conditions at heights of 10,000–12,000 feet. Lilies like *L. martagon* reach as far north as the 60th Parallel, *L. philippinense* to the 16th Parallel, and *L. neilgherrense* as far south as the 10th Parallel.

The area covered by individual lilies varies widely. *L. martagon* spans Europe from the west right across to the extreme east; *L. philadelphicum* reaches from the Rocky Mountains across the American continent to the Pacific. Other lilies, by contrast, are confined to small, isolated areas: *L. mackliniae* grows only on one mountain in Burma, and *L. pitkinense* is restricted to a very small area, a bog on the Californian coast.

The difficulties of planting wild lilies

There are only a few wild lilies which grow well under every condition, even if given the most careful treatment; the majority demand individual and specific combinations of soil, weather, rainfall, frost, environment, companion plants, shade and sun – all of which in their various combinations have provided the correct conditions for wild lilies for thousands of years. Under such difficult circumstances it is always the specialist grower who is the most successful, and not surprisingly the amateur has had many failures, particularly following the rapid spread of plant disease. Considering that Japan annually exports four million bulbs of *L. auratum* and *L. speciosum,* Europe and North America ought by now to have vast areas of lilies under cultivation. But in fact the great majority of these imports either succumb to fusarium during their first year or, as often happens, they are killed by virus diseases during the following years. Another very important reason for the poor acclimatization of these beautiful lilies is the long distance they have to travel before they reach the customer; first, bulbs have to wait weeks for transport, then they travel by rail to the docks, from there by ship to the port of destination, and once again by train to the bulb merchant's store, before finally reaching the gardener. As the lily's bulb lacks the protective skin of the tulip and the hyacinth, it soon dries out, and roots wilt and die. Such bulbs rarely succeed in the long term, particularly when delays during their long journey necessitate late planting, which makes further root development impossible for that season. The bulbs may grow well in the spring, and possibly even flower, but the absence of roots makes it impossible for them to absorb and store the necessary food reserves which are vital if they are to survive for another year. As a result, they become exhausted in one summer, and die off.

Breeding overcomes cultural difficulties

That these difficulties have now been largely overcome is due to the efforts of several parties: the breeders who, by crossing difficult species, have created the hybrid lilies of today; the horticulturists who tested and perfected new propagation methods; the scientists who have learned to recognize diseases, and found and produced antidotes for them; the distributors who have improved their packing methods with the aid of new materials, and who have instituted speedier transport which makes possible in hours what was previously impossible in days.

Let us imagine two lilies, one which prefers calcareous, high pH soils and another which does best under less alkaline, lower pH conditions. If they are transposed, or if their individual soil requirements are changed, they will fail or succumb to disease; but if these two lilies can be successfully crossed, their seedlings will behave in accordance with Mendelian segregation. Not only will the seedlings possess outward differences in shape and colour of flower and leaf, but the parents' individual preferences for alkaline or acid soil will combine to produce a plant which will grow equally well in either or both types of soil.

Another example: if a cross between *L. auratum*, the Golden-Rayed Lily of Japan, with *L. henryi* were successful, the resulting plants, inheriting the virtues of both parents, should have the beauty of the Golden-Rayed Lily of Japan and the robustness of *L. henryi*. Such a cross would produce lilies capable of growing in any temperate climate and in all types of soil, particularly as *L. auratum* prefers the less alkaline soils and an extreme maritime climate with dry winters, while the exceptionally robust *L. henryi* grows well on lime and sandstone in the continental climate of central China. Furthermore, the fact of being a hybrid would give it both stamina and vigour. This would produce lilies which could be grown without difficulty in nearly every soil and in every temperate climate.

Propagation and multiplication methods have also improved. Vegetative multiplication, by bulb scales, used to be the accepted method; scales were carefully broken off the bulb and kept in a warm and constantly damp atmosphere, which caused the scales to form young bulblets that developed into full-sized bulbs over the course of years. Any virus diseases present in the mother bulb were, of course, perpetuated, and fusarium also took its toll. Multiplication from seed is now especially favoured, as it provides two great benefits: virus diseases are not transmitted, while the method also brings out the variations among seedlings and so makes it possible to select only the best and most desirable plants for further seed production. Variations occur in a number of aspects: habit, shape of leaves and flowers, colour, and general structure. It is only a matter of selection to obtain the lilies with the required attributes for further propagation.

Knowledge of this kind, gained over the years not only by scientists but also by horticulturists, provides great opportunity for lily-breeders to produce new lilies for years to come.

The advantages of hybrids

Hybrid lilies have advantages which make them superior to the wild varieties. They are more vigorous, stronger, healthier, grow taller and bear more and bigger flowers. Such results are understandable when we realize that they are only achieved through constant and rigorous selection of seedlings, of which only one to five per cent ever reach the commercial stage – through failure and imperfection of one kind or another, 95–99 per cent of the material is ruthlessly discarded.

Hybrid lilies are less demanding than their parents, and grow well in a wide range of soils. They will flourish if planted among shrubs and bedding plants, and multiply and bloom more freely than their parents; nor is there any need for specially enriched soils or sheltered positions. Climate, too, is of less importance, for it is always possible, by means of careful observation, to select a lily suitable for a particular environment from the many and varied crosses.

The crossing of and selection for disease-resistant hybrids is, of course, similar. Lilies susceptible to fusarium are crossed with varieties less prone to this disease; rigorous selection of the resulting seedlings follows, and only those which have inherited fusarium resistance from one parent and at the same time retained the qualities of the other parent are kept. Disease resistance is of the utmost importance, and the first essential consideration in deciding if a plant is worth growing; with the single exception of *L.* × *testaceum*, all hybrid crosses of the last century have succumbed to disease.

It is now possible to plant lilies in our gardens which grow well and flower satisfactorily – not only for just one season but for year after year. There are lilies for every purpose, for planting in beds with perennials, or in front of shrubberies, or in woods. There are dainty lilies suitable for rock-gardens and others which grow as tall as a man, pushing their flowering heads through shrubs and the branches of trees. Lilies for damp situations and for growing in the shade, lilies for sunny, dry beds along stone walls, lilies which do not suffer from the sun, which in fact flourish best when exposed to it – all are available. There are lilies, too, for growing in pots or tubs, to be displayed at garden entrances, on terraces and indoors. By careful management these magnificent flowers can be in bloom as early in the season as Easter.

As flowers for cutting they are incomparable, and last for as long as 14 days, an ever-changing picture as each bud opens. With their vivid colours, lilies make an excellent decoration for modern houses.

A revolution, the end of which is not yet in sight, is taking place in the lily world; a revolution which we are witnessing, through which we are living and in which we can take part. The real purpose of this book is to impart the new discoveries and methods to lily-growers everywhere, and also to win new enthusiasts for this sweet-smelling and most beautiful of flowers.

2. New lilies for garden and house

The comparatively small number of lilies which used to be planted in gardens has increased rapidly during recent times, owing to the introduction of the far less demanding and more easily grown hybrids. America is ready to supply millions of hybrid lily bulbs every year, but the correct selection of varieties to meet personal requirements and particular environment is important.

Lilies for borders and edging

Formal beds with plants set out in regular rows or in some geometrical pattern are no longer popular, nor do they suit modern house design and garden planning. Garden paths of whatever length, leading to a seat or perhaps to the front door, can be bordered with lilies on either or both sides most effectively. The ideal lilies for the purpose should have a compact habit and be of even height and spread. Until recently the choice would undoubtedly have fallen on the Madonna Lily, but today we can select one of the de Graaff Tigrinum or Midcentury hybrids. Their deep yellow and orange colours attractively show up the path and lead the eye along it. The effect can be heightened and prolonged if a suitable, earlier-flowering companion plant is grown alongside, preferably one with green or silver-grey foliage for increased contrast. Suitable subjects are: *Iberis sempervirens*, *Campanula carpatica* or var. *turbinata*, and *Gypsophila repens*; for later flowering, Phlox or asters.

Lilies for colour

Most lilies prefer abundant sunshine, provided their roots can remain in the shade. They are ideal for planting in groups, but prior selection for colour, height and growth habit are important if the desired effect is to be achieved. The yellow, orange-yellow, orange-red, and vermilion-flowering lilies give emphasis. The Golden Chalice hybrids are recommended if dwarfer plants are needed, and for taller plants one or another of the great number of Midcentury hybrids are most suitable – *Destiny*, for instance (*3*),* a strong chrome-yellow, upright-flowering cup lily which grows to a height of 3–4 feet, or *Croesus* of the same height and form but with clear, golden-yellow flowers. *Harmony*, although only 20 36 inches high, gives beautiful, orange-yellow flowers. (*8*) Gold-yellow *Joan Evans* is another excellent hybrid. Nasturtium-red *Enchantment* (*1*) is unsurpassed for producing a good colour effect from the distance. *Cinnabar* is an equally strong eye-catcher with a deep, glowing, fire-red flower. Darker red *Tabasco* is a little more subdued, but, like the others, grows 2–4 feet high.

The number of lilies which can be used for group planting is legion. There are many varieties in addition to those from de Graaff – for instance varieties from Skinner of Canada, such as *Amaryllis*, *Azalia*, *Cardinal*, *Goldcrest*, *Grace Marshall*, *Lemon Lady* and especially *Dunkirk* with 30 or more shiny red blooms per stem.

Dr S. L. Emsweller's deep-coloured hybrids must also be included: deep gold–yellow *Cavalier*; *Mountaineer*, with dark-red flowers; and the slightly shorter, soft-orange *Brandywine*; also profusely flowering *Fire King*, with deep-red, outward-facing flowers.

Lilies as companion plants

In contrast to the deep-coloured, compact-flowering plants just considered which dominate a garden, another group comprising the mainly

---

* *These figures in italics refer to the illustration numbers.*

pastel-shaded, delicate and recurved flowering lilies should not be neglected for garden use because of their tenderness and lightness. Their blooms are arranged in racemose inflorescence and are not quite as densely placed and on rather taller stems. Clumps of only three to five bulbs can be made to produce the most effective displays, particularly if planted among the leafy background of low-growing shrubs, which these long-stemmed lilies tower over. If a leafy background is impossible, their interestingly varied and colourful flowers appear to best advantage planted near a path. The Jan de Graaff Fiesta and Harlequin hybrids (4–5 feet high), mostly derived from Asiatic hybrids, belong to this group. Fiesta hybrids should always be planted as a mixture, as their colours are particularly striking, ranging from yellow to orange to red and mahogany. The less brilliantly coloured, heavily brown-spotted Harlequin hybrids have slightly recurved petals with pastel shades varying from ochre to the colour of leather and to pink and red. Ideally, these should be grown near a path, where their interesting colours appear to good advantage. The dwarfer lilies from Isabella Preston also deserve garden space for their rich and profuse flowers, as do the Ball strain from the Blackthorne Gardens, which are similar to the Harlequin hybrids. There are many other good lilies which fit into this group: *Skyrocket* – red with brown speckles; and two from Porter, *Rosabelle* – star-shaped, delicate carmine – and *Princess Royal*, with carmine-lilac flowers.

Professor Patterson of Canada has produced several valuable and exquisitely beautiful lilies which deserve a very special place in the garden – a place from which they can easily and conveniently be admired. They are fascinatingly coloured and are derived from *L. cernuum*. Among them are *Edith Cecilia*, *Lemon Queen*, *Rosalind*, *White Gold*, and *White Princess*. All of them flower as June turns into July, an ideal time for bridging the gap between spring and summer flowers.

Companion plants for lilies

There are a vast number of plants to choose from. For a low ground cover, the pale-blue *Campanula carpatica* looks beautiful, and heightens the colour effect of yellow lilies. Dark or light-blue larkspur looks equally well. For a contrast in texture and colour to the strong solid patches of lily colour, gypsophila provides an effective neighbour; thalictrum creates a similar effect, but is more suited to flatter the taller-growing lilies. Too brightly coloured companion plants are likely to weaken the visual impact of lilies, and are best avoided; so too is the use of aubrietia and low-growing Phlox as underground cover – both encourage snails and slugs and, at the same time, hide the irreparable attacks on bulbs and new lily shoots these pests are responsible for.

Tall lilies as dot plants

Not to be missed is the wonderful effect a clump of white, trumpet lilies produces. Plant from 12 to 20 bulbs in an area of about 10 to 20 square feet near the garden entrance or in the vicinity of a terrace; alternatively, plant them in a bed in the lawn, without companion plants, and preferably in a spot where the 40–60 inch tall plants can be seen in outline against the sun, or against a dark leafy background, or even a distant wood. The bulbs will multiply in the course of time and produce ever-stronger and more colourful groups. Suitable varieties are the *L. imperiale* hybrids like the Olympic hybrids *Black Dragon*, *Green Dragon*, *Sentinel* and others. Plantings need not be confined to white lilies only, as clumps of gold–yellow-flowering *Royal Gold* and *Golden Regal* are equally effective.

For planting lilies in shrubberies, the taller Aurelian hybrids have the advantage of flowering above the lower-growing shrubs; the effect is heightened if even taller shrubs and trees are available on the site to provide additionally leafy background. The Aurelian hybrids grow 5–6 feet tall and come in a wide range of colours – white, lemon, chrome-yellow, gold-yellow, apricot, and bright copper. They look equally attractive whether planted singly or in groups, directly in front of shrubs; a charming picture can be created if yellow and gold-coloured lilies are planted next to summer or late summer-flowering helenium, phlox, solidago and rudbeckia, but, again, a leafy background enhances the beauty of the contrast. If the wonderful colours of the Pink Perfection strain and the clones *Damson* and *Verona* are not to suffer, they should not be exposed to very hot sun and should therefore be planted on the northern or eastern perimeter of a wood or shrubbery.

Background for lilies

The white Turk's Caps *L. martagon* var. *album* and *L. taliense* shine magically, like pearls, if given a dark background of rhododendron or fir trees, which they require for best effect. This also holds true for the many lighter-coloured Martagon hybrids available: Paisley hybrids, Terrace City hybrids, and Painted Lady hybrids. *Aruncus sylvester* makes an enchanting background for the dark-red and brown Martagons. If possible, they should be planted near a path, to allow better observation of their jewel-like beauty and delicately shaded colours and markings.

Lilies and rhododendrons

L. auratum and *L. speciosum* and their hybrids are difficult to establish in some areas, as they do not grow on calcareous soils and are therefore best planted with rhododendrons, which have similar requirements. The plant collector Kingdon Ward confirms this in his books where he mentions that lilies and rhododendrons grow side by side in the Burmese and Chinese mountains. The taller-growing rhododendron varieties are, of course, the best for background planting, but for the foreground some of the new and lower-growing hybrids are more suitable, particularly those with *R. williamsianum* or *R. repens* parentage. Both these lilies and rhododendrons grow well in acid, moor-like, peat soils; but Bellingham hybrids (6) and American wild lilies, such as *L. canadense*, *L. superbum* and *L. pardalinum*, which like the same type of soil, need extra moisture. The dark rhododendron foliage provides good background and shelter for the white, trumpet-flowering *L. formosanum*, a lily which reaches 80 inches in height.

The giant Himalayan lily *Cardiocrinum giganteum* needs very specialized conditions which should reproduce as closely as possible the climate of its native, monsoon-swept, Indian and Burmese forests. Not only must the ground be moist; thick ground cover and high trees to give shade and encourage high humidity are also necessary. The reward for success is fine-scented, white-trumpet lilies which grow as high as a man.

Lilies for the rock-garden

Rock-gardens, practical and yet versatile, are becoming more and more popular all the time. A terraced rockery or small soil pockets placed between specially arranged, large, rugged stone boulders hold many more plants than a flat area of equal size. Even the smallest plants – those with trailing stems, mossy tufts and of dwarf creeping habit, including rosettes and small bulbs – can be put on display. Some plants stand erect, others trail over the stones – all attract the eye and are seen to their best advantage. Rockeries present a problem during the summer, when it is difficult to find suitable flowering plants to succeed the alpines, usually at their most colourful during the spring; but lilies can fill this gap and shine forth from between the stones during June and July.

The mountain lily, *L. bulbiferum*, produces wonderful orange-red splashes of colour during June, while orange and yellow-flowering saucer-shaped *L. dauricum* is nearly as effective. Another lily from the eastern steppes that is suitable for rockeries is *L. concolor*, star-saucered in shape, red or yellow in colour.

L. pumilum has sealingwax-red, spherical blooms on elegant pedicels, and the equally dwarf *L. amabile* from the Korean Diamond Mountains displays shiny orange-red or yellow flowers. *L. pomponium* from the Maritime Alps is useful, and loves the sun and stony ground; lilac-coloured *L. cernuum* from the Far East does better in semi-shade. *L. formosanum* var. *pricei*, the dwarf form of *L. formosanum*, produces 6-inch flowers on 12–16 inch long stems later in August. Its jewel-like flowers are finely formed, white trumpets, tinged bronze-red on the outside, with a yellow throat. *L. lankongense*, *L. papilliferum*, and *L. wardii* are some of the scarcer wild lilies from the Himalayas and China and, although eminently suitable for a rock-garden, they require dry loamy soils. *L. lankongense* needs plenty of room, and its roots wander in the soil before it sprouts through the ground. *L. papilliferum* comes from stony ground about 10,000 feet up in China.

Hybrid and tall-growing lilies have, of course, no place in a rockery, as their bright colours and exceptional height only lead to incongruity, but a place might perhaps be found for *L. hansonii*, the yellow Korean Turk's Cap.

The staggered terraces and soil pockets of a rockery automatically provide the well-drained conditions which lilies, particularly the more delicate wild varieties, require. Heavy rain drains through quickly, and yet some moisture is preserved by the surrounding stones. Ground cover and companion plants need careful selection; also, if used, they must only be permitted to provide light cover, or slugs, so fond of new lily shoots, are sure to cause damage.

Lilies for potting

Pot and house plants are becoming increasingly popular; as well as decorating gardens and house interiors, they are to be seen in ever-increasing numbers in parks, outside public buildings and in hotels, banks and schools. Containers made from natural or artificial stone, clay, or plastic are readily available in a wide choice of sizes, colour and shape. Potted plants are convenient: they are easily moved and are therefore always available where most needed at any particular time; they are also quickly and easily replanted once the plants have ceased to flower.

Colourful, scented lilies are excellent subjects for potting, and highly suitable for room decoration. Choice of the correct variety is important: it must flower freely, not grow too tall – unless extra-large pots can be used – and take as little time as possible between planting and flowering. Jan de Graaff recommends his Rainbow, Midcentury and Golden Chalice hybrids for potting, also his gold-yellow *Harmony*, orange-red *Enchantment*, lemon-yellow *Destiny* and dark-red *Paprika*. *Fire King*, so aptly described by its name, is another recommended variety. All these lilies have large, saucer-shaped flowers and provide a glorious focal point in any room. Containers planted with only one variety remain at their best for 14 days, although careful selection of two or three varieties for potting-up together can extend this period to four or six weeks. *L. longiflorum*, the Easter Lily, is exceptionally useful as an indoor pot plant, its long, greenish-white trumpets showing up to perfection against the background of its glossy, dark-green leaves.

The new Auratum hybrids are difficult to surpass for an exotic display, although they are still somewhat expensive. Even a single bulb planted in an all-purpose container can add beauty and grace to garden, terrace, or living-room.

Larger containers are of course needed for the taller-growing Aurelian hybrids and trumpet lilies; a truly beautiful contrast is obtained if the white trumpets are underplanted with red-flowering Pelargonium or salvias.

Lilies should be potted up during the autumn. First make sure that the pot has an adequate drainage hole, and cover it with one or two pieces of charcoal or broken crocks. To permit room for root development, plant bulbs 2–4 inches deep in a mixture of one-third garden soil or leaf mould, one-third sand, and one-third peat, adding one handful of bone-meal to the mixture. The pots are then stored in a coldframe and protected either with a covering of leaves, or with peat, boards or glass. Leave them in the frame until the weather turns warmer, when they should be moved into a warm room with a temperature of 50–59°F (10–15°C). The appearance of the first shoots provides the signal for a further move, this time into the best available light and a room temperature of 54–61°F (12–16°C); possession of a greenhouse or glazed veranda is, of course, an advantage, but it is by no means imperative. The time of planting and the variety chosen determine the flowering period. *L. longiflorum* flowers later than the Rainbow or Midcentury hybrids, which are at their best around the end of April to early May. Regular watering, with an addition of liquid fertilizer every 10–14 days is, of course, necessary; excessive watering is harmful. To help the bulbs to ripen, restrict watering to a minimum as soon as the flowers are past their best. The bulbs can be left in their pots for flowering another year, but the topsoil is best renewed. The process is then repeated, and pots are subjected to the same treatment as already described. Alternatively, bulbs which have just finished flowering can be planted out in the garden and used for potting-up again a year later.

If lilies are to be planted in pots too big for convenient winter storage, or in containers, they can equally well be started off in seed-boxes or smaller pots for transplanting, once they have formed good root balls; transplanting will cause no harm, provided the roots are treated with care. This method is also used to combine the late-flowering trumpet lilies in the same large pot with the less tall and earlier-flowering Asiatics – an attractive combination capable of prolonging the flowering period from four to six weeks.

Potted lilies certainly repay the effort required; not only are they decorative and useful as house plants, but they provide a foretaste of those yet to flower in the garden!

Lily-forcing

Ten million Easter Lilies, *L. longiflorum*, are sold every Easter Saturday in the United States – and have been sold on that day for many years past. Their production and supply has become an industry in its own right. Trade Associations and Government Research Stations issue detailed information, regular reports, and accurate timetables for every stage of production, so that the first blooms will open precisely on Easter Saturday. They advise on the prepreparation of bulbs, the potting date, when forcing is to start and at what temperature the bulbs are to be stored. For instance, if the variety *Croft* is required to flower during early April, it must be planted at the beginning of the previous September, but prior to planting the bulbs are stored for five to six weeks at 50°F (10°C), or ideally at 39–45°F (4–7°C). *Ace*, another variety, requires eight weeks of the same treatment, while *Estate* is put into cold storage during October and November and planted in 6-inch pots at the beginning of December. Drainage requirements are met by putting a layer of coarse sand and broken crocks about $\frac{3}{4}$ inch deep in the bottom of the pot. The loam-based soil is mixed with peat in the proportion of 3:1 or 2:1, and the pH value of the mixture must be at least 6·5; carbonate of lime is added to correct excess acidity. Prior to forcing, the temperature is held at 50–57°F (10–14°C) and increased to 61°F (16°C) during the forcing period. Every two weeks, applications of soluble nitrogenous fertilizers, mostly sodium or calcium nitrate (0·25 per cent) commence when the shoots reach a height of 2–3 inches, and are later followed by an application of a complete fertilizer.

In addition to the Easter Lily, US growers also force Asiatic varieties developed from *L. tigrinum*, *L. × maculatum*, *L. × hollandicum*, *L. bulbiferum*, *L. davidii*, etc., particularly orange-red *Enchantment*, red *Cinnabar*, lemon yellow *Destiny*, light-orange *Harmony* and the two gold-yellow types, *Joan Evans* and *Croesus*, as well as the Midcentury and Rainbow hybrids.

All these umbelliferous lilies have erect, saucer-shaped flowers, grow 2 feet 6 inches–3 feet high and, depending on the exact variety, require forcing from 60 to 70 days. Varieties with outward-facing flowers usually display their blooms to greater effect; among them are orange *Valencia*, light-yellow *Prosperity*, red *Paprika* and fire-red *Fire King*.

The reflexed flowers of the Fiesta hybrids are carried in loose panicles and are derived from *L. tigrinum*, *L. davidii*, and *L. amabile*. They grow taller than the last group and include the three well-known Citronella, Burgundy and Bronzino strains.

A longer forcing period, up to 20 weeks, is needed by the trumpet lilies, which again grow a little taller than the umbelliferous group. The varieties used are *Royal Gold*, Aurelian hybrids in their many forms and colours, Olympic hybrids, and the Centifolium hybrids, which include *Green Dragon* and *Black Dragon*.

Their bulbs are stored for a minimum period of four weeks before planting at temperatures from 33 to 35·5°F (0·5–2°C), unless the bulbs are imported and have already been prechilled. Plantings take place from January onwards and are timed for the first flowers to appear on 1 April. Bulbs are planted in pots or boxes at a density of 3–5 per square foot and covered with $2\frac{1}{2}$–4 inches of good soil; water and fertilizer applications are increased as growth progresses. Forcing temperatures start at 50–55°F (10–13°C) and are later increased to 59–64°F (15–18°C); bottom heat is to be avoided. Adequate ventilation is necessary during hours of sunshine, and increased light is required once the shoots appear, but too much hastens maturity. Bulbs which have been forced are not valueless, and can be usefully planted out in the open.

Forced lilies always find a ready market either as pot plants or as cut flowers, and are in regular demand for special occasions like Mother's Day. As bulb imports from the United States are somewhat expensive, increased multiplication facilities in Europe would be economically justified.

The professional florist or nurseryman selects his lily varieties for the forcing of pot plants or the production of cut flowers from a very different standpoint from that of the amateur gardener. The professional demands a variety with a short forcing time, with blooms which must be not too abundant and of only moderate size, with colour and shape of flower which must impress the customer and with robustness to withstand the journey from greenhouse to shop. Deep colours and the distinctive shape of the flowers make lilies able to compete with other plants.

Lilies for cutting

Lilies are one of the most beautiful flowers for cutting. They are of impressive size, beautifully coloured and decorative, and possess an exotic air almost like that of the orchid; they flower for a long time and have only one small fault – their pollen is apt to stain skin and clothes.

They are best cut during the early morning, just as the first bud is opening, and will last for 14 days if immediately placed in water. Blooms will last longer and be able to absorb water more easily if the main stem is shortened a little each day; removal of fading and spent flowers is also beneficial. Only cut the minimum length of stem with as few leaves as possible to avoid weakening the bulb needlessly for the coming year.

Vases holding the stems of the trumpet Aurelian and some of the Davidii hybrids, which are 3 feet and often more in height, are best placed on the floor. If the stems are not long enough, they can be attached with a piece of wire to a cane or stick, but the end of the stem must reach below the water. An arrangement of a number of stems, with not too many flowers for each, is usually more attractive than a single, densely flowered stem. The light-yellow and copper-coloured Aurelian hybrids lend elegance to any arrangement; nearly as decorative are the trumpet lilies, with their dark stamens and bronze-flushed, white petals. The pale, cool colour of a stem of the white Madonna Lily or of a green-throated trumpet lily, emphasized perhaps with a leafy branch of copper beech or Japanese maple, strikes perfect harmony. Exotic, orchid-like beauty of shape, texture, and colour is achieved by displays of *L. henryi* and *L. speciosum* varieties, and by the Oriental *L. auratum* and *L. speciosum* hybrids.

The short Hollandicum and Tigrinum hybrids look their best in sphere-shaped vases. But there are so many other alternatives: only two or three stems of the nodding Martagon-type lilies – Fiesta, Harlequin or Patterson hybrids – are sufficient to display their full, fresh, and beautifully gay colours. Probably the most elegant of all is a single stem of the red-flowered *L. davidii* var. *willmottiae* in a white porcelain vase. Another remarkably effective combination consists of a few white trumpet lilies mixed with light or dark-blue delphiniums.

Lilies for decoration

Lily blooms make superb table decorations. Red or white *L. speciosum* flowers placed in a fine glass vase or shallow bowl with asparagus fern look charming; so do the Aurelian hybrids, with their wide-open, star-shaped flowers of white, lemon-yellow, and copper.

Some of the most original and strikingly beautiful small displays are produced by following the Japanese flower-arranging art called *ikebana*. Although *ikebana* is full of symbolism and hidden values difficult for Western man to appreciate, many charming and graceful displays are easily arranged with only three raw materials: a porcelain container; a glass vase; and a stone or metal tray to hold either flowers, branches, climbers, creepers or leaves with bamboo, wood, or tree bark. These materials are capable of an infinite number of arrangements: *L. auratum* flowers arranged in a vase with Rex begonia leaves; the bloom of a Japanese Golden-Rayed Lily with a few rushes and one or two white carnations in a bamboo block; a copper plate covered with bronze leaves carrying a few *Sunburst*-type Aurelian flowers mounted on a piece of driftwood; a hosta leaf or two covering the bottom of a shallow bamboo woven basket holding a few white trumpet lilies and a branch of *Cotoneaster horizontalis*. A few simple materials, an artistic touch, deft hands and practice can produce handsome displays to the satisfaction of arranger and beholder alike. Lily arrangements may be used as decorations in shop-windows, on tables, in the hall or the living-room. (*13*)

Corsage is the name of a Jan de Graaff lily which was developed, as the name implies, for use in flower sprays which ladies occasionally like to wear. It is a pink-tinged, ivory-white Turk's Cap Cernuum hybrid which, fortunately for the dress of the lady wearing it, sheds no pollen.

3. The planting of lilies

The structure of the lily bulb

The lily bulb, made up of a number of succulent, fleshy scales, does not have an outer protecting layer like the tulip, hyacinth and crocus, and is therefore unable to tolerate prolonged dry storage. One of the main essentials for satisfactory growth is good, healthy bulbs with undamaged, live roots and fleshy, sappy scales. Bulbs which are displayed without protection in the dry and warm atmosphere of shops, including bulbs which have been stored for too long in polythene bags, are apt to be dried-up and wrinkled, with only a few brown, wizened, lifeless roots. If such bulbs are bought and planted, their chance of success is minimal and their lifespan, because their damaged roots impair their ability to take up nourishment, is reduced.

Bulbs should be out of the soil for as short a time as possible, and ought to be obtained from the nearest possible source to reduce the risks involved during long journeys. For most European growers, as most bulbs are imported from either Holland or the United States, the only practical safeguard is early ordering in the hope that delivery is received from the first consignment, usually during late October or early November. Bulbs usually arrive packed in damp peat inside a polythene bag, and should be stored in a cool place if immediate planting is impossible.

Bulb-planting

As soon as soil preparations are completed, preferably during early autumn, the site should be covered either with leaves, straw or straw mats, to protect it from frost and heavy rain; in this way bulbs, even if they arrive later than anticipated, can still be planted.

If American wild lilies are planted after September, they are unable to develop roots and decay inevitably follows.

Drainage

The native habitat of lilies provides the good drainage they like and which they naturally must also have in cultivation; waterlogged soils mean certain death to them. In their natural surroundings they are found

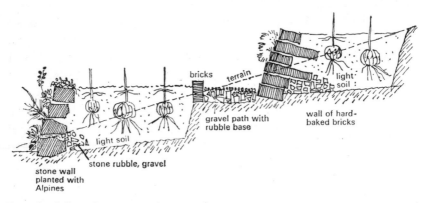

Slopes lend themselves to terracing

growing on slopes, some exceptionally steep, but always on porous types of soils, whether in rock-beds covered with leaf-mould, between boulders in soil pockets rich in humus, or on gravelly, sandy soils with humus cover.

In Japan, *L. auratum* and *L. speciosum* grow on exceptionally free-draining volcanic rubble and ash. The photographs of lilies in their wild surroundings published in the American and English Lily Year Books and also in E. H. Wilson's *Lilies of Eastern Asia* illustrate these points, and always show *L. regale*, *L. henryi*, *L. wallichianum*, or *L. philippinense* growing on steep and often rocky ground. The only exceptions to the rule are the bog-type lilies growing on the Pacific coast of America, which withstand periodic flooding. As lilies are certain to fail in water-logged loam and clay soils, such soils must either be avoided or be well drained before the planting stage is reached.

Selection of planting site

Sloping sites with natural drainage are best, and have the additional advantage of being easily terraced through building up the lower levels with soil dug from the higher parts. Stone walls, or strategically placed, medium-sized rocks effectively retain the soil banks, which should have a barrowload or two of coarse gravel, or builders' rubble, placed at their lowest point to assist drainage.

If planting must be on level ground, it is usually a good plan to raise the level of the bed with additional soil and surround it with stones, bricks or planks.

To satisfy the drainage requirements of the difficult wild Japanese and North American lilies, which must have a soil depth of 20 inches, the planting hole or trench should first be lined with brushwood, topped with stone rubble, and filled with soil previously enriched with additions of sand, peat and leaf-mould.

Soil preparation

Soil conditions are even more important than planting positions. Light, sandy soils need additional nutrients and an improved texture most satisfactorily provided by the incorporation of compost, leaf-mould, or peat (peat is better able to combat difficulties of fertilizer or pH content than soil alone).

Sandy loams rich in humus provide the ideal ground for lilies, but even they are improved, and certainly made more friable, if quantities of peat can be forked in.

Mixing sand and peat with heavy soils lightens them and improves their permeability, while well-rotted turves and leaf-mould provide nutrients for the bulbs.

Heavy soils and clay soils must receive applications of sand, peat and

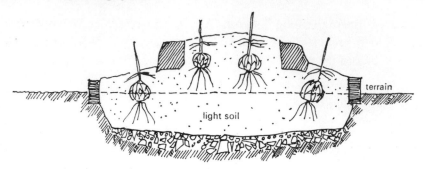

Construction of a raised bed

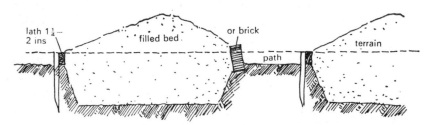

Raised planting beds

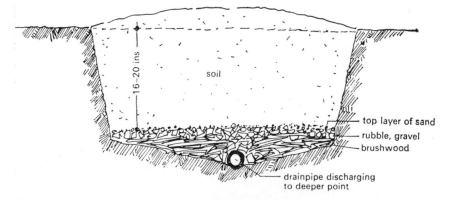

Construction of deep beds with drainage for difficult lilies

leaf-mould, and should preferably be turned several times before being planted. The heaviest soils also benefit from applications of 'Styromull' – flakes of expanded polystyrene. Although these flakes have no manurial value, they help to improve the texture of the soil, solely by their physical properties; they retain water only on their outer surface, and do not become saturated. They lead to permanent loosening of the soil. The flakes of Styromull are scattered over the soil surface from just above ground level, preferably on a wind-free day, and worked into the ground with a spade or a rotary cultivator.

The effectiveness of Styromull applications in improving the texture of soil was demonstrated in 1963 at the International Horticultural Show in Hamburg, where bulbs of irises and lilies were planted in heavy soil with the addition of 20–30 per cent Styromull.

Feeding

Is the soil acid, alkaline, or neutral? If lilies are to flourish, it is important to know the correct answer. It can easily be discovered and measured with the aid of simple and freely available chemicals. Measurements are expressed in terms of pH value: pH 7 is neutral, but lilies prefer slightly acid soils around pH 5·5–6·5. More acid soils, to pH 4, are tolerated by the Japanese lilies, including *L. auratum*, *L. speciosum*, etc., the American bog lilies and also *L. canadense*, while soils of pH values between 6 and 7 are preferred by *L. martagon* and *L. candidum*. Excess acidity of soils is easily corrected by applications of basic slag, lime, or quicklime. Conversely, if acidity is to be increased, liberal dressings of leaf-mould or peat are helpful, as is superphosphate. Certain lilies, like rhododendrons and some Asiatic gentians, require lime-free soils and prefer soft water to hard water containing lime. The Japanese and North American lilies already mentioned also have these preferences.

Dung, when fresh, is poisonous to lilies; it must not be used until at least two years old and then only spread thinly, during autumn or spring, over the topsoil. Dung must never be dug in, nor, if fusarium is to be avoided, must be permitted to come into direct contact with lily bulbs.

Balanced artificial fertilizers are very suitable, particularly the types sold for potatoes, which contain little nitrogen but have a high potash content. The first application is made during early spring, so that rain or melting snow can carry it down into the soil; the second when the first signs of growth appear. If liquid applications are preferred, the fertilizer is easily dissolved in water for a 0·3 per cent solution, about 1 ounce (a fistful) is needed to $2\frac{1}{5}$ gallons of water ($2\frac{3}{5}$ US gallons). Frequent watering with this solution during spells of drought is not only safe but most beneficial, provided that fertilizers are not applied after the flowering period – lilies only absorb potash at this time and no nitrogen; too much nitrogen encourages fusarium. The amount of powder or liquid fertilizer applied is dictated by the level of fertility of the soil, and should not exceed 1 ounce per square foot per year.

As with all bulbous plants, a liberal supply of potash is most important. This is also confirmed in nature, where observations in North America have clearly shown that lilies, during years following a forest fire, always grow more vigorously and produce a greater number of flowers than during normal years – undoubtedly as a result of the extra potash obtained from the burnt timber. According to a South African lily-breeder, additional potash reduces botrytis. Feeding lilies is not complicated; the main essential is to avoid overfeeding.

Mulching

Mulching improves the soil by applications of grass cuttings, peat, or other partly rotted vegetative matter usually applied during the growing period. Ferns, rich in potash, are useful, as are sawdust and wood shavings, which are much used in North America. Chopped or whole straw not only makes a cover against frost, but also good mulch – but it should not be used if there are mice about; they like to nest in it, and live on the lily bulbs. The nitrogen absorbed during the rotting process of the sawdust and wood shavings must be made good by an early spring dressing. Mulch insulates the hot rays of the sun from the soil and therefore keeps lily roots cool; but, conversely, mulching during periods of late frost is disadvantageous, and keeps the ground colder than it would normally be.

Fungus diseases, fully discussed in Chapter 7, must not be ignored; they are apt to attack lily bulbs, which must be protected with a fungicide. Voles, if present, can be kept out by wire netting; wireworms, caterpillars and cockchafers by one or another of the very effective proprietary chemicals (such as benzene hexachloride) on the market. For safety's sake, manufacturers' detailed instructions should always be followed exactly, and chemicals should not be used near vegetable patches.

Planting the bulb

Earliest possible planting is best. To obtain effective distribution and correct spacing, bulbs should first be spaced on the soil surface, with those of a similar kind grouped together. The space between individual

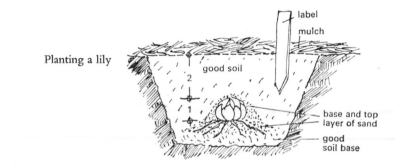

Planting a lily

bulbs depends on the size of the particular bulb and the height the variety is likely to reach. Small bulbs need only 4–8 inches between them, but the larger bulbs, producing the taller lilies, need to be 8–20 inches apart. Considerations of an individual variety's preference for damp or dry, acid or alkaline soils, and shade or sunlight must not be forgotten when siting the bulbs. Many lilies, notably the yellow Aurelian and pink Centifolium hybrids, are inclined to fade in strong sunlight, and prefer positions where they receive only a few hours of sunshine each day.

Bulb size governs planting depth, although bulbs tolerate shallower levels in heavy soils than in light. A good rule of thumb is to plant bulbs at a depth equivalent to three times their height; i.e., a bulb 2 inches high is planted at a depth of 6 inches. *L. candidum* and *Cardiocrinum giganteum* are the two exceptions – the first likes not more than one finger-width of soil above it, while the top of the second should be clear of the soil. As *L. candidum* produces a crop of leaves during the first autumn, it requires early planting, at the end of August or during the beginning of September. Lilies like to have their roots spread out, and the size of the planting hole must always be big enough for this purpose.

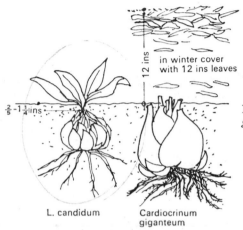

Planting *L. candidum* and *Cardiocrinum giganteum*

L. candidum   Cardiocrinum giganteum

To avoid the threat of fusarium, always place a trowelful of sand, previously mixed with the required amount of a good proprietary fungicide (Terraclor, Ferbam, or Brassicol, for instance) in each planting hole; then place the bulb on this base, spread out the roots, and cover with yet another trowelful of the fungicide-fortified sand.

Additional fungicide treatment, usually only worthwhile when a large number of bulbs are dealt with, is easily carried out by soaking bulbs for a few minutes in water in which fungicide has previously been dissolved. The bulbs are then air-dried for a few minutes and planted in the normal way, but still with a fungicide-sand mixture.

Finally, the bulbs are covered with the soil previously dug out, well firmed down, and labelled. It is wrong to rely on memory, as exact planting positions and names of varieties are often forgotten by the time the following spring arrives. If labels are to last and retain their legibility, they must be made of strong material and be of good size and quality; for lettering, special weatherproof ink is obtainable.

A protective cover of straw, leaves, or wood shavings placed over the planted bulbs guards against possible frost damage and encourages new root formation.

If late delivery of bulbs or early frost prevent planting, bulbs can be safely stored until the following spring in polythene bags filled with moist peat kept at a temperature of 32–43°F (0–6°C). S. L. Emsweller's experience suggests that the best way of keeping bulbs is to pack them in sphagnum moss and store them at 32°F (0°C).

The transplanting of lilies

Satisfactorily established lilies, even if in flower, can be transplanted at any time, always provided that they are lifted without causing root damage and that they can be immediately planted in their new position. Autumn is the best time for transplanting, and September and October should ideally be aimed at; the earlier transplanting can take place, the better for the lily. Any damaged bulb scales should be removed before planting, and the bulb dusted with a fungicide (Arasan, Ferbam, Tersan, Spergon) or dipped in a fungicide solution. As before, the base of the planting hole should be lined with a small quantity of sand on which the bulb is placed; then follows another trowelful of sand which is topped with soil and well firmed down. Lilies can also be transplanted during spring, but special care is needed not to damage roots or any of the fresh-growing shoots – if they are broken off, there is no chance of flowers that year.

Most lilies produce stem-roots to help them to draw nourishment from the soil and to feed the bulb; they must therefore always be covered with soil and be transplanted to a depth which permits this. To encourage the growth of stem-roots and also to allow them to fulfil their function it is important that even the uppermost layers of soil should be enriched with plant nutrients. The effort will be repaid by thick growth, and an abundance of flowers.

4. Botany of the lily

What is a lily?

Botanical knowledge of the lily, without delving too deeply into the scientific aspects, is of equal importance for the amateur gardener, the professional horticulturist and the breeder.

Botanically, the lily belongs to the Monocotyledoneae group, which have only one cotyledon, in contrast to the Dicotyledoneae, which have two. Monocotyledoneae are divided into a number of other families, including one consisting of mainly bulbous plants, Liliaceae, to which the lily belongs. Apart from the genus *Lilium*, a number of other decorative plants belong to the same family: *Allium, Colchicum, Eremurus,* and *Convallaria.*

A genuine lily (*Lilium*) is recognized by a number of features:

1. A bulb built up of a number of loosely overlapping scales but which, unlike the culinary onion (*Allium cepa*), are not covered with an outer membranous, protective skin

2. A leafy stem usually without leaves on the lower portion; one exception is the Madonna Lily

3. Lanceolate or linear leaves with parallel veins, not revolute or heart-shaped

4. A terminal flower or several flowers carried on pedicels, with a small leaf where the flower joins the main stem

5. A seed capsule which opens at the top, splitting down the middle of the three seed compartments and so releases the numerous flat, paper-like seeds for distribution by the wind

10. *L. regale* in an English garden with eremurus, echinops and irises

11. Yellow Aurelian hybrids, strong stems, healthy foliage, lemon, canary, chrome or orange-yellow trumpets
12. Aurelian hybrids from Frietsch with wide-open, delicately frilled trumpets

13. Flower arrangement: a simple board or shallow dish, a few colourful leaves and exquisitely beautiful Aurelian hybrids lend an exotic atmosphere to this display

14. *Coralie*, coral-red, Turk's Cap, nodding flowers on arching stems. A delicately shaped lily with fine, small leaves, not distinguished for the size of its individual blooms but for the overall harmony of the plant. It originates from *L. davidii* var. *willmottiae*

15. Fiesta hybrids also developed from *L. davidii* var. *willmottiae*, and exist in all shades of yellow as well as wine-red and bronze. Strains: Bronzino, Burgundy and Citronella. Clones: *Fury*, dark-red; *Sonata*, orange and salmon; *Tarantella*, saffron-yellow and pink

16. Harlequin hybrids provide a highlight in any garden during June and July; the flowers they bear are comparatively few in number, but are well-spaced

17. *Good Hope.* White trumpet lilies thickly planted in a park. The air was laden with their scent

18. Bellingham hybrids manage to convey their 'Wild West' origin by combining the gracefulness of *L. pardalinum*, the delicate yellow of *L. parryi* and the fiery red of *L. humboldtii*. They multiply rapidly under favourable conditions and can be divided every three or four years

19. *Black Dragon.* The extraordinary beauty of this Jan de Graaff lily is difficult to express in words; it is beautifully shaped, the outside bronze-brown, the inside of the purest white contrasting with the chocolate-brown anthers. *Green Dragon* is similar in shape, rich apple-green outside, greenish-white inside

Near-relations of the genus *Lilium* are; *Cardiocrinum*, *Notholirion*, *Nomocharis* and *Fritillaria*. Neither *Iris* nor *Anthericum* nor *Hemerocallis* are genuine lilies.

Parts of a lily

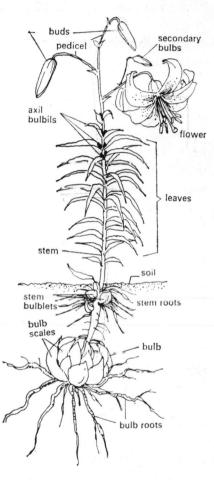

Bulbs and roots

Lilies, like narcissi, tulips or hyacinths, grow from bulbs which store plant nutrients, and can be likened to an underground bud. The bulb is the foundation and the life centre of the plant and consists of the basal plate, a compressed stem, and scales (in reality a form of leaf) from which the flowering stalk, the flowers, and the roots grow. No plant or flower can ever be produced from a vermin-damaged or diseased basal plate.

The bulb scales contain starch particles which are easily seen under a microscope. The starch helps the stem and leaves to burst into growth during the spring, and when the leaves are sufficiently mature, they begin to assimilate. The assimilates (sugar) are returned to the bulb and converted back to starch. In fact, cooked lily bulbs taste like mashed potatoes, and are grown for food in China, Japan, and Siberia. The fleshy, comparatively small lily scales, lacking the protective coating of other bulbs, are easily damaged and apt to dry out quickly; great care must therefore be taken during packing, transporting, and planting.

Every bulb raised from seed illustrates that the bulb scales originate from leaves, in fact from the thicker and lower parts of the leaf sheath. *L. candidum*, *L. formosanum*, and the American *L. catesbaei* show this process exceptionally clearly.

The mostly strong and numerous roots spring from the base of the bulb (the basal plate) and draw both water and nutrients from the soil, in which they also help to anchor the bulb. The roots are contractile and able to draw the bulb deeper into the ground, making sure that it is at all times covered with a sufficient depth of soil. If, for instance, spring-sown *L. regale* seeds are covered with ½-inch of soil, the roots of the young bulbs will have drawn them to a depth of 1½–2½ inches by the following autumn. In its natural surroundings *L. polyphyllum* normally lies about 1 foot below the surface and has especially long roots to enable it to do so. The contractile roots of lilies provide another reason for planting bulbs, especially young, small ones, as early as possible in the autumn; it gives them a chance to root further before the onset of winter and ensures that the bulbs are well anchored in the soil and are not forced out by the cycle of frost and thaw.

The basal roots are usually 12–18 months old. New roots are mostly formed during late spring, although further and regular development takes place up until autumn. If roots break off during transplanting, or bulbs are bought with dry roots or, even worse, with none at all, the bulb is weakened for more than a year of its life.

Many lilies produce stem-roots which grow from the internodes nearest the bulb. In the main they absorb nutrients from the upper soil layers, mostly covered with compost provided by rotting vegetation, and feed it direct into the stem. This habit demonstrates the necessity for stem-roots to be kept covered with rich soil at all times. Stem-roots die off during the autumn and build up afresh during the following spring.

Not all bulbs are alike – there are three different types, and their growth-habits vary accordingly.

The concentric bulb

The scales in most lily bulbs are arranged in a concentric pattern; beginning from the centre of the bulb, scales are spirally arranged against and above each other, similar to the tiles on a house roof. This arrangement, and the ever-increasing size of scales, from the bulb centre outwards, is easily seen in *L. regale* and *L. davidii*.

The development of new bulbs varies. With bulbs of Bulbiferum, Maculatum, and Hollandicum lilies, the growing stem splits the original bulb and the newly developing scales form two separate bulbs. This process is repeated regularly every year and makes it necessary to separate the increasing clumps of bulbs every second or third season. Other bulbs behave like those of *L. regale*, which form a growing centre around the stem for a new bulb that eventually pushes the old scales aside before it dies off, after a year or two.

Stoloniferous bulbs

The North American lilies, *L. canadense*, *L. grayi*, *L. iridollae*, *L. michiganense*, *L. michauxii*, and *L. superbum*, belong to this type; one or two underground stolons grow from a point where the stem leaves the bulb. They are finger-like and fleshy, forming, after $\frac{3}{4}$-$1\frac{1}{2}$ inches growth, new bulbs with scales. In the course of only a few years a whole network of stolons, all terminating in bulbs, is built up, and, unless periodically

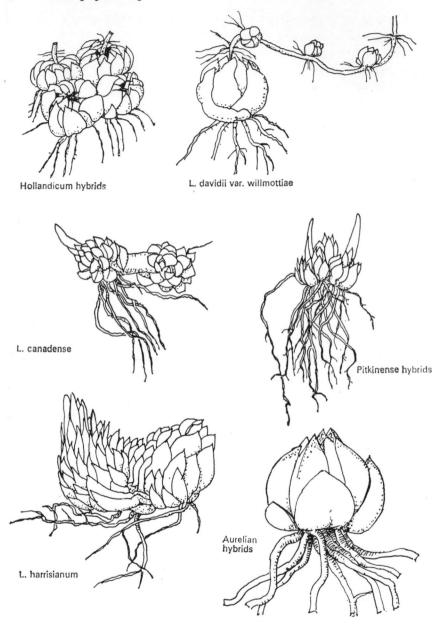

Hollandicum hybrids

L. davidii var. willmottiae

L. canadense

Pitkinense hybrids

L. harrisianum

Aurelian hybrids

Various forms of lily bulbs

divided and replanted, the heavy concentration of bulbs in a small area suffers from lack of space and plant food.

Rhizomatous bulbs

Several Pacific coast lilies grow a mass of scales on a rootstock. Among them are *L. pardalinum*, *L. maritimum*, *L. nevadense*, *L. harrisianum*, *L. occidentale*, and *L. parvum*. New scales grow laterally, adjacent to the old ones, and are sometimes firmly, other times more loosely, connected to the original bulb they spring from. The only satisfactory way of parting them is with a sharp knife, which in the case of the American *L. pardalinum* or *L. harrisianum* has to be done every three to four years if they are not to suffer from lack of plant food on account of their high density. Each of the newly formed rhizomatous bulbs produces a flowering stem during the subsequent growing year.

Rhizomatous lilies must not be confused with, for example, *L. davidii* and *L. duchartrei*. The flowering stems of these plants do not rise vertically from the bulb, but wander around underground before breaking through the soil surface. Bulbs, which produce shoots during the following year, are mostly developed at each node of that part of the stem which remains underground. Some lilies are conveniently multiplied in this way, but if *L. duchartrei* and *L. lankongense* are to be satisfactorily confined to their planting positions, without their flowering stems appearing in inconvenient nearby situations, they must be restricted, with a metal ring sunk into the ground, when they are first planted.

Stems and leaves

The stem grows vertically upwards from the bulb every year and bears leaves which vary in form, colour, and arrangement according to variety. *L. regale* and *L. centifolium* have thickly growing, alternate, lanceolate leaves arranged spirally throughout the length of the stem. Many American lilies carry their leaves like *L. martagon*, which has a few broad-lanceolate leaves scattered on the upper parts of the stem, but the majority encircling it in one to three tiers of regularly spaced whorls. Comparatively broad-lanceolate and opposite leaves cover the stem of the Japanese *L. auratum*, *L. japonicum*, *L. rubellum* and *L. speciosum*. *L. henryi*, too, has similarly shaped leaves. The leaves of most lilies are smooth, shiny and green, but some have foliage with glandular hairs or leaves ciliate on the margins, exemplified by *L. carniolicum* and its variety *jankae* and *L. ciliatum*.

Some lilies with small, grass-like leaves come from the dry, sunny steppes or from arid mountains. Good examples are *L. pumilum*, *L. cernuum*, *L. callosum*, and *L. concolor*. By contrast, lilies native to wooded areas and mountains subject to monsoons, like the Japanese varieties, have shiny, green, broad leaves.

The leaves soak up energy from the sun and, through photosynthesis by means of the chlorophyll, absorb carbon dioxide from the atmosphere; this, together with water, produces a new substance, similar to simple sugars. The plant uses the substance partly to maintain itself, and also to build up reserve nutrients in the bulb for future development. Excessive damage to or plucking of the leaves so vital to the plant's food supply damages the bulb and jeopardizes its continuity. When cutting flowers, two-thirds of the leaves should be left on the growing plant. Botrytis, which attacks lily leaves and prevents them from functioning properly is for this reason very detrimental to growth and bulb development.

Flowers

The stem from a sound and healthy bulb produces one or more flowers. The floral envelope (perianth) consists of two groups of three tepals; the three outer ones correspond to sepals, and the three inner to petals. The similar outer and inner petals in monocotyledonous plants are more correctly termed tepals, although for convenience they will, in the following chapters, be referred to as petals. They radiate from their base in symmetrical hexagonal form.

Flower display

Flowers are arranged in one of two ways, racemose or umbellate.

In the first case each flower in the head is arranged in a series; in *L. davidii* the flowers are arranged to look like a long candle; *L. martagon* and its hybrids look like a loose bunch of grapes; while in *L. leucanthum* var. *centifolium* the outline is the shape of a pyramid.

In contrast, the pedicels of the umbellate types all arise from the same level (*L. bulbiferum*, *L. dauricum* and Rainbow hybrids) and consequently show a larger and more concentrated area of colour.

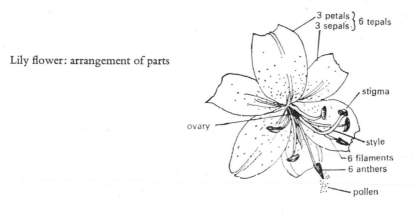

Lily flower: arrangement of parts

There are deviations, notably among hybrids and varieties that give a mixture of both classes. The best effect is achieved by lilies with long, widely spaced, horizontal pedicels which permit full development of the individual blooms. *L. regale* flowers are positioned like a wheel in circular form on the extremity of the stem, and the plant seldom produces another one or two flowers at a different level. The similar *L. sargentiae* or, a better example, *L. leucanthum* var. *centifolium*, produces attractive, pyramid-shaped flower spikes. The delicate, slightly arched pedicels of *L. canadense* and of some other wild lilies of American origin create a truly beautiful and graceful picture. For the lily-breeder it is interesting to know that the umbelliferous flower arrangement is dominant.

Flower shapes

Flower shapes are divided into three classes: the Turk's Cap, the saucer-shaped, and the funnel or trumpet-shaped.

L. martagon is the Turk's Cap lily, but many Asiatic lilies bear flowers of the same shape, including *L. davidii*, *L. cernuum*, *L. callosum*, and *L. henryi*. So, of course, do the Bellingham hybrids and the American *L. pardalinum* and *L. superbum*.

Turk's Cap or Martagon   Saucer shape   Funnel or trumpet shape

Among the saucer-shaped, flowered types, with always erect and upright blooms, are the Asiatic *L. dauricum* and *L. concolor*, the European *L. bulbiferum*, and the American *L. philadelphicum*.

Funnel or trumpet-shaped flowers are borne by many Chinese lilies, *L. regale*, *L. sargentiae*, *L. sulphureum*, and *L. wallichianum*. The funnel-shaped flowers of *L. nepalense* show this form but are wide open. Flowers are mostly horizontal or slightly pendant, with overlapping, recurved, or reflexed petals flaring out from a pipe-like tube into a funnel or trumpet shape.

Colour of flowers

The pigment available in the petals determines their colour. Varying shades of yellow are produced by carotene and flavine; carotene is present not only in the epidermis but also in the mesophyll, while flavine confines itself to the upper epidermis. Red and blue are produced by various anthocyanins.

Carotene is capable of stronger and deeper pigmentation than flavine, and is responsible for the deep, sumptuous, yellow and orange colours. The many nuances of shades so admired in lilies are produced by a mixture of carotene, flavine and anthocyanin. Paper chromatography easily detects the presence of the different pigments in the flower.

Breeders are, of course, most interested and need to know if colours and individual pigments are inheritable and also if they are dominant (i.e., visible) or recessive (i.e., not apparent in the present generation but with a tendency to appear in a subsequent one).

The nectary furrows, occasionally surrounded by papillae as in *L. henryi* and *L. speciosum*, are shallow troughs at the base of the flower which secrete nectar in minute quantities.

The structure of the epidermis determines whether the flower has a shiny or a velvety appearance; the shiny petals have their cells evenly arranged in one plane, the velvety petals are in palisade form.

Stamens and carpels

The lily flower has six stamens, arranged in the shape of a hexagon. Each stamen consists of the filament growing from the base of the flower, and bears a pollen-filled anther at its apex. The vividly coloured stamens often project over and above the corolla; anthers usually open a few hours after the flower has begun to bloom, and release their pollen.

The female part of the flower, the pistil, consists of the ovary at the base of the flower, which contains three double-rowed seed cells, and the style and stigma. The style, like the filaments, is very long, and projects far outside the bloom. The stigma placed at the apex of the style shows its readiness to receive pollen by its damp, sticky appearance and often even drops of secretion. Pollination is effected by insects, particularly butterflies and moths that suck the nectar with their long proboscis, by shaking, by wind or through accidentally knocking the plant.

When the pollen is deposited on the stigma a long pollen *tube* travels down through the style to the ovules in the ovary and fertilizes the female egg cells. In order to fertilize every one of the 300–500 egg cells, an equal number of pollen grains must be deposited on the stigma and find their way to the ovary. If the pollen comes from more than one plant, egg cells are likely to be differently fertilized, and any subsequently produced seed will not be of uniform progeny.

Seed and seed capsules

Lilies have fairly large seed capsules of cylindrical or spherical shape, a few with wings along the ribs. The very large, elongated capsules of Cardiocrinum look most decorative when they open and reveal their

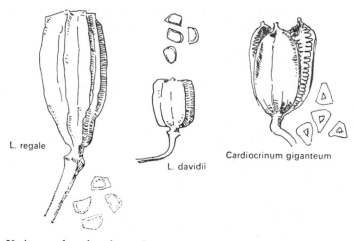

L. regale

L. davidii

Cardiocrinum giganteum

Various seeds and seed capsules

toothed edge. The seeds of most lilies are thin and light, and easily distributed by wind as soon as the capsules split open into three parts, from the apex downwards. Cardiocrinum has the lightest and thinnest seeds, with a broad border of papery membrane around the periphery; those of *L. martagon* and the American lilies are more substantial, with no border of papery membrane; the seeds of the trumpet lilies are very thin and transparent, with a membranous border.

One seed capsule can contain 500 or more seeds, although some, because of unsuitable pollen, may contain only infertile seeds. The weight of seed varies widely; 700 *L. henryi* or *L. martagon* seeds weigh ¼ ounce, but it takes twice as many *L. davidii* var. *willmottiae* seeds or 10 times as many *L. regale* seeds to make this weight.

Seeds are easily examined for quality by holding them against a light and looking for the embryo which, if present, appears in the form of a dark, slightly curved nucleus; if such an embryo is absent, the seed is infertile, and is not able to germinate.

5. The multiplication of lilies

Few gardeners are satisfied just to grow lilies: they want to do more than that; they want to multiply them. Two methods are possible – either from seeds, or vegetatively.

Vegetative multiplication

Vegetative reproduction means taking a part of the living lily and growing it on, with care, to produce another plant exactly like its parent. The process is carried out in a number of ways, and is the only certain method of obtaining plants identical to the original stock and the only method by which hybrids, to be identical, can be multiplied.

Multiplication by bulb division

Bulbs of Tigrinum, Umbellatum, and Davidii hybrids double every year; during the first year they are divided into two parts by the main stem growing from the centre, and by the second year each of the easily parted sections is capable of producing a flowering lily. Bulbs of Mid-century and Tigrinum hybrids, and some others, are therefore best lifted and divided every year to keep the ever-increasing clumps of bulbs from weakening plant growth and flowering ability. Work of this nature should always be completed before new growth has started, during autumn and spring, which is not only the correct time for separating the easily parted bulbs, but also for transplanting the surplus.

The Bellingham hybrids and also the American *L. canadense*, *L. pardalinum*, *L. harrisianum*, *L. superbum*, *L. washingtonianum*, etc., are either rhizomatous or stoloniferous, and develop new bulbs on their underground stem system. A sharp knife soon separates them, followed by individual replanting, but if they are to be kept vigorous, regular lifting and division are necessary every four years, particularly with the rhizomatous *L. pardalinum* and *L. harrisianum*.

Multiplication by underground bulblets

When spring growth first commences, some lilies, including *L. davidii* var. *willmottiae*, *L. wardii*, *L. duchartrei*, and *L. nepalense*, produce underground stems which, after wandering along below ground, suddenly break through the soil surface, but not before bulblets have started to build up on the internodes. Bulbs also form on the parts of the stem which remain underground – particularly if the bulb has been planted fairly deeply – and often provide a very prolific means of increase. Stem-bulblets are regularly formed by lilies which split their bulbs annually; this is also the case with trumpet lilies, *L. henryi*, the Aurelian hybrids, and especially *L. longiflorum* (37). Autumn is the best time for lifting and replanting stem-bulblets.

Multiplication by axil bulbils

A number of lilies produce bulbils in their leaf axils: *L. bulbiferum*, aptly named on account of this habit; *L. tigrinum*; *L. sargentiae*; *L. sulphureum*; and many hybrids. Axil bulbils are small and should be planted in pots after removal from the parent plant during summer or autumn; they often produce leaves during that very same autumn, and certainly during the following spring. Removal of, or accidental damage to, flower buds on the upper parts of the flowering stem aids both axil bulbil and underground bulblet production. This is a remarkable phenomenon well worth remembering, as it provides the only means of retaining a valuable lily if its main stem has been accidentally damaged. But axil bulbils and stem-bulblets can also be produced if the stem is cut into several pieces and each part, including leaves, is planted vertically in a mixture of sand and peat and kept at a temperature of 68–77°F (20–25°C). This method is, of course, particularly valuable for the propagation of lilies where stem damage has taken place close to ground level.

Some lilies which do not normally produce axil bulbils can be induced to do so provided they show no flower buds at the time: eminently suitable are the hybrids of *L. leucanthum* var. *centifolium*: *L. sargentiae*, *L. sulphureum*, and *L. tigrinum*. Seedlings or young plants of such hybrids raised from bulblets kept in the warm and very humid atmosphere of a closed greenhouse, produce numerous bulbils at all the internodes of the stem which remain above ground level. Most of the newly formed bulbils grow short roots and leaves, and are easily removed from the parent plant for immediate planting. This rapid method of multiplication is often used if a new lily is to be quickly brought onto the market. If the plant produces a flower, the formation of axil bulbils does not take place.

Multiplication by bulb scales

This is the usual and normally the most rewarding method. As soon as flowering stops, the lily bulb is lifted, and some of the scales (often up to 50 per cent of them) are carefully severed from the lowest possible point of attachment to the bulb plate. After allowing the wound to dry, the scales are treated with a suitable proprietary fungicide (scales and a level teaspoonful of fungicide are put in a tin and well shaken) which should be based on either Captan, Ferbam, Maneb, or Thiram (TMTD). The bulb, prior to replanting, should also be dusted with fungicide. Scales are nearly as easily removed from bulbs left *in situ*, provided a hole is first dug at their side; the scales are then carefully removed, and on completion of the operation the bulb is dusted with fungicide and the soil replaced.

If scales are to produce satisfactory bulbs, they must be subjected to a humid, warm atmosphere. In Oregon, scales are scattered in shallow drills on open land and lightly covered with soil. Within four to six weeks the small, newly developed bulbs produce leaves, and they continue to grow until late autumn. Other methods must unfortunately be used in regions not favoured with the Oregon climate, where heavy autumn rains terminate the necessary period of warm, humid conditions too early in the growing season.

Scales previously treated with fungicide are put into a sufficiently large polythene bag which contains damp peat, damp vermiculite, or sphagnum moss. The closed polythene bag is then stored at a temperature of 68–72°F (20–22°C) in a warm cupboard or in the kitchen; for

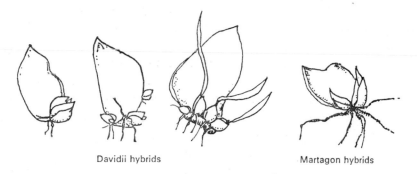

Davidii hybrids   Martagon hybrids

Bulb development from bulb scales

native American lilies a temperature of 59–68°F (15–20°C) is sufficient. With some varieties, the small bulbs growing from the callus occasionally take months to develop; others take only four to six weeks, but normally the newly developing bulbs reach pea to hazelnut size within a few months.

Bulbils must be subjected to a period of cold treatment to induce leaf growth if they are to be planted in the open or in pots or boxes during the following spring. This is achieved simply by storing the plastic bag in a cool cellar or in a coldframe, or even in a refrigerator, for two to three months at temperatures ranging from 36° to 46°F (2–8°C). Unless young bulbs and axil bulbils receive this treatment, leaf development is likely to be very poor or even nonexistent. Before the bulbils are planted they need to be most carefully separated from the now-exhausted scales to avoid root damage. If, however, some of the scales are still sound, healthy and sappy, they can again be subjected to the warm treatment to produce still further bulbils.

An alternative method is to grow the fungicide-treated scales in boxes or pots filled with vermiculite or a peat and sand mixture. The long side of the scale – or, the side with the broken edge – should be pressed into the growing medium, and the container should be covered with a sheet of polythene well tied round the sides and placed, as previously, in a warm position. Although pots and boxes need more storage space than plastic bags, the method is ideal if a warm greenhouse is available. It also has the additional advantages of reducing root disturbance to a minimum, and postponing the operation of planting-out until the first summer.

Scales can be encouraged to produce more numerous, though small, bulbils is they are lightly cut along the broken edge with a sharp knife. Particular care should be taken that the growing medium, of whatever kind, is not too wet; it should be only slightly damp, so as to feel almost dry if touched with the back of the hand – excessive moisture invariably gives poor results. Peat is undoubtedly the best material to use, as it seldom leads to failures, and retains moisture more evenly and for longer periods than most other growing mediums.

Multiplication by scales can take place at any time of year, but the provision of a rest period, after two to three months of warmth, is important. Finally, a warning – the scales of some hybrid lilies can take longer than six months before they start to produce bulbs.

Multiplication by seed

The sense of achievement and pride obtained by raising lilies from seed is far greater than that given by vegetative reproduction from bulbs. This is only natural, for even if lilies raised from seed do not always 'come true', they quickly make up for what they lose in beauty by numbers and vigorous growth. If a garden is to be filled with lilies, raising them from seed is certainly the least expensive method and, given a little luck, some of the new plants will excel the mother plant in every respect. Growing lilies from seed is not complicated, provided particularly difficult varieties are not chosen; but patience is certainly needed, as it is usually three years before efforts are rewarded with blooms!

Growing plants from seed has two advantages. Firstly, virus disease cannot be transmitted to the new plant as is the case with vegetative reproduction. Secondly, home-grown bulbs can be planted out immediately and, unlike bought ones, their root growth is intact; in addition, they need not be kept out of the soil for any length of time.

Germination categories

Before sowing lily seed it is necessary to establish to which of the four different groups, all different in their mode of emergence, a particular variety belongs. Seedlings belonging to the first group emerge above ground (epigeal), from between two to six weeks after sowing (immediate epigeal), or after several months (delayed epigeal). Seeds which germinate from below ground level, without producing a cotyledon, fall into the second group (hypogeal) and are similarly subdivided into immediate hypogeal and, in the case where germination can take up to one year, delayed hypogeal.

1. *Immediate epigeal*

Most of the trumpet lilies and the Asiatic Maculatum, Davidii and Tigrinum groups fall into this category; individually they are as follows:

amabile	*formosanum*
bakerianum	*lankongense*
callosum	*leichtlinii* var. *maximowiczii*
cernuum	*leucanthum* var. *chloraster*
concolor	*longiflorum*
dauricum	*neilgherrense*
davidii	*nepalense*
delavayi	*nobilissimum*
duchartrei	*papilliferum*

philadelphicum	Tigrinum hybrids
philippinense	Trumpet lily hybrids
primulinum	*wardii*
pumilum	*wilsonii*
regale	
sargentiae	
speciosum var. *gloriosoides*	
sulphureum	Aurelian hybrids
taliense	Cernuum hybrids
tigrinum	Davidii hybrids
wallichianum	Midcentury hybrids

After a four-to-six-week incubation period, the embryo produces a downward-growing root – a little thicker in one part than elsewhere – from which the future bulb grows. Finally the upward-growing, loop-shaped shoot, full of chlorophyll, pushes the seed case through the soil until the cotyledon stands erect. The first true leaf emerges approximately four weeks later.

2. *Delayed epigeal*
Sowings of freshly harvested seeds of lilies in this group often give the same quick results as varieties in Group 1.

candidum	*leucanthum*
carniolicum	*pomponium*
chalcedonicum	*pyrenaicum*
henryi	*sargentiae*

Although embryo development is exactly the same, seeds may take one year (often two years in the case of *L. carniolicum*) before they germinate. Seeds of *L. candidum* germinate unevenly, and can take as little as four weeks or as long as two years. Harvest-fresh seeds of *L. henryi* germinate immediately, but if the seeds are brown and dry, germination is usually delayed.

3. *Immediate hypogeal*

This is the smallest of the four groups, and consists of the following varieties and hybrids:

brownii var. *australe*	*philadelphicum*
dauricum	*speciosum*
martagon var. *album*	
parryi	Golden Chalice hybrids

After being subjected to a temperature of 68–77°F (20–25°C), the root emerges from the seed and produces a small bulb. After a short rest-period, the first true leaf pushes through the soil without any cotyledon having appeared.

4. *Delayed hypogeal*

Martagon, Japanese, and nearly all North American lilies belong to this group:

alexandrae	*japonicum*	*polyphyllum*
auratum	*kelloggii*	*rubellum*
bolanderi	*maritimum*	*rubescens*
brownii	*martagon*	*speciosum*
bulbiferum	*michiganense*	*superbum*
canadense	*monadelphum*	*tsingtauense*
columbianum	*nevadense*	*washingtonianum*
distichum	*occidentale*	
grayi	*pardalinum*	Auratum-Speciosum hybrids
hansonii	*parvum*	Bellingham hybrids
humboldtii	*philadelphicum*	Martagon hybrids

The mode of lily-seed germination is suited to the life-cycle of the plant and depends on the climate of its native habitat. Wild *L. martagon* drops its seed onto the warm soil at the beginning of September and produces embryos below ground. The small embryos withstand low winter temperatures, snow, and ice, and produce their first leaf immediately the soil becomes a little warmer during the following spring. If the seed is saved and not used for immediate sowing, the vital autumn seed-germination and bulb-production periods are missed, and if sowing is delayed still further the temperatures become, in any case, too low. *L. auratum* seeds ripen too late to be germinated during autumn, and it is impossible to produce bulbs until the following spring; the first leaf cannot therefore emerge until another 12 months have passed – that is, during the subsequent spring – because the underground bulblets must first pass through a cold period to stimulate leaf formation.

It is essential always to remember the lily's natural life-cycle when sowing seed of lilies in this group. It does not matter if the seed of lilies in this group is sown during late autumn or in the spring, as germination and leaf production cannot take place in the following summer but only during the subsequent one.

Delayed hypogeal: Warm and cold treatment

The Americans have shown that the germination period and the growing cycle can be shortened if the warm conditions in which seeds are normally kept for three to six months are interrupted by a brief period of cold storage. Breeders, nurserymen, and gardeners have welcomed the system, and use it widely.

When dealing with Group 4 lilies, the most practical method of propagation is to use jam-jars or large preserving jars, preferably the type with screw-top lids. Seeds, first dusted with fungicide, are placed in a jar together with the previously sterilized and lightly damped growing medium, which can be either peat, sphagnum moss, vermiculite, or perlite. The jar is sealed with either the screw cap or a piece of securely tied polythene or foil, before being stored in a temperature of 59–70°F (15–21°C); American West coast lilies only require 50–59°F (10–15°C). Three to six months later the root, mostly with a tiny bulb, pushes through the seed case; this is the signal for the cool-storage period to begin. A refrigerator kept at 36–39°F (2–4°C), or a cellar or other suitable cool place up to 46°F (8°C), provide the best conditions for the following two to three months, after which the seedlings are planted out into warm quarters and produce their first leaf within two to four weeks. The timetable works out very well in practice; the freshly harvested seeds are put into warm storage during October, November and December; the cold storage period occupies January, February and March; then the seedlings are ready for planting out just as spring is about to commence, and have ample opportunity to develop with the whole of the summer before them. The timetable is, of course, subject to variation, depending on whether new or old seed is used, if cold storage takes place in a refrigerator or cellar, and also on the particular variety. Newly sown seed of *L. auratum* can be obstinate, and some may lie dormant for a long time; remarkable, too, is their uneven habit of germination with some seed germinating either long before or long after the main bulk. This is not necessarily a disadvantage; it is perhaps even one of nature's protective devices, for if circumstances suddenly turn unfavourable for the germination of the variety, not all seedlings will be destroyed. Breeders usually segregate the early-emerging seedlings for use in breeding in the hope that this trait can be genetically fixed.

If glass jars are not used, boxes, pots, or even polythene bags make alternative containers, though they lack the versatility and transparency of glass, which aids accurate control. As in the case of bulb-scale multiplication, it is important that the growing medium should be only slightly damp, never really wet, and that it should be sterilized before use.

The fortunate gardeners of the United States are able to buy already germinated lily seeds for immediate planting in their gardens, but usually only of the Auratum and Speciosum types.

Sowing seeds

Seeds are obtained from home-grown plants or through exchange or purchase.

As soon as the seed capsules open, they are carefully removed from the plant and dried in a warm room. The 200–500 seeds are later put into a bowl. Unsuitable seeds are not as heavy as the others, and consequently are easily separated from those containing an embryo (a dark nucleus in the centre of the seed) by blowing lightly into the bowl.

Old seeds often give only poor results. In general, lily seeds stored in a warm room retain their germination for only two years, after which time it drops to nil. If seeds, after being dried in a desiccator over a drying agent, are stored in an airtight container at room temperature, they

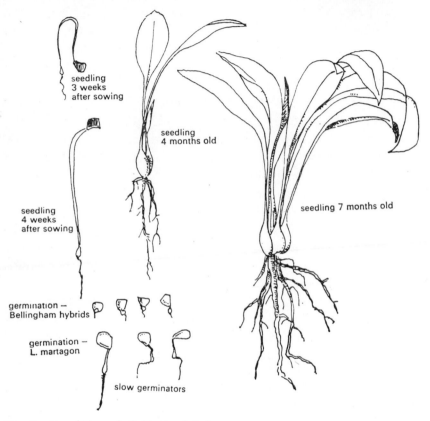

seedling
3 weeks
after sowing

seedling
4 months old

seedling 7 months old

seedling
4 weeks
after sowing

germination –
Bellingham hybrids

germination –
L. martagon

slow germinators

Germination of lily seeds (half natural size).

remain viable for five years, and 30 per cent of them even germinate after seven years. Still better results are obtained if, after desiccation, the airtight jam-jars can be stored at a temperature of 41°F (5°C); an experiment with *L. regale* seed so treated and stored has confirmed that, even after 15 years' storage, 93 per cent of the seeds remain viable.

The seed, like bulb scales, should be treated with a fungicide before being sown; to apply the dressing, both seed and the prescribed amount of fungicide are put into a tin, and shaken well until the seeds are completely coated.

Sowing in the open
For optimum results, it is advisable to sow only the quick-germinating seeds of lilies in Group 1 in the open, and then only between the end of March and mid-May. The seed bed must not be too firm, and should preferably consist of light soil rich in humus which, if necessary, can be improved with a peat dressing. If the soil is not in very good condition, an application of low-nitrogen fertilizer will prove beneficial, provided it is worked well into the ground. Seeds should be sown $\frac{2}{5}$–$\frac{3}{5}$ inch deep, $\frac{2}{5}$ inch apart with 6–10 inches between rows, and watered immediately with a fine spray. Never allow the seed bed to dry out.

To keep seedlings growing after they have germinated, applications of 0·3 per cent solution of a liquid fertilizer every two weeks are beneficial. Of particular importance is the scrupulous removal of weeds as soon as they show; if they are not removed at once, there is every likelihood that the small, newly formed lily bulbs will be loosened or, worse still, pulled out together with the weeds.

The young plants also appreciate a mulch of either peat or sawdust during the winter months. This also avoids the possibility of their being lifted out of the ground by alternate frost and thaw. Mulching materials such as leaves, grass-cuttings and straw provide too dense a cover, and are best avoided.

Seedlings ought ideally to be left in their original beds until the autumn of the second year or the spring of the third year, when they can be safely transplanted to their permanent positions. Occasionally, one of the seedlings in the quick-germinating group provides a pleasant surprise, and flowers as early as the second year.

Unfortunately, open sowings usually suffer from heavy seedling losses, through a variety of causes – weed competition, flooding as a result of heavy rains and thunderstorms, and bad overwintering during the first year. Open sowing perhaps has advantages in maritime climates, but is hardly to be recommended in a continental climate subject to dry summers and sharply alternating frost and thaw conditions.

Sowing under glass

Notably better results are obtained if seeds can be raised in a coldframe. Good weather permits sowing as early as the end of February, seeds germinate more quickly, seedlings develop better and remain protected through the winter months. Ventilation and the provision of shade during sunny weather are, of course, important.

Even earlier sowings are possible if seed-boxes or pots are stored in a veranda, on a window-sill or anywhere in a heated room, provided sufficient light is available. When the weather turns warmer, the seed containers are transferred to a coldframe.

If a greenhouse is available it, of course, provides all these advantages and more. Sowings can be brought forward to January, management is more efficient, weather has less influence, and pests and disease are easier to control. Rare and difficult seeds or precious seed from first crosses are more safely raised in a greenhouse than anywhere else.

Soil-less culture

This term signifies the raising of plants in inert materials which conduct water to the plant but are devoid of all plant nutrients. Nitrogen, phosphate, potash and other necessary nutrients and trace elements must be continuously or regularly supplied to plants in aqueous solution.

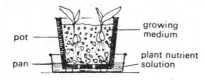

growing medium

pot

plant nutrient solution

pan

Hydroponic cultivation in pot or frame

A small-scale arrangement is quickly and easily put into operation. A flower pot with drainage holes, or a seedbox, is filled with either pumice gravel, vermiculite or perlite, and stood in a watertight tin or similar receptacle. The seed is sown in the vermiculite and watered with a suitable plant nutrient solution; any excess drains into the tin, and is drawn up by the porous vermiculite as and when required.

It is only when this method is used on a larger scale, in a coldframe for instance, that its real advantages become apparent. The first task is the removal of the old soil from the frame and its partial replacement with a thin layer of sand arranged in such a way as to allow a fall of 1–2 inches towards the middle, or one corner. Next, the entire floor and sides (up to a height of 6–8 inches) of the frame are lined with a sheet of polythene. To facilitate free drainage, a brass or copper plate fitted with a pipe

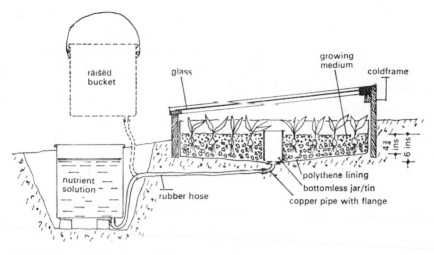

Hydroponic cultivation in a coldframe

flange is securely glued to the polythene sheet at its lowest point; a heated nail or knitting needle neatly cuts the polythene to fit around the outlet flange, to which in turn is attached a rubber tube sufficiently long to hang down outside the frame. To prevent the growing medium, still to be put into the frame, from blocking the water outlet, it is first covered with a bottomless jar or tin. The growing medium, whether pumice gravel, vermiculite, or perlite, is sieved with a $\frac{1}{4}$-inch mesh; the larger particles are then used to fill the lower portion of the frame, the fine particles to top it up to a height of $4\frac{1}{2}$–6 inches.

Pumice gravel, a natural, porous and volcanic mineral, is ideal for this purpose. Though it is always moist, it does not retain excessive water.

Its porosity, and the air space between the particles, favour good root development. Vermiculite and perlite are both exfoliated minerals, also light and porous, but with less or no air room between the particles.

Provided the frame area is no larger than 10 square feet, a semi-automatic watering device is easily arranged. A bucket with a capacity of $4\frac{1}{2}$–$6\frac{1}{2}$ gallons ($5\frac{1}{4}$–8 US gallons) is connected to the rubber tubing and filled with plant nutrient solution. On lifting the bucket, the solution flows into the growing medium and is absorbed; when the bucket is lowered, the excess fluid flows back into the bucket. The liquid requirements of frames of more than 10 square feet would necessitate a liquid container which, when full, would be too heavy to lift; the alternatives are watering by hand with a fine-rosed can and permitting any excess to drain away, or installing a pump.

One or other of the generally available proprietary brands of completely balanced liquid manures are suitable for making the plant nutrient solution, although its analysis should be checked first. A few additional drops of phosphoric acid may be necessary to adjust the pH around 5·5 to 6·5 (slightly acid). Correct pH values are easy to determine, either with a pH meter or with one of the specially prepared test papers.

Frequency of watering can vary from once a week to once every second day, depending entirely on the weather, and duration and strength of sunshine. Watering must cease completely during the autumn, and can only be resumed in the spring, when the warmer weather returns.

Frames should be closed during periods of rain to prevent the nutrient solution from being leached out, while moisture losses due to evaporation are easily made good through extra watering. To guard against fusarium, a fungicide watered over the whole of the frame area once every four weeks proves beneficial. The nutrient solution must always be renewed at regular four-weekly intervals; any old solution which may be left is best discarded.

Sowings can be made as early as February, March or April. Seeds are sown in shallow drills and covered with a layer of vermiculite $\frac{1}{2}$ inch thick. The space between rows need not be wide, as the nutrient solution is able to provide for a larger number of plants even if Iris, Hemerocallis, or alpines are sown at the same time – all of which will do equally well under the same conditions. Normal treatment along the lines of the usual coldframe culture is all that is necessary, but frames should be kept

Hydroponic cultivation in the green-house

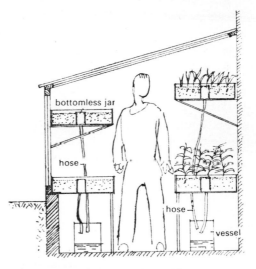

closed after the seed is first sown; once germination has taken place, shade and ventilation are essential to prevent the temperature inside the frame from rising too high.

The advantages of soil-less culture are as follows:

1. Healthy growth in a clean growing medium
2. Satisfactory, quick, high germination
3. Controlled fertilizer application of selected plant nutrients
4. Consequent strong and quick seedling development
5. No losses due to fungi
6. No worms, insects or slugs
7. No weeds or weeding, therefore no physical damage to seedlings
8. Impossible to water to excess because of porous growing medium
9. Therefore first-class root development
10. Exceptionally easy to lift without damaging roots

The same growing medium can be used again, but must first be disinfected with formalin, once the seedlings have been removed. The formalin solution should be left *in situ* for several days, and then well washed out of the growing medium, prior to its being air-dried.

The same method is also used for greenhouse work; it is clean, simple, labour-saving, and capable of producing seedlings which flower as early as the second year.

Recent experiments and trials in the United States have established that good aeration of the growing medium is essential for successful germination and seedling development; the better the aeration and drainage, the better the germination and seedling growth. This in itself is yet another recommendation for soil-less culture.

6. Breeding new lilies

New lilies can be obtained by cross-fertilization, mutation, and through polyploidy.

The term 'cross-fertilization' refers to the fusion of male and female gametes of two specially selected but different varieties or species. Seed resulting from such a cross produces a hybrid lily, which may have two parents utterly different in appearance, character, and growing habits.

Mutations are usually spontaneous, but can also be artificially induced; they are transmissible to the progeny. If, however, a whole complex of cell tissue changes genetically, it is termed a 'sport'. Artificially induced mutations are created by subjecting plant tissue to gamma-rays or x-rays: results are mostly negative, i.e., plants or their offspring are deformed or sterile.

A polyploid plant has more than the usual number of chromosomes; again, the process is artificially induced, and usually leads to stronger and more vigorous plants as well as flowers of larger than normal size.

The cross-fertilization of lilies

The ever-increasing popularity of lilies in our gardens during recent years is undoubtedly due to the development of hybrids, their enhanced beauty, and their universal adaptability – wild lilies do not unfortunately possess the latter virtue, and have individual and often difficult requirements which can only rarely be satisfied in the average garden.

Wild types continually and frequently crossed with each other produce more suitable lilies for garden culture, because they have lost some of their parents' undesirable characteristics, but breeders can only obtain such results provided they rigorously select the progeny of these crosses and ruthlessly discard any which fall short of requirements. Thousands of lilies are discarded in this way, certainly many thousands more than those few which eventually reach the stage of a variety.

Selection takes account of every characteristic of the plant – not only the shape, size and colour of the flowers, but also their number and spacing, the length of pedicels, whether the flowers are pendulous, erect or horizontal, the number of leaves, their colour, the height of the main stem. Every detail is considered – many of them never noticed by a non-specialist. The essential aims are vigour of growth, health, and disease resistance. The ability of a lily to multiply quickly is also of the greatest commercial importance; a lily which multiplies by axil bulbils and/or bulb scales is of greater value than a plant without bulbils or one which produces relatively few bulbs from scales. Only if a breeder is satisfied that his new plants possess the maximum number of desirable attributes will he make arrangements for large-scale multiplication.

The raising of new lilies is an expensive process – the success of one cross has to compensate the professional breeder for the heavy expenses incurred for the thousands of initial crosses and subsequent raising of plants in expensive greenhouse space, most of them ruthlessly discarded for failure of one or another characteristic.

Relationship and incompatibility

Not every lily crosses with every other lily. Lilies only cross with each other if they are closely related, and even then success is not inevitable; the only means of determining compatibility is by trial – visual observation or academic knowledge is of no use in this matter. Whether a cross 'takes' or not is often influenced by uncontrollable circumstances. As a rule fair and dry weather and a warm summer contribute greatly to a cross's success whereas many a cross has been spoilt by a cold and wet summer.

One failed cross between two lilies does not necessarily prove that they are incompatible, and many crosses of the two particular varieties need to be made before the case is proved one way or the other; to be absolutely certain, numerous parent plants of the same variety or species need to be used (also reciprocally) and, if possible, under differing circumstances and weather conditions.

The use of the word 'reciprocal' in this context means the interchange of plants as male and female parents. If in the first case plant A was fertilized with pollen from plant B, then in a reciprocal cross plant B must be fertilized with pollen from plant A. The use of reciprocal crosses often enables breeders to overcome anatomical and genetical insufficiencies, e.g., sterile pollen of one parent.

Successful crosses between widely different species are rare, and are mostly brought about by sheer good luck; E. Debras of Orléans succeeded in 1925 with *L.* × *aurelianense* from *L. sargentiae* × *L. henryi*.

To cross two lilies, the pollen (male) of one plant is transferred to the stigma (female) of another. The pollen absorbs the nutrient secreted by the stigma, and the protoplasm in the pollen grains produce tubes which grow through the style to the ovary, where they fuse with the female nucleus. To obtain the maximum quantity of seed in the autumn, enough pollen is necessary to fertilize the several hundred available egg cells in the ovary.

Two lilies of the same species cross in the same manner as closely related species. It is possible to cross, for example, *L. davidii*, not only with another plant of *L. davidii*, but also with its near-related *L. davidii* var. *willmottiae*. But a cross between *L. davidii* and *L. auratum* or *L. speciosum* will not succeed, because the relationship between them is too slight, and they belong to another section.

Self-pollination – that is, the fertilization of a plant with its own pollen – is only rarely possible. This barrier is described as self-incompatibility or self-sterility. If self-sterile plants are multiplied by bulb scales to the clone stage, all further plants obtained from the clones are self-sterile, i.e., they are unable to cross-pollinate, and therefore produce no seeds. The term 'clone' refers to all those plants which are vegetatively reproduced from one original parent.

In addition to the genetical prerequisites, the pollen must always be viable, and capable of fertilizing the female egg cells; old or rain-damaged pollen is of little use.

For the female organs, too, certain conditions are essential to successful fertilization. The stigma must be ripe to take the pollen. This stage is reached after the flower has opened, and only when the stigma has secreted a gummy, sugar-containing substance, although previously deposited pollen also 'takes'. Rain spoils the receptivity of the stigma.

Once the stigma has been dusted with pollen, it is useless to attempt to fertilize again; but a self-sterile plant, although already dusted with its own pollen, is able to produce seeds if pollinated with another plant.

Another possibility is the fertilization of various lilies with a mixture of pollen. This method is of advantage in an attempt to break through quickly the incompatibility barrier between lilies only distantly related, and speeds determination of the fruitful pollen, which can be identified later by single crosses between individuals.

The use of pollen mixtures, combined with the fact that pollination fertilizes a great number of ovules, always results in nonuniform seed.

Cross-incompatibility and self-incompatibility can occasionally be overcome by the use of growth hormones. According to Dr S. L. Emsweller, the ovary is treated with growth hormones previously dissolved in lanolin. One per cent of naphthalene acetamide is dissolved in previously heated and liquefied lanolin until the mixture turns dark in colour. The cold fat is applied to the base of the ovary, which in trumpet lilies can only be reached by first removing one of the petals.

This technique, limited in use and impracticable for large-scale work, induced *L. longiflorum Croft* and some other lilies to set seeds through self-fertilization.

Pollination technique

Crossing lilies artificially is not difficult; the flowers and reproduction organs are large and accessible. The style, topped by the stigma, grows from the ovary and emerges through the centre of the open flower. Around the ovary and the stigma stand six filaments, each one with an

20. *Ralph*, a 51-inch-tall, redcurrant-coloured, star-shaped, upright lily. White trumpet lilies grown as companion plants provide an effective contrast
21. *Rosenfinger*, a charming, pink trumpet lily, very graceful; light shade is more suitable than full sun

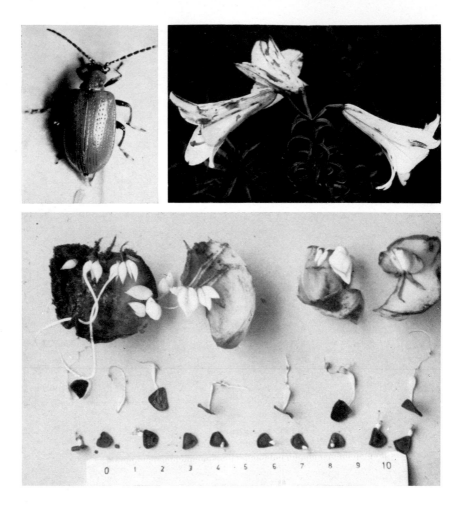

22. Lily beetle, a red-backed insect which in common with its larvae destroys leaves, flowers and buds

23. Botrytis, a fungus which attacks flowers, leaves, stems and even the seed-capsules, eventually destroying the seeds. Excessive rain and damp situations encourage the disease, which is best prevented and controlled with a Bordeaux mixture

24. *First row*: development of bulbs from bulb scales. *Second row*: germinating seeds of *L. martagon*; the thicker portions indicate future bulbs. *Third row*: *L. canadense* seeds germinating; the seeds have already produced their first shoots, from which bulbs develop. Leaf development, not yet present, is only triggered off after seeds have been subjected to a period of cold for three months

25. *L. amabile* comes from Korea. Reliable, long-living, with glistening red or yellow flowers. The Fiesta hybrids have inherited its beauty and glistening petals

26. Aurelian hybrids. Midsummer-flowering trumpet lilies

27. *L. auratum*, the Gold-Rayed Lily of Japan, perhaps the Queen of Lilies

28. *L. canadense*, probably the most graceful of all wild lilies, requires careful siting and only reaches perfection on damp, acid, peaty soils

29. *L. candidum* requires a sunny corner in loam, and dislikes disturbance. Its faultless, immaculate, white flowers have been regarded as symbols of purity and innocence since medieval times

30. Red Auratum hybrids, perhaps the most sumptuous of all flowers

anther pivoted at the top which contains the pollen. If the flower opens during the early morning, the anthers are still closed, and remain so until warm sunshine releases their pollen. At the same time the secretions of the stigma are brought into action, making it ready to receive the pollen, i.e., receptive for the pollen tubes to grow into it.

Insects, wind, and physical shaking of the plant are the natural means of pollination.

Artificial cross-pollination should be timed to take place earlier than it would do in the natural way – this ensures that only the chosen pollen is used for fertilization, and so prevents stray and undesired pollen and the plant's own pollen from spoiling the cross.

Most lily-breeders use their own preferred and often personally evolved pollination method. The following describes my own technique of controlled pollination:

The flower which is to receive the pollen is first emasculated, that is, the still-closed anthers are removed with tweezers before or as soon as the flower opens, usually during early morning. An anther is next removed (again with tweezers, but now they must be previously disinfected with alcohol) from the partner plant and used to dust the stigma of the first flower. To avoid further and unwanted cross-pollination, the dusted stigma is protected with a small aluminium foil hood (chocolate wrapping formed around the point of a pencil), and gently sealed with finger pressure around the style. The cross (mother and father) is entered in the breeding book and preceded with the number of the cross, e.g.

No. 147   18.6.1966   *L. martagon cattaniae* × *L. hansonii*

A label bearing the same number is fastened to the stem of the pollinated flower. Paper labels are soon spoiled by the weather, and do not provide as permanent a record as the foil of an empty toothpaste tube which has the number 'engraved' on it by a typewriter.

Two to three weeks after the flower has faded, the ovary begins to swell, becomes erect, and so confirms that fertilization has taken place.

Other breeders use fine paint-brushes or pipe-cleaners for the transfer of pollen, but risk contamination from unwanted pollen unless a new instrument is used for every cross. The Americans use artificially produced drinking straws, instead of foil hoods, for the protection of the pollinated stigma; straws of various diameters are necessary if the stigma, particularly big in trumpet lilies, is not to be damaged.

The pollen employed for a cross can either be freshly gathered from a flower or be a few days or even weeks old provided it has been air-dried. Pollen keeps for a month if stored in a desiccator at 28·6°F (−2°C). Lily pollen packed in glass tubes or aluminium foil travels well, and facilitates

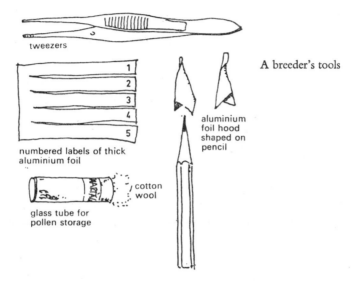

tweezers

1
2
3
4
5

numbered labels of thick aluminium foil

glass tube for pollen storage

cotton wool

aluminium foil hood shaped on pencil

A breeder's tools

not only the crossing of home-grown lilies with those overseas but also the cross-fertilization of lilies of different flowering periods.

Other methods are open to breeders who wish to cross early and late-flowering lilies. Certain varieties are greenhouse-forced for early flowering like their partners; in the case of others, the bulbs are kept in cold storage for longer than the usual period in order to delay flowering.

If breeding is to be successful, several essentials must be observed: cleanliness during pollination, use of flowers only just opened, rich cover of pollen on the stigma, pollen uncontaminated with that from other flowers, cleanliness of pollen storage containers and their correct labelling, and complete and safe protection of the stigma to prevent 'foreign' pollen from reaching it. The penalty for insufficient attention to these important details is wasted time and seedlings unrepresentative of the original cross.

Purpose of artificial pollination

Artificial pollination achieves two aims. Firstly, it ensures the true reproduction of a lily species without being spoiled by 'foreign' pollen. Secondly, it enables hybrids to be produced by crossing two different lily species or varieties. The second possibility, called hybridization, opens the door to an influx of a host of lilies of various colours and shapes which have been unknown and which grow better in cultivation than their wild forms.

The characteristics inherited as a result of a cross are as per Mendelian segregation. The first cross between two different lilies produces fairly uniform plants (F_1). Back-crossing of the F_1 generation with their parents or their F_1 brothers and sisters produces a great number of varied and interesting form and colour variants (F_2). Generations obtained from further crosses are termed F_2, F_3, and so on (F stands for filial).

The back-crossing (one or more times) of the F_1 generation with their parents increases and strengthens the desired characteristics in the following generations.

The art of the breeder lies in the selection of plants which through further breeding produce the characteristics which he aims at and which he hopes to strengthen and to fix (selection), or to breed a lily which combines the many and various attributes obtained from crossing differently constituted types (combination).

Polyploidy

We know that lilies normally have 24 chromosomes, a pair each of 12 types, contained in each cell nucleus. We call such a plant a diploid. In 1935, four American research workers, A. F. Blakeslee, A. G. Avery, B. R. Nebel, and M. L. Ruttle, were successful in doubling the number of chromosomes in each cell nucleus by treating seed or seedlings with a colchicine solution. Colchicine is a highly poisonous alkaloid obtained from the autumn crocus (*Colchicum*), which acts only on dividing cells or tissues in growth. The action of this poison during the cell division, and especially during division of the chromosomes, ensures the successful doubling of their numbers. If during subsequent cell-splitting the double number of chromosomes can be retained, a tetraploid is formed.

To ensure the production of tetraploid plants from even a single tetraploid cell, it is essential that the colchicine contacts the growing point as cell division takes place there, as indeed does the whole growing process. If other cells are treated, it could happen that only one leaf or even only part of one leaf develops tetraploidy. Treatment with colchicine is therefore a shot in the dark, a shot which very seldom hits the target.

A tetraploid lily has twice as many chromosomes as a diploid plant, namely $2 \times 24 = 48$ chromosomes. The difference is noticeable in the bigger and thicker leaves, the taller and stronger stems and the blooms, which are appreciably larger with significantly improved flowers – exactly what the breeder aims for, stronger plants with bigger blooms.

Several tetraploids with noticeably larger and more vigorous flowers have already been bred from *L. longiflorum* (Easter Lily). S. L. Emsweller has treated his diploid hybrids *Cavalier*, *Mega*, and *Brandywine* with colchicine, and produced significantly stronger tetraploids.

The doubling of chromosome numbers is also used to induce fertility in sterile hybrids. It usually makes the plant fertile and set seed, if dusted with the pollen of another tetraploid plant. The pollen from tetraploid plants is bigger than that of diploid lilies, and so are the stomata on the undersurface of leaves. Crossing diploid lilies with tetraploids can also result in seed being produced, which when grown produce triploids, usually sterile, of $36 (3 \times 12)$ chromosomes.

To induce polyploidy artificially, previously separated bulb scales are treated with colchicine. To stimulate cell division, the bulb scales are first stored under warm conditions for several days. The broken edge of the bulb scales, where a callus always forms, is immersed in a colchicine solution (0·2 per cent) for approximately two hours. After drying and dusting with a fungicide, normal bulb-scale multiplication methods are followed under damp and warm conditions. Treatment with colchicine, as already mentioned, is a shot in the dark; comparatively few targets are hit – less than 1:100. To make sure of securing some success, it is advisable to treat as many bulb scales as possible.

In addition to bulb scales, sprouting seeds or seedlings can also be subjected to colchicine treatment. An exposure of between two and 10 hours in a 0·2 per cent colchicine solution has proved the most suitable.

Breeding

A basic knowledge of inheritance is essential to the serious breeder. In fact, it is only during the present century that science has begun to grapple with the problem and discovered the chromosomes in the cell nucleus (and the genes in the chromosomes) which are the carriers of inherited characteristics. Each gene is responsible for the transmission of a particular characteristic to the future generation. The almost countless number of characteristics collectively make up the picture of the plant and influence every part of it. Examples are: shape of bulb, plant and flower; number and colour of bulb scales; pendant, erect or horizontally held flowers; small, broad, pointed or blunt petals; colour of flower – red, dark-red or mahogany-red; colour of the centre; speckles on the flower petals – their colour, size, number, pattern of distribution – and so on. The number of these and other characteristics reaches into many thousands, and also includes the less visible attributes of a plant, such as ability to withstand disease, susceptibility to frost, preference or dislikes for certain types of soil, etc.

At least one gene is responsible for each characteristic, and often more than one, as is the case in increased intensity of colour.

The breeder must learn to recognize and differentiate between even the smallest characteristics, whether advantageous or disadvantageous, and to try and select parents for further crosses so that they are always superior to previous generations. These small, almost imperceptible changes often lead to greater overall improvement than a spectacular colour variation or other big change: for instance, the length of pedicels (long pedicels give the plant an air of elegance), or if petals are flat and broad instead of reflexed (flowers with flat, broad petals seem larger). Details such as these enable new crosses to supersede older varieties and enhance their value – but only if they lend themselves to comparatively trouble-free multiplication. A most beautiful lily may be capable of taking many prizes at flower shows but be commercially useless and unlikely to ever reach the stage of distribution, if for any reason it is only capable of slow and therefore costly multiplication.

Breeding necessitates keeping meticulous records and numbering, in sequence, every seedling, otherwise it is quite impossible to establish and to review, with hindsight, from which parents desirable characteristics have been inherited and, even more important, to eliminate those which have only contributed negative characteristics.

Breeders devote particular care to the raising of seedlings, as undue losses nullify much of the laborious work of crossing. For example, E. Debras obtained only two seeds from his successful cross *L. sargentiae* × *L. henryi*. Although both seeds germinated, one seedling was later lost; if both had succumbed we would probably have had to wait for many more years before obtaining a hybrid like *L.* × *aurelianense*.

It is possible that freshly harvested seeds from a cross are not capable of germination even though they may contain embryos. Dr S. L. Emsweller found this when crossing *L. speciosum* with *L. auratum*, but solved the problem by removing (from the same cross) the embryo from the still-green seed. The embryo was treated like orchid seed and germinated in previously sterilized test-tubes filled with an agar-agar growth medium. The lack of viability in seeds of this cross was due to growth inhibitors forming tumours which, in turn, killed the germ; subsequent analysis established that the growth inhibitors consisted of three organic acids which can be partially removed by washing the seed for 15 hours in continuously changing water.

Hybridization is undoubtedly the most interesting part of lily-breeding. The lifelong work of the man who is the best-known lily-breeder not only in the United States, but in the world, Jan de Graaff, demonstrates what remarkable success can be achieved. Not only has de Graaff produced lilies less demanding in their individual requirements which grow well in gardens under a wide range of conditions; he also dominates the world lily market through planned and scientifically controlled large-scale breeding.

The enthusiast can also create new lilies. However many beautiful lilies there may be in our gardens, it is difficult to contain one's patience for the first home-crossed lily to open and to see it with amazement one sunny morning for the first time – face to face! The feeling of having created something new gives real satisfaction.

The breeding on a wide front as practised by Jan de Graaff, the largest commercial producer, has advanced tremendously. But we must also be grateful to nonprofessional lily enthusiasts for both the small advances and indeed for some of the big forward steps in lily-breeding. E. Debras, of Orléans, is to be thanked for *L.* × *aurelianense* – our gardens would be very much poorer without it and the many thousands of its varieties. Australia's Roy M. Wallace bred the unique Auratum-Speciosum hybrid *Jillian Wallace*, which combines the beauty and majestic colour of two Japanese lilies, and excited world-wide admiration among breeders. Professor Patterson, of Saskatoon, Canada, was the first to cross successfully *L. cernuum* with the Davidii-Umbellatum-Elegans complex and thus brought new colours and pastel shades of mother-of-pearl into the colour range of lilies.

Hundreds of breeders set themselves the task of producing a completely yellow Regal Lily, but none succeeded until L. N. Freimann, of Bellingham, United States, raised one in his small garden. His professional knowledge of breeding and selection, a sure intuition, the will to succeed, and the patience of the born breeder, combined with many years of continuous crosses, helped him to produce *Golden Regal* after 14 years of work!

The potential of new crosses is vast, and certainly not yet exhausted. The hereditary characteristics dormant in lilies make countless new combinations possible. Amateur breeders have thousands of possibilities open to them and the chance, through controlled and purposeful breeding, of producing a lily which is as good as any now available; nor will the more serious and scientific find any difficulty in satisfying their creativity in this field.

7. The enemies of the lily

Pests

Voles

Voles seem to consider all bulbous plants a delicacy, and invariably attack them. It is difficult to eliminate voles completely, as they usually invade gardens from neighbouring fields, but their numbers can be effectively reduced with poisoned bait, gas, or traps.

A paste of red lead painted onto the outer surface of the bulbs also affords some protection, as does wire netting placed round the bulbs and buried in the soil; some nurserymen sell specially-made wire baskets for this purpose.

Field-mice

Damage is likely to take place during the winter months, and usually only when bulbs are covered with the thick layers of straw or leaves in which mice like to overwinter. Any one of the good and numerous proprietary poison baits will control them effectively.

Slugs and snails

Unless slugs and snails are kept in check, they can cause considerable damage to young, growing shoots. The leading shoot is usually the first to suffer, but seedlings, even if kept in a coldframe, are often attacked. Bulbs, too, suffer from slugs, which during the autumn and winter months retreat into the soil. Fortunately, both slugs and snails are easily controlled if one of the various slug baits produced from a base of metaldehyde is scattered on the lily beds. Bait application should commence as soon as the weather turns warmer during early spring, and be repeated frequently throughout the growing season.

Nematodes

These microscopic worms penetrate the roots, leaves, and buds of plants from the outside. Nematode development is dependent on soil moisture and rather high temperatures. The amateur has little to worry about, and will hardly know of the existence of nematodes, but they can be a serious nuisance to the commercial producer, who may suffer great and severe losses, particularly as nematodes multiply rapidly wherever monoculture without rotation is practised.

As far as lilies are concerned, only two types of nematode need receive attention: leaf and flower nematodes, and root nematodes.

Leaf and flower nematodes enter the leaf through the stomata, but require damp weather to enable them to do so. Leaves and flowers become discoloured, lifeless, malformed and eventually turn brown. To combat leaf nematodes (mainly of the type *Aphelenchoides fragariae* and *A. ritzemabosi*) the bulbs are immersed in a formalin solution (one part 45 per cent formalin plus 200 parts of water) for 60 minutes, and must be held at exactly 111°F (44°C). It is vital that both temperature and timing should be exact if the treatment is to be successful. Bulbs are subsequently dipped in a fungicide solution and air-dried, and should be planted within three days of treatment. Protection must be maintained to control those nematodes which may have wandered to the extremities of the plant – either the stem or the leaves – by spraying plants three times during the growing period (allowing four to five days between each application) with a systemic insecticide, Metasystox or Nemafos.

Root nematodes, the free-living *Pratylenchus penetrans* and *P. pratensis*, are chiefly concerned with lilies, and are not to be confused with nematodes causing gall formation on roots. They are more difficult to control than the leaf and flower nematodes, and live in the soil, from where they enter the lily bulb. Attacks are recognized by yellowing and dying of leaves and severe destruction of roots until only a few stumps are left. In the larger lily beds attacks are usually confined to a few isolated patches.

Care must be taken only to plant nematode-free bulbs in nematode-free soil. If attacks do take place, the damaged roots of affected bulbs should be cut back to healthy tissue which automatically removes some of the pests. Infested ground has to be treated by chemical means, and proprietary products such as Basamid, Shell-DD, Di-Trapex (WN 12), Larvacide, Terabol, Trapex, and Vapam are all useful. According to manufacturers' instructions, the chemical should always be applied to freshly forked ground, which is then sealed either with polythene foil or by flooding. Root nematodes are often the cause of secondary infection, namely fungi. Dutch findings indicate that certain plants are nematode-resistant; Tagetes is an enemy of free-living nematodes.

Millipedes

Recent US observations have dispelled the once prevalent idea that millipedes do not damage lily bulbs; on the contrary, they eat the bulb scales and cause considerable damage. Aldrin or Gamma pellets provide effective control if scattered over the soil surface and also if buried in the ground; systemic insecticides applied in water solution are equally effective.

Lily beetle (Crioceris lilii Scop.)

This pest (22) only attacks lilies and Lily of the Valley. It is $\frac{1}{3}$ inch long, sealingwax-red, and lays red eggs, neatly arranged in rows, on the underside of lily leaves during May and June. The yellow larvae soon emerge and continue the damage by feeding on leaves, buds and flowers. Lily beetle damage is characterized by a series of semicircular notches on the leaf margins. These pests are fortunately confined to certain locations, but if present they unerringly find their way to the nearest available lily. Remedies are numerous: physical removal of beetles and larvae from the plant, dusting with parathion, repeated spraying with DDT or Meta-systox. Plants need to be watched carefully during the autumn for a second generation of beetles.

A close relation, which attacks lilies and onions, is *Crioceris merdigera* L.

Lily thrips (*Liothrips vaneecki*   Priesner)

Lily thrips are small insects, $\frac{1}{16}$ inch long at the most, and shaped like a comma; they are either black, brown, or milk-white according to their stage of development.

Thrips live in the spaces between lily scales on which they feed, severe attacks causing flower malformation. Thrips mainly damage and puncture the outer skin of the bulb scale, which in turn make it prone to fungal attack. Lilies with a loosely formed bulb system, like the Asiatic varieties and also hybrids, are more likely to be attacked than the firmer-bulbed trumpet lilies. Thrips-damaged bulbs can always be easily detected by their most disagreeable smell! Thrips attacks are fairly widespread in the United States, both among wild and cultivated species, also in Japan and Europe. The Dutch method of repelling these attacks is to immerse the bulbs for 15 minutes in a solution of 4 cubic inches parathion (25 per cent) to $2\frac{2}{5}$ gallons ($2\frac{9}{10}$ US gallons) of water, followed by a cold-water rinse. The ground must also be treated with $\frac{1}{4}$ pound of aldrin to every 80 square feet. The Americans advise hot-water treatment, whereby the bulbs are kept in water at 110°F (43·5°C) for one hour. It is important that the water should remain at this exact temperature throughout the period of treatment. The spraying of growing plants with a systemic insecticide, parathion or Metasystox, is beneficial. Dusting the bulbs when they are planted with DDT is also deadly for thrips.

Aphides

In addition to damaging stems, leaves and flowers, aphides are also responsible for the spread of virus diseases; particularly dangerous in this connection are the green peach aphis (*Myzus persicae*) and the potato aphis (*Macrosiphum solanifolii*). The winged forms fly from plant to plant, puncture the surface to feed, and so transmit virus diseases, if present, from one plant to another.

Three-to-four-weekly spraying with a systemic insecticide, such as Metasystox, is recommended. All plants susceptible to aphides, e.g. roses, in the vicinity of lilies, as well as the lilies themselves, should be sprayed to avoid rapid reinfestation. Systemic insecticides are absorbed by the plant and remain in their sap stream for up to three weeks; spraying, therefore, not only kills the aphides on the plant at the time but also all those which try and feed on the plant up to three weeks after spraying.

Fungus diseases

Botrytis and fusarium are the most prevalent fungus diseases, and they can both cause severe damage. US growers also have to cope with a number of other fungal diseases, but these two are the main ones.

Botrytis

This fairly common and widespread fungus (23) damages leaves, blooms and stems. It is most prevalent in summer during humid and warm periods when sunshine and rain, mostly as a result of thunderstorms, alternate. The first signs, usually on the leaves, appear in the form of small round or elliptical-shaped brown areas (*Botrytis elliptica*), but during the later stages a second fungus (*B. cinerea*) attacks leaves, stem, flowers and seed capsules. Clusters of spores cover the whole plant with a greyish mould.

Botrytis develops quickly among wet petals, which after blooming and during storms drop onto the ground and from there reinfect hitherto healthy plants. Leaves and stems die off in turn. Although botrytis does not directly attack the bulb, it retards or even stops its development, as leaves are no longer able to assimilate nutrients, and are therefore unable to nourish the bulb. Seed capsules are of course also affected, and seeds loose their viability.

Spraying every two weeks from the end of May onwards with either captan (orthocide) or thiram (TMTD) (Pomarsol) is useful. The Americans, including Jan de Graaff, find that Bordeaux mixture is difficult to improve upon as a control material. It is made as follows:

To obtain 2 gallons (2⅖ US gallons) of spray material, 2½ ounces of slaked lime is stirred into 1 gallon (1⅕ US gallon) of water contained in a plastic bucket (a metal bucket is liable to be holed by the mixture). Similarly, and again using a nonmetal container, 2½ ounces copper sulphate are dissolved in 1 gallon (1⅕ US gallon) of water. The copper sulphate solution is then poured into the well-stirred lime solution (never the other way round). Finally a spreading agent or ⅘ cubic inch of Alginure is added.

The spraying of lilies against botrytis should take place every 14 days, particularly where lily plantings are fairly dense, for under such circumstances plants remain damp for longer periods, and provide ideal conditions for botrytis to spread.

Fusarium

Probably more lilies – up to 80 per cent – are lost from this fungoid disease than from any other cause. Practically all Auratum bulbs imported from Japan die after a year or two from this very trouble.

Bulb scales and bulb basal plates are attacked, and show signs of brown or black-coloured injuries which spread outwards to the roots and cause them to die off. Further progress of the disease breaks up the bulb scales until often only their tips remain. The fungus *Fusarium oxysporum* f. *lilii* is the cause, although other fungi and bacteria are also partially responsible for this destruction. It is found in most soils, and builds up rapidly if lilies continue to be grown on the same ground.

To avoid infection, beds should be chemically treated before lilies are planted out. Formalin, Vapam, Trapex, and Larvacide, in addition to other proprietary chemicals, are used. Always follow the manufacturers' instructions exactly, as many of these chemicals are poisonous and corrosive.

Good results are being obtained in the United States from bulbs disinfected with either Terraclor, Captan or TMTD. Healthy bulbs are immersed, for 10 minutes, in a solution consisting of ⅓ ounce Terraclor plus $\frac{1}{3}$ ounce Pomarsol (TMTD) or Orthocide 50 (Captan) in 1 gallon ($1\frac{1}{4}$ US gallons) of water. They are then lightly dried and planted immediately. Brassicol may also be useful for disinfecting soils prior to lily-planting – one spoonful per bucketful of soil.

Virus diseases

Almost all plants are prone to virus attack of varying degrees of severity. Lilies are no exception, and the almost complete destruction of *L. longiflorum* in Bermuda during 1919–25 led to a detailed investigation of the problem.

It is impossible to give a detailed account of all the virus diseases which occur in lilies – in any case, they are not only confined to these plants. It is only during the last few decades that significant scientific progress has been made, and not all the facts are yet known.

After the *L. longiflorum* disaster in Bermuda, F. P. McWhorter and Philip Brierley investigated the virus disease complex and fully reported their findings in the North American Lily Society Year Books of 1955 and 1963. They differentiated between the following viruses:

Virus	Lily disease	Other known hosts
Rosette	Rosette	None
Cucumber Mosaic (CMV)	Mottle	Vegetables, gladioli, tulips, many others
Symptomless	None	None
CMV and symptomless	Longiflorum fleck	None
Echinocystis	Streak	*Echinocystis*, cucumber
Speciosum fleck	Speciosum fleck	Corn
Mosaic viruses	Mosaic	Tulips

Viruses react differently on different lilies. Some lilies are completely destroyed, others are hardly harmed and barely show visible effects. Some viruses are described as symptomless, and plants only show effects after they have received a second virus infection. Vectors are mostly aphides and, according to latest scientific evidence, also thrips.

The rosette virus only affects *L. longiflorum* and is transmitted by the melon aphis. The leaves distort and curl, in rosette-like manner, and plants invariably die.

The fleck virus is easily recognized by the formation of fine, long, light or white streaks along the leaves. Longiflorum fleck arises as a result of the combined attacks of Cucumber mosaic virus and the symptomless virus – but again only in *L. longiflorum*.

Speciosum fleck only attacks *L. speciosum* var. *rubrum* and also maize. The pest responsible for transmitting the virus is the green peach aphis.

Longiflorum streak originates as a result of Echinocystis-Mosaic virus, found on *Echinocystis oreganus*, of cucumbers and watermelons. It apparently affects only *L. longiflorum*, and then only in north-western parts of the United States. The vector seems to be the 12-spot cucumber beetle.

Mosaic virus disease is clearly recognized by the mosaic pattern changing the leaf colour from dark to light green. Young, not yet fully unfolded leaves also show the change of colour pattern quite distinctly in the form of spots or lines.

Tulips are apt to suffer from the same disease and show similar symptoms. In fact all striped tulips suffer from mosaic virus. They are differentiated as follows:

1. *Colour-adding virus.* Tulip colours gain in intensity, lily leaves bear the typical mosaic patterned lines
2. *Henryi – mottle virus.* Mottles the flower of tulips, causes mosaic in *L. henryi* and one or two other lilies; apt to destroy *L. regale*
3. *Mild lily colour-removing virus.* Produces contrasting colour patterns in tulips; causes the typical mosaic pattern in several lilies, including *L. auratum, L. speciosum, L. tigrinum,* and *L. × umbellatum*; blooms of *L. speciosum* and *L. × umbellatum* become flecked
4. *Severe lily colour-removing virus.* Changes the colour of tulips to white and kills them; often present without symptoms in *L. longiflorum, L. candidum,* and *L. tigrinum*
5. *Lily vein-darkening virus.* Changes the colour of veins in tulip blooms; present in healthy lilies, particularly in the *Ace* varieties of *L. longiflorum*

The nonprofessional finds it difficult to distinguish between the different symptoms, but the disease is easily recognized on close examination of the young shoots. If they are carefully unrolled they reveal a light and dark-green mottled pattern if the disease is present.

The observance of the following points aids the prevention and reduction of the incidence of virus diseases:

1. Virus-infected plants, including the bulb, must be dug up and burned
2. Aphides transmit virus, and lilies have to be protected from them. Preventive spraying at minimum four-weekly intervals is advisable, preferably with a systemic insecticide (e.g., Metasystox)
3. Particularly susceptible lilies (*L. formosanum, L. auratum, L. speciosum, L. tigrinum*) should be planted on their own, as far away as possible from other lilies
4. Lilies should not be planted in the vicinity of virus-carrying tulips
5. Lilies should be grown from seed. Seed, even if obtained from a virus-infected plant, cannot transmit virus

Not all virus-infected plants succumb. There are lilies which continually carry a symptomless virus and are perfectly healthy – e.g., *L. tigrinum, L. longiflorum Ace*, and *L. candidum*. But virus-infected plants present a great danger, as vectors can so easily transfer the virus to a healthy plant. Virus infections progress gradually, and debilitate plants over a period; first the shoots and flowers become malformed, later their vigour decreases, until the plant eventually dies. During the later stages, the weakening plant is also often attacked by fusarium or botrytis, which hasten its end. So far, no effective means of curing virus-infected lilies has been discovered.

8. Lilies in the wild

The classification of lilies

Lilium is an old genus which apparently developed in the temperate and subtropical zones of the Northern Hemisphere. It is, indeed, confined to these zones – no lilies are known south of the Equator.

Many species were lost during the evolution of the genus: some species were unable to adapt themselves to changing geological and climatic circumstances; others only colonized comparatively small regions, and were overtaken by unsuitable conditions before they could spread into surroundings more congenial to their preservation. Precise details are lacking, and the available knowledge of wild varieties is rudimentary and full of gaps. The origin of some isolated lilies reaches very far back, while other groups developed much later and are therefore still closely related today.

The first classification of lilies was made in 1836 by the Austrian botanist, Stephan L. Endlicher, and was revised in 1925 by E. H. Wilson in his book *The Lilies of Eastern Asia*. This classification was unfortunately both unsatisfactory and unnatural, because it was based only on the shape and bearing of the flower, and consequently split several closely related lily groups, particularly groups of American origin.

A recent classification, put forward by H. F. Comber in the Royal Horticultural Society Lily Year Book for 1949, does not confine itself to the flower shape only, but includes a host of other characteristics, notably germination of the seed, arrangement of leaves, and shape of bulbs and scales. It led to a new, more logical classification of the species, one which on the whole corresponded more closely to their evolution.

Diagram of new classification by Harold F. Comber

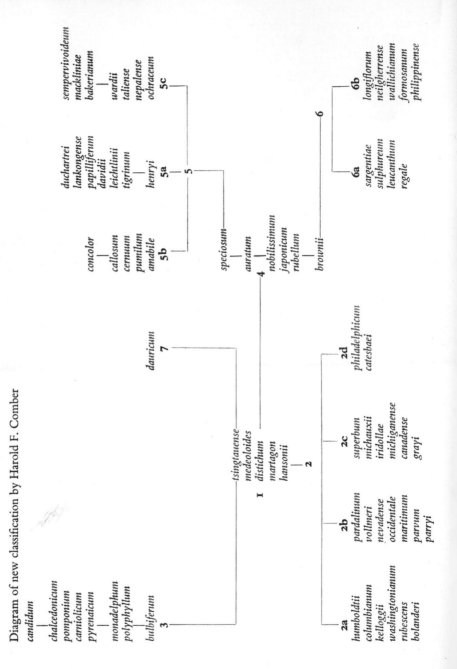

Each of the seven sections in Comber's diagram (some of which have subdivisions) comprises closely related lilies:

1. Martagon section   5. Asiatic section
2. American section   6. Trumpet Lily section
3. Candidum section   7. Dauricum section
4. Oriental section

The Austrian botanist, F. Buxbaum, illustrated the evolution of the genus and its divergence from *Fritillaria* as follows:

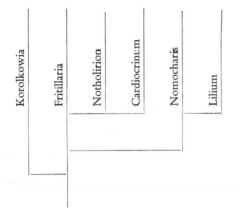

Recently, in the Royal Horticultural Society Lily Year Book for 1968, Dr R. W. Lighty produced a diagram of the evolution of the genus *Lilium* which takes into consideration all the different characteristics and also the migration of lilies. It gives a complete picture of the genus and the interrelationships between its species (*see* page 88).

Lilium   Linnaeus

L. alexandrae   Wallace 1893

Named *Uke-Yuri* in Japan, where it is confined to the valleys and fields of one or two small islands lying south of the Ryukyu Islands.

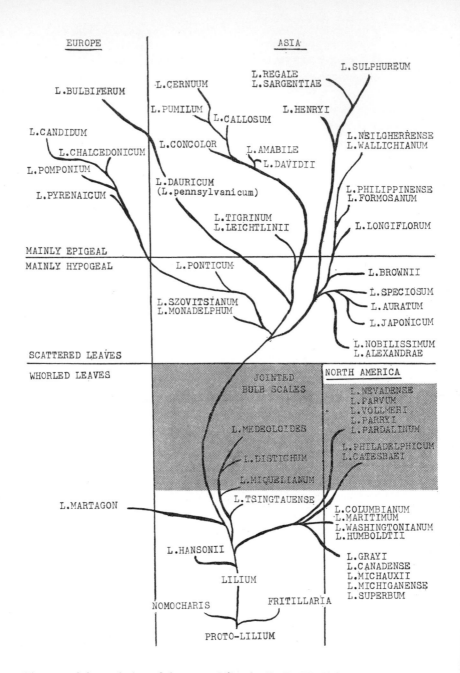

Diagram of the evolution of the genus *Lilium* by Dr R. W. Lighty

The Japanese botanist Moto'o Shimizu corrected the error in Woodcock and Stearn's *Lilies of the World*, where *L. alexandrae* is wrongly described as *L. nobilissimum*. The large, very fragrant, pure-white and occasional pale-pink blooms are borne horizontally, or slightly erect, on stems about 3 feet long. Stigma and pollen are purple-brown, the flowering period extends from May to July.

Seeds germinate within 6–12 months, provided the soil temperature is 68°F (20°C). This exceptionally beautiful lily can only be grown in the greenhouse in Europe; it is very susceptible to virus (NALS-LYB 1952, Moto'o Shimizu).* Crossed with *L. japonicum*, like pink Easter lilies.

L. amabile Palibin 1901

Native in Korea and Dagelet Island, grows in sandy loam among grass and woody undergrowth. The globe-shaped but pointed bulbs are white. Grows to a height of 16–39 inches, bears fairly numerous, narrowly lanceolate leaves marked with a brown spot at their apex. Produces between one and six nodding, black-spotted, Turk's Cap blooms of shiny orange-red. The anthers are dark chocolate-brown, the pollen is vermilion. Long, oval-shaped seed capsules, quick-germinating seed. Flowers June–July. (*25*)

Although this lily was introduced comparatively late – E. H. Wilson only sent seed to the United States in 1918 and 1919 – it was rapidly distributed throughout the West. It is remarkable for its shiny, orange-cinnabar-red flower; even a few plants provide an effective splash of colour. Tolerates full sun and dry soils, does not fade, but has an unpleasant scent.

L. amabile var. *luteum*. English and Dutch-grown seedlings of *L. amabile* produced a variant with shiny, orange-yellow flowers. Both yellow and

---

* *This and similar references are to articles in the Lily Year Books, with the name of the author appearing after the date of the book.* NALS-LYB = *North American Lily Society Lily Year Book*; RHS-LYB = *Royal Horticultural Society Lily Year Book.*

red-flowered varieties were crossed to produce hybrids which retained the gloss on the upper leaf surface in addition to the pronounced colours.

The resulting hybrids are *Duchess* (with *L.* × *maculatum*), *Waxwing* (with *L. philadelphicum*) and *Cardinal* (with *L. tigrinum*). J. C. Taylor, of Guelph, Ontario, is the breeder of the last two.

L. amabile was also used by Jan de Graaff in the breeding of his Fiesta and Midcentury hybrids.

L. amoenum   Wilson 1920

A delicate lily, 6–12 inches tall, with nodding, deep-pink flowers, bell to saucer-shaped, similar to *L. rubellum*, and discovered at a height of 6,000–7,200 feet in the Chinese province of Yunnan. Jan de Graaff has raised this lily from seed in an attempt to acclimatize it.

L. arboricola   W. T. Stearn 1954

One of Frank Kingdon Ward's last finds before his death, this curious lily grows on trees in the woods of northern Burma.

Ward found it in 1953 and sent it to England during the following year for exhibition at the Chelsea Flower Show. He described it as an enchantingly coloured Martagon type, with nutmeg fragrance and rounded, reflexed petals of silk-textured nile-green contrasting with the cinnabar-orange-coloured stamens. It is unfortunate that this rare and singular lily is now again lost, as none of the bulbs which flowered at both Wisley Gardens and Liverpool survived the second winter.

L. armenum (Mishch.)   Mandenova

P. L. Mishchenko previously classified this lily as a variety of *L. szovitsianum* Fisch. and Lall., var. *armenum* Mishch.

A Caucasian lily from the Dirachichag, Kirovokan and Goktscha sea region growing at elevations of 6,000–6,500 feet in light woodland among long grass and on shaded, north-facing sites. The outside scales of the broadly ovoid bulb, which measures about 3 × 4 inches, are golden-yellow; so are the 10–12 bell-shaped blooms supported on the stem, about 6 feet 6 inches high. The stem is densely leaved, the flower segments are strongly marked along the keel with either dark-purple spots or papillae, the anthers are deep-yellow, the pollen dark-yellow or rust-red. During the June flowering period the blooms exude a strong, unpleasant smell. (RHS-LYB 1966, V. Eremin)

L. auratum Lindley 1862, Golden-Rayed Lily of Japan

A beautiful, elegant, colourful and sweet-scented lily. The best of all wild lilies, much sought after in its natural state, although difficult to grow. (*27*)

Called *Yama-Yuri* in its native Japan, it extends over the whole of the main island of Honshu (with the exception of the western point), and also over some others. Prefers the eastern side of mountain faces up to a height of 5,000 feet; it is occasionally found growing in the fissures of vertical rocks but mostly among low-growing grass, bamboo, and rhododendrons; it is often found growing in the company of *L. japonicum*, *L. maximowiczii*, and *L. medeoloides* on volcanic ash and thin, stony ground. The bulbs are bigger than those of other lilies, in cultivation 3–4 inches in diameter, flat-round, yellow with pink spots. Strong purple stems 3–8 feet high, dark-green, short-stemmed leaves, small to broad lanceolate and up to 8 inches long. Large, outward-facing flowers, 10–12 inches wide, very fragrant, flat bowl-shaped, slightly reflexed, wax-white, rayed golden-yellow with carmine-red spots, papillose; chocolate-brown pollen. Under good cultivation the flowers, which in the wild only number six at the most, can be considerably increased. The flowering period is from August to September; 300–400 seeds in oblong seed capsules; slow germination, stem-rooting.

Grows best in temperate maritime climates, including England, Oregon and Washington, particularly well in Victoria, Australia, and New Zealand. Should be planted in light, lime-free, peat soils.

A. and R. Buckley, of Langley Prairie, British Columbia, recommend that *L. auratum* be planted no deeper than 3–4 inches, increasing to 4–6 inches in light soils. Bulbs should be planted in slightly acid soil of pH

5·5–6·5, well surrounded with sand and topped with leaf-mould. Compost must be well rotted and only applied as a top dressing.

L. *auratum* consists of a number of varieties in the wild which have been used to introduce several new lilies into cultivation. Work on a massive scale, conducted by the Buckley brothers, has enabled them to produce 60 clones from which the Esperanza seedlings originated and found their way into commerce.

L. *auratum Crimson Queen*. One of the best varieties with large flowers, rayed in broad crimson along the centre of the flower petal.

L. *auratum* var. *platyphyllum* is hardier and broader-leaved than the type, with numerous large flowers, up to 1 foot wide. E. H. Wilson notes that this form is native in southern Japan.

L. *auratum* var. *rubro-vittatum*. The yellow median band in this form is continued in dark crimson right up to the segment point; heavily spotted in red.

L. *auratum* var. *rubrum*. Crimson median band rarely found in the wild in Japan, only in the ratio of one red-rayed type to 100,000 of the others.

L. *auratum* var. *tricolor*. Similar to *platyphyllum*, with yellow band, and slightly speckled.

L. *auratum* var. *virginale*. Pure-white, golden-rayed with yellow speckles. Successfully crossed with L. *speciosum* (L. × *parkmannii*). Other lilies crossed into this complex are the Japanese L. *japonicum* and L. *rubellum* (Dr N. E. Pfeiffer, Boyce Thompson Institute, New York, 1942).

L. *bakerianum*   Collett and Hemsley 1890

Discovered in 1888 in upper Burma by the English botanist, John G. Baker, who was an enthusiast of lilies and devoted much of his time and writing to their popularization. It is widely distributed, and consequently variable; in fact, five different forms have been described. It is not winter-hardy in Europe, and is best grown in a cool greenhouse. Comparatively rare, spectacularly coloured, and found up to 4,000–12,000 feet above sea leavel in the eastern Himalayas of western China. One typical form is pendulous, with up to eight bell-shaped, pleasantly scented, greenish blooms with red-brown, speckled throat. Plant height 12–39 inches.

Other forms have white, pink, yellow or light-green, bell-shaped flowers with chestnut-brown to purple to carmine-lined throats.

L. bolanderi   S. Watson 1887

A lily 1–3 feet tall, with bell-shaped flowers, from the 3,000–6,000 feet-high Siskiyou Mountains of southern Oregon and northern California. The greenish-yellow bulb has loosely jointed scales; blue-green oblanceolate to lanceolate leaves arranged in three to six whorls clothe the stem. Up to nine delicate, silk-textured flowers from brick to wine-red on the outside and fine, red-spotted, pale-crimson on the inside, are arranged in a racemose inflorescence.

July-flowering, *L. bolanderi* grows in stiff loam in its natural habitat, on rocks and stony ground; it receives 50–70 inches of rain each year, most of it during the spring, and also survives the dry autumns of the region as well as winter snows. As it belongs to the western American land-type, it must receive the best possible drainage, and must always be provided with a damp subsoil, which under some circumstances may necessitate subterranean irrigation. It flowers within four years if raised from seed; hybridizes with *L. pardalinum*. (RHS-LYB 1951–52)

L. brownii   F. E. Brown 1845

The type is *L. brownii* var. *brownii*. This exceptionally beautiful funnel-shaped lily, without known place of origin, was probably exported to England from Canton in 1835. It grows 3–4 feet high from a white-yellowish, broad-scaled bulb. The trumpets, about 6 inches long, arise horizontally from the stem, bloom during July, and are cream-white inside; the purple-pink to chocolate-coloured outside is occasionally flushed with green. A moderately hardy stem-rooter which does not set seed and can only be vegetatively multiplied.

L. brownii var. *australe.* Occurs in the southern Chinese provinces of Fukien, Hong Kong, Kwangtung, Kwangsi and Yunnan. A strong-thriving, almost continuously growing plant, but with a smaller bulb and leaves than var. *viridulum*; not winter-hardy in Europe. (NALS-LYB 1959)

L. brownii var. *viridulum* (var. *colchesteri* Wils.) is found in the wild at an elevation of 5,000 feet throughout almost all of the western Chinese provinces. The large and cream-white bulb is used as food by the inhabitants; the stem grows 39–78 inches high; the leaves are linear lanceolate; the strongly scented flowers are 6 inches long and, although pale-yellow when they first open, soon turn white; their back is marbled in green and purple and the inside outlined with green nectary-furrows.

Although also found in the northern Chinese provinces, it is not very easy to cultivate; it flowers during August/September, and sets seed.

L. bukozanense   Honda 1942

First discovered as recently as 1942 at an elevation of 2,000 feet on the Japanese mountain Buko, 38 miles north-west of Tokyo. Grows in the soil pockets of near-vertical rock faces, with downward-hanging stems which bear large, erect, heavily spotted, orange-red, saucer-shaped flowers. The stem continues to retain its pendulous habit, even if the plant is grown in a pot. (NALS-LYB 1960, Moto'o Shimizu)

L. bulbiferum   Linnaeus 1753, Fire Lily

This famous European lily was already known to sixteenth-century writers of old herbals, and illustrated in woodcuts: Leonard Fuchs, 1542, or Hieronymus Bock, 1546, described it as '*Goldt Gilg*'. Two forms are, however, known under the name *L. bulbiferum* – the typical axil bulbil producing *L. bulbiferum*; and var. *croceum* which lacks this characteristic – but even then the two species overlap and some plants under exceptional circumstances, particularly if their main shoot has been damaged, produce axil bulbils nevertheless. The distribution areas also overlap. (4)

L. bulbiferum var. *chaixii*. A dwarf variety with red-tipped orange flowers from the French Maritime Alps (Var valley, Val di Minera). (RHS-LYB 1957)

L. bulbiferum var. *croceum*. Described as a variety by Woodcock and Stearn, it extends north and southwards from its native Alps. It likes the Föhn-swept valleys of the northern Alps and is also found in Austrian Carinthia and Tyrol, Switzerland, eastern France, northern and central Italy and Corsica – usually among rocks, in fields and on stone spoil heaps.

Stronger in appearance than *typicum*, with yellow-orange, less red, heavily brown-spotted blooms. According to Hegi the upper surface of the segments is not shiny as the type, but papillose and therefore dull.

L. bulbiferum var. *giganteum* is a particularly large variety, 5–6 feet tall, occurring chiefly south of Naples, on the Vesuvius and Cigliano craters.

L. bulbiferum var. *typicum*. Now very rare, but occasionally found in upper Bavaria, Thüringia, and the Erz and Adler Mountains.

Round, white bulb; 2–4 foot stem with numerous lanceolate leaves; bulbils form in the upper leaf axils during the summer.

The erect, orange-yellow, saucer-shaped flowers, up to 20 in number, have slightly spotted, red-orange petal tips, and are borne in an umbel. Stem-rooter, round seed capsule.

Has been crossed with *L.* × *maculatum*, *L.* × *hollandicum*, *L. davidii*, *L. concolor*, *L. monadelphum* and *L. pumilum*.

L. callosum Siebold and Zuccarini 1839

China (Hupeh), Manchuria, Japan (island of Kyushu and Tsushima), Formosa. A delicate lily, 1–3 feet tall, July/August-flowering, bearing up to nine little Turk's Cap flowers on slender pedicels that end in a narrow funnel. The black-spotted flowers are an unusual tone of brick-red. The leaves are thicker at the tip, and the plant derives its name from this characteristic (*callosum* means thick-skinned). Suitable for rockeries, quick-germinating, and easily multiplied from seed. R. W. Lighty reports the existence of unknown, large-flowered types in Korea.

L. callosum var. *flaviflorum* grows on the Japanese island of Okinawa.
    Crosses with *L. concolor* = *Evening Star* (Skinner), *L. callosum* var. *flaviflorum* × *L. concolor* var. *coridion* = *Sugekime* (Myodo)1963.

L. canadense   Linnaeus 1753, Canada Lily

An American lily first brought to Europe in 1620, described by Parkinson in 1629 and named by Linnaeus in 1753. Native over a wide range of North America from the 50th Parallel in the north to the 35th in the south, but only east of the Rocky Mountains. As its American name, Meadow Lily, implies it prefers damp meadows and grassy situations along dykes, road verges and railway banks, as well as light woodland. (*28*)

L. canadense

The fleshy rhizomes continuously build new bulbs from which, during the following year, grow stems 2–5 feet high covered with leaves in whorls. The long and gracefully arched pedicels end in up to 20 pendant blooms during June/July. They are usually yellow with black-purple spots, of Turk's Cap type with slightly reflexed petals, forming an elegant bell shape. An aesthetic feast!

The Canada Lily requires damp, acid, well-drained soils of sandy loam with ample peat. A layer of rubble below soil level assists drainage. Seeds germinate slowly, and plants raised from them flower after three or four years. Cross-pollination between the various forms of *L. canadense* is, of course, possible, as it is with *L. superbum*, *L. michiganense*, *L. michauxii* and *L. columbianum* – an obvious reason for the existence of such a large number of variants.

L. canadense var. *coccineum* has a heavily spotted, dark brick-red flower with yellow throat.

L. canadense var. *editorium* is confined to the dry Appalachian mountain regions, and distinguished from other types by its broader leaves and more beautiful red flowers.

L. canadense var. *flavo-rubrum*. Spotted, deep-orange-coloured flowers with yellow throat; speckled.

L. canadense var. *flavum* is the most widely distributed variety of this species, with chocolate-coloured speckles on pure-yellow flowers.

L. canadense var. *immaculatum*. Unspotted light cadmium-yellow blooms. Mrs J. Norman Henry collected a whole range of them for planting in her Pennsylvania garden.

L. candidum   Linnaeus 1753, Madonna Lily

Known throughout mid-Europe for a long time, the white Madonna Lily is a symbol of innocence, purity and chastity, has been the attribute of many saints, the Virgin Mary and Joseph, and is depicted on many altar-pieces. It is thought that the Crusaders brought it to mid-Europe from Asia Minor and Palestine during the twelfth century, but it is perhaps more probable that the Romans had already previously brought it over the Alps. Its place of origin is uncertain, but it was certainly already being cultivated 1,000–2,000 years earlier in the Mediterranean area by the Egyptians, Cretans, Greeks and Romans as a medicinal plant. It has also been associated with Herat in Afghanistan, the Lebanon, Israel (Haifa), Beirut and the country surrounding Izmir. The First World War saw the var. *salonikae* discovered by an English soldier during 1916/17 on the Salonika front; it has smaller perianth-segments and smaller and more waved leaves than the type. It is also found growing among thickets and on cliff faces in the valley of the Vardar of Greece near Dojran as well as near the Albanian frontier at Krystallopegae. (*2, 29*)

Strong basal roots several years old grow from the broadly ovoid, white or yellowish bulb. The glabrous, oblanceolate basal leaves appear during September and retain their greenness throughout the winter. The stems arise during the spring to a height of 2 feet 6 inches–4 feet – also higher on occasions – and carry during June/July, 5–20 pure-white, wide-open, funnel-shaped, scented blooms in panicled inflorescence. Yellow pollen. Unfortunately it does not set seed in the cold Northern European climate, but occasionally succeeds in doing so under the warmer conditions of France and Italy; the wild forms of Turkey, Greece and Israel are all seed-setters. The seeds are dormant for the first two years and germinate irregularly. This lily has retained the life cycle of its native south, where it is exposed to summer droughts and autumn rains and must therefore always be transplanted immediately the flowers and stem have withered and in sufficient time to allow it to develop its basal leaves during the same autumn in preparation for the following year's growth.

If it is to do well it needs calcareous soils and as little disturbance as possible. It is well known that this lily flourishes for decades in old cottage gardens, but always provided it is grown on good calcareous loams and silt soils, is not disturbed, is not planted deeper than 1¼ inches and in full sun with adequate ground cover. (RHS-LYB 1954)

L. candidum var. *cernuum* has a black stem and small, pointed segments; is reputed to set seeds.

L. candidum var. *salonikae* occurs in the wild near Salonika in Greece, has small flowers with pointed segments, sets seed.

Cascade strain. A selection of crosses with *L. candidum* of various origin from which Jan de Graaff has selected a number of tall and dwarf-growing forms for commercial release.

The best-known hybrid is *L.* × *testaceum* = *L. candidum* × *L. chalcedonicum.* Crosses with *L. parryi* and *L. ledebourii* are reported to be possible.

L. carniolicum   Bernhardi 1837, Carniola Lily

The varieties of this species grow in the Balkans from Carniola (Krain) to Istria, Dalmatia, Croatia, Albania, Greece, Bulgaria, and Rumania. This lily, so variable in appearance, has led to disagreement among botanists, and some have even classed the variety *L. jankae* Kerner as a species in its own right.

The same environmental conditions are common to all forms, mostly mountain meadows, stony, scrub-covered, hard loam, with little humus overlying free-draining, calcareous rocks.

Yellow bulbs about $2\frac{1}{2}$ inches in diameter. Stems 1–3 feet long with scattered, lanceolate leaves growing horizontally from the stem with upward-pointing leaf tips. The Turk's Cap flowers, supported by short, thick pedicels, appear during late May/June.

According to W. B. Turrill (RHS-LYB 1954) varieties can be differentiated as follows:

	veins of lower surface of leaves	
colour of flower petals	hairy	glabrous, or nearly so
orange or red	*carniolicum*	*bosniacum*
yellow	*jankae*	*albanicum*

L. carniolicum var. *albanicum* is a low-growing form with glabrous leaves, one to four amber-yellow flowers, and vermilion-red pollen. Occurs in the mountains of Montenegro, Albania, northern Greece, and Macedonia.

L. carniolicum var. *jankae*

L. carniolicum var. *bosniacum* Beck has red flowers and glabrous veins and occurs on the alpine meadows of the Bosnian Trescavica mountains, at an elevation of 4,500 feet. Its distribution area overlaps with those of the varieties *jankae*, *bosniacum*, and *albanicum*.

31. *L. davidii* from western China. Its strong stem and general robustness have been inherited by many hybrids. It grows fairly tall, has yellow-orange flowers, and enhances any garden. Selection can produce several different varieties

32. *L. davidii* var. *willmottiae*, also from western China. Ideal for cutting because of its elegant appearance

33. *White Excelsior*, a *L. formosanum* flower grown in the greenhouse for cutting. Its greenish-white, elongated trumpets only appear during late autumn

34. *L. hansonii* from Korea. Nearly all Martagon hybrids arise from this exceptionally disease-tolerant, yellow-gold Turk's Cap; prefers rich soil and partial shade

35. *L. harrisianum*, previously known as *L. pardalinum* var. *giganteum* and also as the Sunset Lily. Multiplies very well if grown on damp soils in full sunlight. Vermilion, carmine, chrome-yellow flowers with brown spots. Looks most effective if planted with Asiatic primulas at its base

36. *L. mackliniae*, a new Kingdon Ward discovery; bell-shaped, pink-tinged, white flowers

37. *L. longiflorum* bulblets forming on the underground stems

38. *Mount Everest*, a *L. longiflorum* flower, is only suitable for growing in a greenhouse; millions of them are sold in the United States at Eastertime

39. *L. duchartrei* comes from China, and bears marble-white, red-spotted blooms

40. *L. superbum*, a wild lily from America; orange-yellow flowers, a little difficult to grow in Europe

41. *Formobel*, an English-bred, triploid, Longiflorum hybrid with very long, pure-white trumpets

42. *L. pyrenaicum*, an interesting yellow or red lily

43. *L. pumilum,* a small-flowered, glistening-red species ideally suited to the rock garden
44. *L. nobilissimum* comes from the Ryukyu islands; a white-flowered trumpet lily
45. *L. nepalense* from the Himalayas, beautifully coloured and only hardy in mild areas

L. carniolicum var. *carniolicum*. An alpine to subalpine plant growing between rocks and scrub on alpine meadows, with mostly calcareous subsoils, stretching from the Karawanken Mountains in the north through Istria to Dalmatia. The leaf veins are ciliated below; one to six Turk's Cap blooms with colour ranging from red-orange to pale red; red pollen.

L. carniolicum var. *jankae* has ciliated leaf veins and margins, mostly one to four canary-yellow Turk's Cap flowers with finely black-spotted throat and cinnabar pollen. Occurs at elevations of 2,000–4,000 feet in Bosnia and Croatia as well as Bulgaria (Rhodope Mountains) and Serbia and Rumania.

L. catesbaei Walter 1788

North America, Florida, Louisiana, Carolina. Grows in coniferous woods and on marshland.

L. catesbaei

Bulbs are white, and built up of loosely connected, small scales. The long-lanceolate leaves growing from the base of the 12–20 inch high stem are perennial; all leaves are scattered, acute, and gradually become smaller and narrower on the higher parts of the stem. The August-flowering, mostly single, erect, and saucer-shaped scarlet blooms are of distinctive shape on account of their long-stemmed petals, and bear yellow markings strongly mottled with brown.

Not all varieties of this lily have yet been written about. Its natural habitat of acid soils or marsh makes cultivation very difficult; it is best planted in pots containing a layer of sphagnum topped with a wet mixture of sand and peat; pots to stand in water continually. Germinates within 40 days. Cross-pollination with other lilies has, so far, been unsuccessful.

L. caucasicum   A. Grossheim (*L. martagon* ssp. *caucasicum* Mishch.)

Caucasus, north-eastern coast of the Black Sea in Abkhaz and at Tuapse, in oak and beech woods, among bracken and in meadows at heights of 1,000–1,500 feet.

Short, broad-oval bulb, yellow scales, $1\frac{1}{2}$–2 inches, rather strong stem furnished with hairs, 2 feet 6 inches–5 feet high (reaches 7–8 feet in cultivation), stem-rooting, leaves mostly in two whorls, smaller, hairy leaves scattered along upper part of stem. Broad, wide-open, but short, funnel-shaped flowers, petals $1\frac{1}{4}$–$1\frac{1}{2}$ inches long, lilac-pink. Buds covered with glandular hairs. Dark-purple anthers, brick-red pollen. Flowers between the end of June and July. Seed ripens during mid-September, germinates slowly. Likes sunlight and calcareous soils.

L. cernuum   Komarov 1901

A small, pretty lily with nodding, fragrant Turk's Cap flowers of unusual lilac-pink, lightly spotted with carmine. Native of Korea, Manchuria, and the Russian region of Ussurysk (Vladivostok).

L. cernuum

The comparatively large, white bulb consists of only a few thick scales. Stem 1 foot–2 feet 6 inches high; bears small grass-like leaves and carries up to eight sweet-scented blooms – in cultivation even more. The pollen is orange in colour. Wild forms colonize on sandy loams, alluvial soils, and stony ground, and among grass and woody under-growth, usually in full sunlight or light shade. It is not very long-living, but a succession for garden use is quickly built up if raised from its easily propagated seed. Quick-germinating and stem-rooting. The white-flowering *L. cernuum* var. *candidum* comes from the Diamond Mountain area of Korea. Professor C. F. Patterson recently bred some strong, pastel-coloured hybrids from *L. cernuum* and *L. davidii* crosses.

L. chalcedonicum Linnaeus 1753

Greece: Euboea, Mount Kandyli, Tirphys Mountains, at 3,000 feet, calcareous soils of dry valleys, among grasses and conifers.

White to yellowish, broad bulbs. Stem 2–4 feet long with many scattered lanceolate leaves – the lower long and spreading, the upper small, erect, and bunched around the stem. Up to 10 Martagon-type flowers with fleshy, mandarin-red segments, without spots in the type. Deep, red-orange pollen. Flowering period: July/August.

It is unfortunate that this, one of the most beautiful of European lilies, which grows so well on warm calcareous loams, is very vulnerable to botrytis.

L. chalcedonicum var. *maculatum* is densely spotted with black. *L. chalcedonicum* and *L. heldreichii* are often classified as one and the same lily, but are more likely to be two distinct varieties.

Crossed with *L. candidum*=(*L.* × *testaceum*). (RHS-LYB 1954)

L. columbianum Hanson 1874

First found on the banks of the River Columbia, from which it derives its name, in the state of Washington. It has the widest distribution of any lily on the west coast, and occurs from northern California through

Oregon and Washington, all the way to British Columbia. Usually found at heights up to 6,000 feet, mostly in damp meadows or light woodland and under the most varied climatic conditions.

Small, white bulbs about 1½ inches wide, slender stem 2–5 feet high, broad lanceolate leaves growing in whorls from the lower part. Six to 10 small, nodding, strongly recurved funnel-shaped flowers of bright-yellow to red-orange, with numerous, small, purple speckles in the centre of the bloom. Flowers during June/July/August.

L. columbianum var. *ingramii* is a strong plant, probably one of nature's hybrids, and belongs to the American land-type lilies which prefer well-drained, sandy loams. Wild hybrids with *L. occidentale* have also been reported, and so have successful crosses with *L. canadense* and *L. kelloggii*.

L. concolor   Salisbury 1806

L. concolor

At home in central China (Hupeh, Hunan, Yunnan), scattered in Japan at elevations of 1,000–4,000 feet, mostly on limestone subsoils and growing in pockets of humus, in loam and among grass and scrub.

Its extreme variability has given rise to a number of differing descriptions, which E. H. Wilson found difficult to classify. Certainly a pretty, but small, June/July-flowering lily carrying one, and on occasions up to 10, erect, unspotted scarlet blooms. Scattered, linear-lanceolate leaves spread horizontally from the stem, 1–3 feet long. The small, round, white bulb is short-lived, and has only a few broad scales. Rapid germination, prefers full sun.

L. concolor var. *coridion* is the best form, with lemon-yellow, finely brown-spotted flowers.

L. concolor var. *partheneion* has black-spotted, red flowers with green and yellow streaks.

L. concolor var. *pulchellum* comes from Korea, Manchuria and Siberia vermilion to orange-red, spotted flowers.

L. concolor var. *stictum* originates from Shantung. Black-spotted, scarlet flowers.

L. concolor Dropmore is a hardy and thriving, orange-red hybrid raised by Dr F. L. Skinner from the red type crossed with *L. concolor* var. *pulchellum*.

L. concolor Okihime has pure-yellow, unspotted flowers bigger than *typicum*, is a bulb-splitter, and has been crossed with *L. dauricum*. *L. callosum*, and *L. pumilum*.

Ideal for cutting, much used in floristry; its bright colours create a focal point in any garden. (NALS-LYB 1959)

L. dauricum Ker-Gawler 1809 (*L. pensylvanicum Ker-Gawler 1805*)

Ranges widely throughout north-eastern Asia, Altai, Mongolia, Amur region, northern Manchuria, northern Korea, Sakhalin and Kamchatka (Japan). It is called after the old names for Siberia, i.e., Davuria, Dahuria or Dauria.

The globose bulb, $1\frac{1}{4}$–3 inches in diameter with jointed scales, is white and produces long stolons before emerging from the ground. The June-flowering blooms, one to six in number, chalice-shaped, orange to scarlet-coloured, and heavily spotted, are borne in an umbel on the stem, 1 foot–2 feet 6 inches high and usually ribbed. It is clothed with scattered lanceolate, erect, dark-green leaves with the upper half, like the flower buds, very cobwebby. Saliwski reports the presence of 12–15 flowered, giant plants (6 feet tall) in Khabarovsk, Russia. Very hardy, likes rich, damp, lime-free soils.

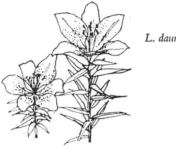

L. dauricum

Varieties: only *alpinum*, 4–8 inches high, and the bright-yellow, black-spotted *luteum*. Also var. *citrinum* (*Makino*) in Japan (Shimizu).

Breeders have used *L. dauricum* a great deal. Isabella Preston (Canada) used it for her famous Stenographer and Fighter hybrids, and Jan de Graaff for his Midcentury hybrids; Dr F. Skinner crossed it with *L. philadelphicum*. According to Moto'o Shimizu, the hybrid *L.* × *elegans* is the result of crosses with *L. maculatum* made by Japanese gardeners as long as 200 years ago. (NALS-LYB 1960)

L. davidii   Duchartre 1877

Armand David, after whom this lily is named, was a French missionary who collected its bulbs in Szechwan, China, and sent them to Paris in 1869. It is distributed throughout western Szechwan and north-western Yunnan, where it is cultivated as a vegetable and grows at heights of 5,000–10,000 feet. (*31*)

L. davidii is one of the most beautiful Martagon lilies, with a stiff, erect stem, bearing upright to horizontally held leaves with slightly inrolled margins on the lower parts, and an impressive pyramidal head of flowers with horizontal pedicels, which often carry from six to 20 and even up to 40 flowers. They are vermilion to scarlet-red, spotted black in the centre and without scent; the pollen is scarlet. The leaves, 3–4½ inches long and ¾–1 inch wide, have hispid margins, the stem and buds are often hairy. The white bulb, 1¼–2 inches, assumes shades of red when exposed to the air and is usually broader than it is high. Rich supply of seed in the elongated, round seed capsules. Quick germination. Easy to grow in most types of garden soils. As a result of crosses with var. *unicolor* and var. *willmottiae* and also selection, more profusely flowering plants, with larger blooms, and even secondary flowers on the same pedicels, have been produced.

L. davidii var. *macranthum*   Rafill 1938. Stem up to 5 feet tall with two to three orange flowers per pedicel.

L. davidii var. *unicolor*   Cotton 1938. Introduced into Italy by the Italian missionary Giraldi as *L. biondii* in 1895; the Dutch knew it as *L. willmottiae* var. *unicolor* and the English as *L. sutchuenense*. Weaker than the original type, it barcly reaches 3 feet in height and carries only 10–15 pale orange-red flowers weakly spotted with red; seedlings are similar. Grows in every type of soil.

L. davidii var. *willmottiae*   Rafill 1938. A very elegant lily, on the whole similar to type, more wiry stem, longer but gracefully upward arched, and closer-spaced pedicels, longer, broader and also more closely spaced leaves, smooth stem and buds. Chestnut-spotted, orange-red flowers. After the main stem emerges from the bulb, it sometimes wanders about below ground level and produces bulblets on the internodes. The cylindrically shaped seed capsules have rounded ends, and provided pollination is satisfactory, produce an abundant supply of seed. Rapid germination. Alexander Steffen, of Erfurt, Germany, selected a much improved, richly flowering and strong-growing type which Pfitzer of Stuttgart, Germany, introduced into commerce. Improved forms also exist in both Holland and England. Suitable for cutting. (*32*)

Although first discovered as early as 1868 by A. Henry and Père Farges, it was not until 1908, when E. H. Wilson sent bulbs to America and England, that its distribution was increased. A good garden-type lily, amenable to all kinds of soils, which can be multiplied without difficulty from either seed or daughter bulbs. It comes from the mountainous Chinese provinces of western Hupeh, eastern Szechwan, and southern Shensi, growing at heights of 4,000–8,000 feet. (RHS-LYB 1949)

L. davidii Maxwill. Dr F. L. Skinner is responsible for this variety, which arose in 1928 from a cross between *L. davidii* var. *willmottiae* and *L. leichtlinii* var. *maximowiczii*, or possibly *L. davidii*. Its stem, as strong as that of *L. davidii*, bears a beautiful pyramidal inflorescence. Its stiff stem, strong growing habit, and profuse flowering ability make it a particularly good lily for use as parent material.

Hybrids of *L. davidii* and the var. *willmottiae* have been produced with *L. bulbiferum* var. *croceum*, *L. cernuum*, *L. dauricum*, *L. amabile*, and *L. tigrinum*. The Preston hybrids were bred by crossing the hybrids *L. dauricum* × *L.* × *maculatum* with *L. davidii* var. *willmottiae*. *Dropmore Gold*, *Lady Lou*, and *Lemon Lady* are hybrids or selections of *L. davidii*, bred by Dr Skinner.

L. distichum   Nakai 1915

Another lily from Manchuria (Amur, Ussuri, Vladivostok) and Korea belonging to the Martagon section and not dissimilar to *L. medeoloides*. The stem, 1–3 feet tall, carries one leaf whorl and three to eight fleshy-petalled, orange flowers with dark spots in a raceme. Flowers in July, stem-rooting, grows best in damp, shaded, wooded situations; difficult to cultivate.

L. duchartrei   Franchet 1887

Occurs on damp, often boggy ground, on the margins of woods and glades, and in mountainous meadows at elevations of 8,000–11,500 feet in China – north-western Yunnan, western Szechwan and south-western Kansu. (*39*)

The ovoid bulb is white, 1–1½ inches in diameter, and stoloniferous. The stem is 1 foot 6 inches–5 feet high, with lanceolate leaves. The marble-white, red-spotted, nodding blooms have erect pedicels, usually between two and 12, in an umbel form. Strong, pleasant scent, orange anthers, yellow pollen.

This fine, attractive lily requires light, damp, shaded ground rich in humus to give the stoloniferous stem room to spread. Dislikes being transplanted. First found by the French missionary Armand David and named after Duchartre, a French professor of botany. (RHS-LYB 1957)

L. fairchildii   M. E. Jones 1930

A rare North American lily from the Palomar, Cuyamaca and Laguna Mountains in San Diego County, which must not be confused with *L. ocellatum* ssp. *bloomerianum*. Grows from a bulb with incurved scales to a height of 4–6 feet in the shade of conifer woods; small leaves with a shiny-green upper surface. The pale-orange segments are strongly reflexed, chrome-yellow near the base, and spotted black. (RHS-LYB 1957)

L. fargesii   Franchet 1892

A small, delicate lily with grass-like leaves and small, greenish-white, pink mottled Martagon flowers. Named after the French missionary Paul G. Farges (1844–1912), it is native to central China (Hupeh, Shensi, Szechwan, and Yunnan) and has, seemingly, never been introduced to cultivation.

L. formosanum   Wallace 1891

As the name indicates, this lily comes from Formosa, where it grows among grass and bamboos in the volcanic and sandstone soils of the northern parts of the island. Distributed from sea level up to 10,000 feet, the height of the plant varies according to the altitude at which it is growing: at sea level its stem is 6 feet 6 inches long, decreasing to only 1 foot at an altitude of 10,000 feet – in fact, it is called var. *pricei* in this form. In the subtropical lowlands, flowering follows unfailingly six to eight months after sowing, irrespective of season. But when it is grown in Europe the blooms do not appear until late October and the rather small, exhausted bulbs rarely overwinter and are often destroyed by frost. (*41*)

The very small bulbs, about 1¼–1½ inches thick, are either white or pale-yellow; grass-like, leaf-covered stems of dark-purple grow to a height of 4–5 feet, although selection makes it possible to produce plants up to 10 feet tall. Nodding, white, funnel-shaped flowers, 4½–6 inches long, narrow throat, wide-open mouth, tinged with pink along outside-centre rib, yellow pollen. Mostly only one or two flowers (selections with 30–40), long, cylindrical seed capsules, thin seeds with membrane around margins. Immediate germination. Easily recognized by its small bulb, which continually produces fresh shoots enabling the plant to flower throughout the year – unless damaged by frost! It is therefore best grown in a cool greenhouse, but if open sites are the only ones available, they must be chosen to provide maximum warmth and shelter. Even then, this lily is short-lived, but replacements are easily and quickly raised from seed.

Because of its high susceptibility to virus infections, it is often used as a test plant. For this purpose it is inoculated with the sap of a lily which is suspected to have virus but shows no visible symptoms. Results are judged by whether the inoculated *L. formosanum* survives or dies.

Various types are commercially available and listed below.

L. formosanum var. *pricei*

L. formosanum var. *pricei*. A dwarf, high mountain range type, grows only 1–2 feet high and bears one or two narrow-throated, white, funnel-shaped flowers, suffused with red on the outside. Winter-hardy and suitable for the rock garden. Flowers during July/August.

Crosses are:

L. formosanum × *L. philippinense* (RHS-LYB 1949)
L. formosanum × *L. nepalense* (*Formolense*, New Zealand)
L. formosanum var. *pricei* × *L. longiflorum* (*L.* × *zalivskii*)
L. formosanum × *L. longiflorum* Tetrabel.

L. georgicum   J. Mandenova 1942 (*L. ponticum* C. Koch)

Caucasus, Georgia, north of Tbilisi by Gudermes military road, in the long grass of mountain meadows up to a height of 7,000–8,000 feet.

L. georgicum is perhaps identical with *L. ponticum* – the bulbs are broad-oval with pale-cream scales, the narrow stem grows about 2 feet 6 inches high, lanceolate leaves heavily marked with stiff hairs along leaf veins and margins, four to seven deep-yellow flowers with deep-orange anthers. The flower is shaped like a campanulate, and the petals, 2–2½ inches long, are purple at the base and mottled along the centre rib with the same colour. Sharp, unpleasant odour.

L. grayi   Watson 1879

First collected by the American botanist Asa Gray, after whom it is named. Similar in habit to the closely related *L. canadense*, and confined to the comparatively small area of North Carolina, Tennessee and Virginia. Its flowers differ from *L. canadense* in their number – one to eight – smooth funnel shape, and nonrecurved segments. The outside of the flower is deep-carmine, the inside orange, strongly speckled with red-purple. Orange-brown pollen. Grows in the Allegheny Mountains at heights of 3,000–6,000 feet. Rhizomatous bulbs with yellow-white scales similar to those of *L. canadense*, but lacks its vigorous growth. Germinates only slowly.

L. hansonii   Leichtlin 1871

Distribution: Dagelet Islands off the Korean coast (Takeshima), Diamond Mountains, Negita Mountains in Korea. Japanese name *Takeshima Yuri*. Grows on the rocky cliffs of Takeshima Island at heights up to 3,000 feet, in leaf-mould and light woodland. June-flowering. (*34*)

L. hansonii

Bulb yellow-white, 2–2½ inches, flat and sphere-shaped; stem green, strong but hollow, 2–5 feet tall with several leaf whorls and a few scattered leaves on upper part; leaves are long lanceolate, approximately 5 × 1¼ inches. Strongly scented Turk's Cap flowers, nodding, with very thick, revolute, orange-yellow petals spotted brown. Rarely produces seed when grown in Europe, but good pollen donor for breeding work. Easy grower, lasts for a decade, likes damp soil rich in leaf-mould and light shade, tolerates calcareous soils, and withstands most lily diseases.

Dr S. L. Emsweller proved that *L. hansonii* is the only virus-resistant lily, a characteristic that the Hansonii hybrids, which are seldom found to suffer from virus attacks, have inherited. It is thought that virus-transmitting aphides avoid *L. hansonii* and its hybrids.

Cross-pollinates easily with *L. martagon* and Martagon varieties, as well as *L. medeoloides* (*Redman*). A number of beautiful, coloured hybrids of a delicate yellow were bred with *L. martagon* var. *album*. This colour also combines well with the dark wine-red of *L. martagon* var. *cattaniae*. (*L.* × *marhan*, *L.* × *dalhansonii*, Paisley hybrids from de Graaff, Painted Lady hybrids from E. L. Kline.)

L. harrisianum   Beane and Vollmer 1955 (*L. pardalinum* var. *giganteum* Woodcock and Stearn)

This lily was at one time considered to be a giant form of *L. pardalinum* or a natural hybrid between *L. pardalinum* and *L. humboldtii*; it is now listed in American catalogues as *Sunset Lily* or *Red Giant*. Jan de Graaff

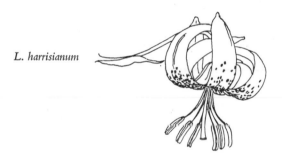

L. harrisianum

considers it as a 'volunteer' plant originated from Luther Burbank's breeding work. In the meantime, Beane and Dr Vollmer located its place of origin along the banks of the Van-Duzen River in northern California, where flowering is entirely dependent on the vagaries of the weather; rhizomes are often washed away by the rain-swollen river, and buried deep under sand and rubble. (*35*)

It is a magnificent lily bearing numerous blooms of a Martagon type, 3–4 inches wide, on a stem 5 feet–6 feet 6 inches clothed with strong, green leaves arranged in whorls. The shiny carmine-red of the perianth segments reaches inwards from the petal tip and changes to chrome-yellow midway, and again into a shade of green towards the base of the flower; the whole of the petal area is marked with large, yellow-framed, chocolate-brown spots. It does well in cultivation, but only if placed in moist soil rich in humus, with its base in the shade and head in the sun. The rapidly multiplying rhizomes necessitate lifting and division at intervals of three or four years. Slow germination. Has been crossed with *L. pardalinum* and various other American lilies. (RHS-LYB 1957)

L. heldreichii   Freyn 1904

Greece: Mount Parnes north of Athens, Mount Parnassus near Delphi, Mount Olympus, Pindus Mountains, Peloponnesus and Jablanitz mountain range on the Yugoslav–Albanian border. Prefers the stony, calcareous humus of mountain slopes, and is only rarely found in cultivation. This orange-red, strongly recurved, Turk's Cap-flowering lily is named after the German botanist Theodor von Heldreich (1822–1902), who was, at one time, Director of the Athens Botanical Gardens. Some botanists consider it a form of *L. chalcedonicum*. (RHS-LYB 1954)

L. henrici   Franchet 1898

South-east China: Yunnan, Mekong–Salween, and Salween–Shweli watershed, at elevations of about 10,000 feet on the margins of thickets in a damp monsoon climate. Discovered by Prince Henry of Orléans in 1895, it was at one time included in *Nomocharis* on account of its flat, open, outward-facing, cup-shaped flowers. Blooms 3–4 feet high, white, crimson to purple-spotted, with green nectary furrows. Flowers during July. Red-flushed bulb 4–4½ inches in diameter. With proper care, it grows well in a damp climate – Scotland and northern England suit it. (RHS-LYB 1965)

L. henryi   Baker 1888

A hardy, indestructible lily, with large, orange, Martagon flowers, from the central Chinese mountains (Hupeh, Kweichow). (57)

Although it bears only one to three flowers in its natural habitat, between 10 and 20 blooms, displayed on a stem 5–8 feet tall, are obtained under cultivation. The large, spherical bulb increases to fist size with age, turns dark-purple when exposed to the light, and produces strong

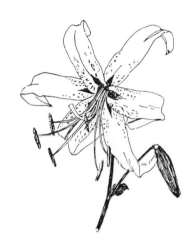

L. henryi

and deep-reaching roots. The strong, slightly arching, purple-brown stem is covered with numerous fairly broad, dark-green leaves. Raceme inflorescence, horizontal or slightly upward tilted pedicels often carry two heavily brown-spotted, orange flowers of Martagon type – some with prominent papillae and green nectary furrows. The pollen is orange, and the flowering period extends from the end of July to August.

The shape of the seed capsules resembles that of inverted skittles; the seeds are large and brown, and germinate quickly, but are best sown immediately after being harvested. Bulblets are freely produced on the underground stem of this stem-rooting lily, but if the bulbs are planted lying on their side the production of daughter bulbs is even more prolific. A virtually indestructible and long-living plant which likes to have its bulb planted deeply in calcareous soils without the addition of peat.

Augustine Henry, who in later life became a professor of forestry, was the first to discover *L. henryi* in China.

L. henryi var. *citrinum* is a mutation with lemon-yellow flowers later than the type.

L. henryi Improved reproduces true from seed. Stiff, upright stem; first entered commerce from the United States.

   L. henryi var. *citrinum* and *L. henryi Improved* are ideal parent material for hybrid production, the first on account of its lemon-yellow colour, the second because of its upright and stiff stem.

   L. henryi has been used a great deal for breeding with *L. sulphureum* (*T. A. Havemeyer*), with *L. sargentiae* (Aurelian hybrids) and with *L. speciosum* (*Black Beauty*).

L. humboldtii   Roezl and Leichtlin 1870

Discovered by A. Roezl in the Sierra Nevada, mid-California, on the hundredth anniversary of A. von Humboldt's birth. It grows at heights from 2,000–4,000 feet, usually in the half-shade provided by the margins of woodland, or among woody undergrowth and fern.

   The large, yellow-white, scaled bulb is usually deep in the ground and grows from only one side. The stem, 4–6 feet high, carries numerous shiny, ribbed, oblanceolate leaves and 10–15 June-flowering blooms arranged in the shape of a pyramid. The shiny, orange flowers are spotted in purple or chestnut-brown, nodding, and of the Turk's Cap type. Dark-orange pollen, slow germination.

   L. humboldtii is most variable, and rarely do two of its 1,000 seeds produce the same result. A land-type lily which prefers to grow on hard dry ground and should receive a covering of mulch during autumn and winter to protect it from excessive wet. Bulb production from scales is impossible; var. *bloomerianum* and var. *ocellatum*, previously considered as *L. humboldtii* varieties, are now included under *L. ocellatum*.

   Crossed with *L. pardalinum* and *L. parryi*.

L. iridollae   M. G. Henry 1947

North America, south Alabama and north-western Florida. Grows in peaty meadows and sphagnum marshes.

Small, white bulbs growing from thin stolons. The upper half of the stem, 3–5 feet high, is almost devoid of leaves, while the lower portion bears whorls of lanceolate leaves. The nodding, recurved, Martagon-type flowers are usually borne singly, although up to eight blooms have been observed. The warm, golden-yellow, heavily brown-spotted flowers appear during June/July, and are marked with green nectary furrows.

L. iridollae was first discovered in the swampy ground of southern Alabama by Mrs Mary G. Henry during 1940; it is related to *L. canadense* and *L. superbum*, and seed germinates within one or two months from sowing.

L. japonicum Thunberg 1780

The Japanese call this lily *Sasa-Yuri* (Bamboo Lily). It grows on Honshu at 3,000 feet above sea level, mostly on east and north-facing slopes among bamboo and rhododendron.

The ovoid, cream-white bulbs, approximately $1\frac{1}{2}$ inches in diameter, consist of small, long, sweet-tasting scales, and are used as food. Few lanceolate leaves arise from the thin stem, 1–3 feet high. It has between one and three short, bell-shaped trumpet flowers, pure-pink or white in colour, which appear from May to August, depending on altitude. Red-brown pollen, self-fertile, slow germination.

Although plentiful in nature, *L. japonicum* proves difficult in cultivation; even the Japanese grow it in only minor quantities. The mature plants, as well as bulb scales used for multiplication, are very prone to fusarium attack. The temperature of the soil should not exceed $59°F$ ($15°C$). To emulate this natural habitat the bulb should be planted very deep in a soil consisting of sandy loam with liberal additions of powdered charcoal and leaf-mould, on slopes facing north in half shade between grass and shrubs. Ralph Warner reports that the best results are obtained if the bulb is planted near a ditch through which cold water continually flows. It crosses with *L. rubellum*, *L. auratum*, *L. speciosum*, and apparently also with *L. cernuum* and *L. wallichianum* – all lilies without carotenoid content. (NALS-LYB 1956, Moto'o Shimizu; NALS-LYB 1962)

L. kelleyanum   Lemmon 1903 (*L. fresnense* Eastwood)

The existence and distribution area of this variety was established by Lawrence Beane in 1952; it belongs to the *pardalinum* group and was at one time known as *L. fresnense*. Up to 70 fragrant flowers 6 feet 6 inches tall in pyramid-shaped inflorescence. Blooms, Martagon type, nodding, cadmium-yellow, light purple spotted, flushed in green towards the inner half. The perianth segments are completely recurved, and give the appearance of a crown; flowers from June to mid-August.

The rhizomatous bulb has many small, jointed scales. *L. kelleyanum* is a bog type found up to 9,000 feet above sea level from Oregon southwards to Tulare County, Kings River and Fresno County, California.

Hybridizes with *L. parvum* in nature. (NALS-LYB 1952)

L. kelloggii   Purdy 1901

A very fragrant and smaller version of *L. rubescens*, which it closely resembles. It ranges from the north-western Californian redwood belt to southern Oregon. Small, 2–4 inch bulbs; stem 18 inches–4 feet tall (sometimes as much as 8 feet), with pale-green leaves arranged in four to eight whorls. Up to 30 nodding, Turk's Cap blooms with strongly reflexed petals form a pyramid around the stem. As the flowers age, the fine, ivory-white, pink-tipped petals turn completely pink, and later to magenta-red with brown to wine-red speckles. Characteristic is a lemon-yellow median band on every petal. Slow germination, land type, flowers during July, needs best possible drainage with ground shade.

Hybrids have been obtained with *L. parryi* and *L. martagon* (Kelmarsh, Wyatt). (NALS-LYB 1952)

L. kesselringianum   Mishchenko 1914

Western Transcaucasia: Sukhumi and Batum, 5,000 feet. It differs from the similar *L. monadelphum* in several easily recognized respects: it only grows 2–4 feet tall; has paler, straw-coloured, cinnamon-spotted, less-reflexed and smaller flower petals; shorter and separated stamens. Eight to 10 cinnamon-spotted flowers, loose raceme inflorescence, scent can be unpleasant, brown anthers, seed capsules $1\frac{1}{2}$–2 inches, slow germination (Saliwski). Bulbs rather large.

Named after W. Kesselring, who before the 1914–18 war was proprietor of the well-known Russian Regel and Kesselring nurseries. (NALS-LYB 1965)

L. kosa (L. cossii)   Orekhovs and Eremin 1957

A vigorous and thriving lily which was discovered by Yuri Kos in northern Caucasia as recently as 1957. The broad, ovoid, large bulb $5\frac{1}{2}$–7 inches and often weighing up to $4\frac{1}{2}$ pounds) has numerous small, pink-yellow scales. Closely set leaves $4\frac{1}{2}$ inches long and 1 inch wide, linear lanceolate, alternately but closely spaced on the 5–6 feet high stem. Between two and five, sometimes up to seven, flowers, trumpet to bell-shaped, outward-facing, bloom during the second half of June, pale-yellow and flushed with pink in nature. Small, cinnamon-red spots mark the centre of each segment. Shiny, yellow anthers, rust-yellow pollen, scent like *Hesperis*, seed ripens late August. (RHS-LYB 1966)

L. lankongense   Franchet 1892

Occurs at heights of about 10,000 feet in the alpine and subalpine areas of north-western Yunnan. Delavay first found it in 1886 at Lankung, about 20 miles north-west from the Tali lake, similar to *L. duchartrei*.

L. lankongense

White, ovoid bulbs measuring 1¼ inches; two-foot stem, stoloniform at base; up to 15 fine-scented, delicate-pink, pendant, practically unspotted Turk's Cap flowers, which darken with age; racemose inflorescence, flowers during July.

Not difficult in cultivation, but needs partially shaded position in light, damp soils.

L. ledebouri (Baker) Boissier 1898 (*L. monadelphum* M.B. var *ledebouri* Baker)

Found from the Talysh area of eastern Caucasus to the Iranian border. Grows in mountainous terrain and wood clearings at elevations of 3,000–4,500 feet. Perhaps a relic of European lilies, as *L. pyrenaicum* is considered to be its nearest related variety.

Broad, ovoid bulbs of 2–2½ inches, with white scales. Stem 3–4 feet high with narrow to broad, small, linear leaves, each with three to five veins. One to three vanilla-scented, May/June-blooming, Turk's Cap flowers 2–2½ inches in diameter, pale-green to yellow-white with dark-purple spots on the lower half of the petal margins. Orange pollen, self-pollinating, seeds ripen July/August, slow germination. Should be planted in loam; transplanting during autumn. A cross with *L. candidum* may be possible. (RHS-LYB 1966, Saliwski)

L. leichtlinii Hooker 1867

Indigenous to Japan and named after Max Leichtlin, a botanist and plant collector from Baden-Baden. The stem, 2–4 feet high, bears up to 12 pure lemon-yellow, red-purple speckled flowers. They are of the nodding, Martagon type with recurved segments, and bloom during July/August; hardly ever develops seed capsules.

This radiant yellow lily is now very rare, and hardly ever found in cultivation. It is even difficult to find it within its native Japan, where it used to grow at heights of about 4,000 feet on the Yatsugatake mountain in mid-Honshu, mostly among the grass of damp, sloping meadows rich in humus. The orange-flowered variety, by way of contrast, is found almost throughout Japan. *L. leichtlinii* could, in fact, be a mutation from the original stock *L. leichtlinii* var. *maximowiczii*.

L. leichtlinii var. *maximowiczii*, Baker 1871. Distributed over the same area as *L. leichtlinii*; also reported from Korea and Manchuria, where it flourishes among the tall grasses of damp meadows.

The bulb is white, the stem runs underground before emerging, rises 2 feet–6 feet 6 inches high, and is covered with numerous linear-lanceolate leaves. Its irregular inflorescence carries up to a dozen nodding, Turk's Cap, brown-purple speckled flowers of cinnabar-orange – similar to *L. tigrinum*, with which it is often confused. Flowers in Japan from mid-April (on the south coast) till the end of August (in the mountains at 6,000 feet).

If grown under cultivation, where it prefers damp soil rich in humus, it does not usually flower until August, although plants raised from seed of different origin may flower from mid-July to the end of September, and some plants are even capable of producing a second crop of blooms. (NALS-LYB 1949, Dr Emsweller.) The flower buds are hairy, a characteristic which is transmitted to the hybrids.

Has been successfully crossed with *L. × hollandicum* and *L. × maculatum* hybrids. Isabella Preston's well-known hybrid *Tigrimax* is the result of *L. leichtlinii* var. *maximowiczii* × *L. tigrinum*. *L. × maxwill* is probably a form of *L. davidii* rather than a hybrid.

L. leucanthum   Baker 1901

The original lily of this name, first brought to England from the Chinese province of Hupeh by Augustine Henry during 1889, is now lost; only two varieties still exist – *centifolium* and *chloraster*.

L. leucanthum var. *centifolium* Stearn 1935 (*L. centifolium* Stapf). Reginald Farrer found the first two specimens, as garden plants, during 1914 in southern Kansu; he brought two seed capsules back with him, from which all known plants of this name originate. The stem, up to 10 feet tall, carries 10 to 17 large, white, scented, funnel-shaped, horizontally held flowers disposed in a raceme which are pale-yellow inside and carry pink-purple or brownish markings on the outside. The anthers and pollen are red-brown, the pistil and filaments slightly downy, the stem covered with numerous dark-green, linear leaves. Round bulbs of average diameter 2¾ inches, red-brown scales, winter-hardy, needs better than average drainage and overhead protection from excessive wetness during the winter months. Flowers during July and August.

L. leucanthum var. *chloraster* Wilson 1925. Introduced by A. Henry from Hupeh. Grows about 3 feet tall with white, funnel-shaped, green-keeled flowers. Red-brown pollen, July/August-flowering.

Both varieties cross with *L. regale*; var. *chloraster* crossed with *L. henryi* gave the now-lost *L.* × *kewense*.

L. longiflorum   Thunberg 1794, Easter Lily

Named Easter Lily in the United States, where millions are annually raised for sale as pot plants around Easter. Like *L. alexandrae* and *L. nobilissimum*, it comes from the Japanese Ryukyu Islands (particularly the islands of Okinawa, Oshima, Takushima, and Kawanabe), where it grows in humus pockets between coral near the sea. *L. longiflorum* was brought to England in 1819, and was propagated on a large scale in Bermuda throughout the second half of the nineteenth century until severe outbreaks of virus put an end to production. Japan then continued to provide supplies, and delivered 26 million bulbs annually until the outbreak of the Second World War, when production again moved, this time to the United States, particularly Oregon. (*37, 38*)

The bulbs, 2–2¾ inches, are spherical and white-yellow. Stems 1–3 feet long, with many tightly crowded, broad-lanceolate leaves, carry one or more horizontal, pure-white, long, funnel-shaped blooms, size 5–7 inches. The pollen is yellow and the seed germinates quickly. Provided the climatic conditions are ideal, flowers can be produced within six months from seedling stage. *L. longiflorum* does not last very many years when grown in the open in Europe, and is best treated as an indoor pot plant. Flowers from August to September. Prolific producer of bulblets.

This lily has many forms, some of which have been specially raised and selected for quick maturity to meet commercial needs.

L. longiflorum Creole is a clone propagated in the New Orleans area for cut-flower production; grows taller than other forms.

L. longiflorum Croft, another clone. Only 6 inches–2 feet tall and mostly used for potting in the United States. Introduced by Sydney N. Croft in 1928 and propagated on a massive scale.

L. longiflorum Estate, again a clone from S. N. Croft, raised from *Croft*; although a little taller, it is mostly used for cut-flower production.

L. longiflorum Slocum's Ace was discovered in a garden by Clark Slocum of Longlois in 1935. *Ace* is only exceeded by *Croft*, as far as its use as an Easter Lily is concerned, and differs from the other clones, as the width of the funnel-shaped flowers exceeds their length. Other forms have either been superseded or are confined to certain regions, as for instance in Holland, where the taller-growing *Holland's Glory* and *White Queen* are preferred. Dr S. L. Emsweller of the US Department of Agriculture, made a close study of the production of the Easter Lily and conducted a series of strictly controlled experiments in multiplication, disease resistance, propagation, etc. Bermuda produces perfume from this lily.

L. longiflorum Tetrabel. Colchicine treatments carried out by Dr S. L. Emsweller enabled him to introduce three tetraploid clones of *L. longiflorum* ($2n = 48$). *Tetrabel* was raised in England from tetraploid seed and produced triploid hybrids when crossed with *L. formosanum*. (RHS-LYB 1957, NALS-LYB 1964)

L. mackliniae Sealy 1949

Captain Kingdon Ward first found this plant in 1946 in Burma when searching for missing aircraft. Earlier classed as *Nomocharis*, it was actually found on Sirhoi peak, near Ukhrul, at an altitude of 7,500–8,000 feet. Bulbs cream-white, 1–2 inches in diameter; stem usually about 16 inches long, but can be as much as 3 feet. Mostly one to two flowers, certainly never more than seven per stem, pendant, bell-shaped, wide-open, white suffused with pink, 2 inches in diameter. Flowers June/July. *(36)*

Reports from Oregon and England confirm that this plant grows well in open gardens provided it is given acid soil, good drainage and semi-shade. Multiplication by scales or by rapid-germinating seed. (NALS-LYB 1958; RHS-LYB 1946, 1949, 1957, 1966)

L. maculatum   Thunberg 1794

According to the Japanese botanist Moto'o Shimizu (NALS-LYB 1960) this name belongs to a lily growing on the Japanese north island of Hokkaido. It grows, nearly without exception, on the island's Pacific coast on sand, among rocks and grass, and always in open situations. From the east coast, where it flowers earlier, it penetrates a little deeper inland and up to a height of 3,000 feet, but its normal flowering period extends from the end of May until the beginning of August. The three to 12 blooms are relatively large, and are supported by a stem 1–3 feet long. The saucer-shaped flowers are mostly orange-red and heavily speckled. When this lily grows on rock faces, the stem is often in a horizontal position, and bears the flowers in erect form. It seems that this lily likes acid soils, because the companion plant is *Eriophorum vaginatum*.

L. maritimum   Kellogg 1875

A small-flowered lily from mid-California (Mendocino and Sonoma Counties) growing along the coast from San Francisco to Fort Bragg on sand and sandstone soils, at about sea level, and used to being flooded.

Small rhizomatous bulb; stem 20 inches–4 feet; one to eight small, bell-shaped, dark-orange flowers. Very difficult in cultivation on account of the near-impossible growing conditions it requires. (NALS-LYB 1958)

L. martagon   Linnaeus 1753, Turk's Cap Lily

Spread throughout most of Europe and parts of Asia, from the River Rhône in the west to the east of Lake Baykal in Siberia, but avoiding the Siberian Plain. It extends from the 59th Parallel in the north, with the exception of the German lowlands, as far south as the Po valley, Dalmatia, northern Greece and the Hungarian plain. It is found at elevations of 8,000 feet in the northern and southern Alps, likes calcareous soils, beech woods and meadow margins, and only grows in areas undisturbed by agricultural activity and grazing cattle. On the whole, these situations offer good drainage, but even then this lily is also found on moraine, through which water constantly percolates. (73)

The bulb is round and yellow, with numerous pointed scales; the round stem, with dark markings, rises vertically, and usually has only one whorl of spatulate leaves, the rest scattered. It reaches a height of 2–4 feet, and bears three to 12 blooms – but up to 50 flowers and a height of 6 feet is more usual if grown in cultivation. The flower buds are so hairy that they appear to be covered with 'white wool'. The colour of the flowers is variable and depends on location; in the lowlands they are mostly of a light or brown-tinged pink, among mountains a strong, dark, not very clear carmine. The brown-violet spotting is also extremely variable. Some blooms, even if growing within the same location, show no spotting at all, while others are spotted only along the centre of the tepals and others still are heavily speckled over the whole of the segments. The pendulous flowers have fleshy, strongly recurved petals with nectary furrows at the base. The stamens protrude very noticeably from the flower; the pollen is brown-yellow. The style is longer than the stamens, the stigma is dark-red, and the seed capsules are largish-round with angular edges. The light brown-coloured seeds germinate slowly, but if sown immediately after being harvested they usually germinate quickly, although the first leaf only appears after several months of cool conditions. Easily raised and maintained in fertile gardens, particularly if located under light shade of trees, where it can produce self-sown plants.

L. martagon var. *albiflorum* has white flowers with carmine-pink speckles; occasionally found growing wild.

L. martagon var. *album* produces pure-white flowers, usually a little larger and more vigorous than type. Very pretty, particularly if positioned in front of dark-green evergreens. Breeds true from its light-coloured seeds.

L. martagon var. *cattaniae* comes from Dalmatia (whence the old name var. *dalmaticum*). A spectacularly beautiful lily with a large number of dark wine-red, unspotted blooms.

L. martagon var. *hirsutum*. Both the stem and undersides of the leaves are thickly covered with white, cobwebby hairs. Southern Alps.

L. martagon var. *pilosiusculum*. A geographical race with smaller leaves from the Urals and also Siberia, Angara, the Lena region, and Mongolia. Stems, pedicels, buds, and flowers are covered with woolly hairs.

L. martagon var. *daugava* (syn. var. *koknese*) has been described from Russia and Latvia and grows on the banks of the River Daugava between Koknese and Plavinas. Several features distinguish it from *typicum*: its taller growth (up to 6 feet 6 inches); short hairs on the stem; and broader leaves (up to 2 inches). The three to 10 blooms have spotted, strongly recurved, light-purple segments, with a few red hairs. Contrary to type, the seed germinates immediately.

   Both white and wine-red forms of *L. martagon* have been crossed with *L. hansonii* (*L.* × *marhan, L.* × *dalhansonii*). It crosses successfully with *L. pumilum* and *L. medeoloides,* and also, according to C. Bonstedt, with *L. umbellatum.*

L. medeoloides   A. Gray 1859

The Japanese call this variety *Kuruma-Yuri* (Wheel Lily); it is distributed northwards from the main Honshu Islands to Sakhalin and Kurile

Islands to Kamchatka. It is also found on Quelpart Island off southern Korea, in Chekiang, a Chinese east coast province, and in Russia on the lower Amur and on the coast near Vladivostok.

Like *L. martagon*, it carries its leaves in whorls (wheel-shaped), and also resembles it and *L. distichum* in shape and bearing. Grows on volcanic soils at heights of 650–8,000 feet, but prefers the half-shade provided by trees if growing at low altitudes.

Snow-white bulb with jointed scales; green stem 10 inches tall at high elevations and up to 2 feet 3 inches at lower levels; four to 10 broad, lanceolate leaves in each of four whorls; small, nodding, recurved, orange to apricot, black-spotted flowers 1½ inches in diameter which bloom during July/August.

There are several varieties in existence, some without speckles. Cultivation seems to be somewhat difficult; a gravel base 4 inches deep below leaf-mould, provision of winter cover, and semi-shade are recommended. (NALS-LYB 1952, Moto'o Shimizu)

The following hybrids are known: *Marmed* from England (*L. martagon* var. *cattaniae* × *L. medeoloides*), and *Redman* from Canada (*L. hansonii* × *L. medeoloides*).

L. michauxii Poiret 1813 (*L. carolinianum* Michaux)

Occurs at elevations up to 2,500 feet on well-drained, dry ground in south-eastern North America, southern Virginia, North and South Carolina, Georgia, Alabama, and Florida.

Stoloniferous bulb, stem 1–3 feet long, broad lanceolate leaves with waved margins arranged in whorls. Umbellar inflorescence, one to five strongly scented, nodding, shiny orange-red, yellowish-white throated flowers. A stem-rooter which requires planting 4½ inches deep in lime-free, sandy, peat soils. Does not appear to be winter-hardy in Europe.

Professor Showalter, of Harrisonburg, Pennsylvania, has numerous crosses from *L. michauxii*, as with *L. canadense* and *L. harrisianum*. The hybrid *L.* × *harrichauxii* can be crossed with *L. michauxii*, *L. harrisianum*, and *L. superbum*. (NALS-LYB 1961)

L. michiganense   Farwell 1915

Closely related to *L. canadense* and distributed in North America around the Michigan lakes and to a point where the Mississippi and Ohio rivers join at the Kentucky border.

Like *L. canadense*, it has a stoloniferous bulb; other features are a stem 2–5 feet tall with elliptic leaves set in whorls, one to eight red-orange flowers on long, upright pedicels, pendulous, richly spotted red-brown and of the graceful Turk's Cap type, although with more recurved segments than those of *L. canadense*. Reddish-yellow pollen; flowers during June/July; flourishes in loam soils (pH 8–5), and is usually found in meadows; likes full sun. Germinates slowly. Crosses with *L. canadense* and *L. michauxii*.

L. monadelphum   Marschall von Bieberstein 1808

Mostly found growing in the black leaf-mould of beech woods, up to an altitude of 7,000 feet in north Caucasus, from Maikop to Kuban.

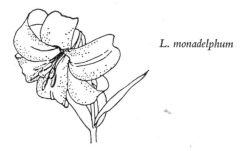

L. monadelphum

It is one of the earliest lilies and already in flower during mid-June. The stem only rises 2 feet–2 feet 6 inches in nature, but up to 4 feet in cultivation; short pedicels carry 5–20 strongly scented, pendulous, wide-open, pure-yellow, pale-lilac, spotted, trumpet-shaped blooms. The unusual arrangement of the conjoined stamens around the ovary gave rise to its Latin name *monadelphum*, which means single brother-hood. The fairly large bulb is egg-shaped. Free-draining loam soils which have been enriched with leaf-mould provide the best growing medium for this lily, which dislikes being transplanted – in fact suffers as a result of it. If it has to be moved, autumn is the best time; an alternative is to raise it from its readily germinating seeds. Reports state that crosses with *L. bulbiferum* and *L.* × *maculatum* are possible. (RHS-LYB 1966, Saliwski)

L. nanum   Klotzsch and Garcke 1862

A small-leaved alpine lily, only 6–16 inches high, with pendulous, bell-shaped, pale-lilac or also cream-yellow flowers with purple speckles. Distribution: the Himalayas from Bashahr eastwards to Garhwal, Kumaon, Nepal, Sikkim; south-eastern Tibet to Bhutan and west Szechwan; north-western Yunnan at heights of 9,000–15,000 feet. In cultivation since 1852, although rare. (RHS-LYB 1951–52, 1962)

L. neilgherrense   Wight 1853

Grows further south (as far as the 10th Northern Parallel) than any other lily, and comes from the southern Indian mountains Nilgiri, Pulney, and Cardamon (6,000–8,500 feet).

The round bulbs of 4-inch diameter have brown-margined, yellow scales. Dark-green, lanceolate leaves grow from the three-feet-long stem, which carries one or two heavily scented trumpet flowers, 7–10 inches long, positioned at right angles to the main stem. They are pure-white with yellow throat, reflexed, and at their best between August and September.

Unsuitable for growing in the open – should be reserved for pot culture or the cool greenhouse. The stem runs underground, and produces bulblets. Prefers pure leaf-mould and damp atmosphere.

L. nepalense   D. Don 1821

A genuine trumpet-type lily, even if the trumpet is wide-open and the petals strongly recurved. There are one to five drooping, pea-green flowers dark-purple within, loosely arranged on the stem, 4 feet tall, which also bears broad lanceolate leaves. The bulb is flat and round, with broad, overlapping and tightly closed white scales, slightly tinged

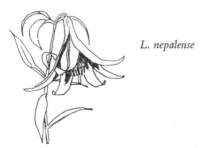

L. nepalense

with pink. The stem runs up to 5 feet underground, and forms bulb-lets on the internodes before rising to the surface. A comparative late starter, which does not produce shoots until May, but nevertheless flowers during July. (45)

L. nepalense is not winter-hardy in northern and central Europe, al-though it overwinters, without surface protection, in Scotland and Oregon. Surface protection from autumn and winter rains is necessary. This very exotic lily is a native of Nepal, Bhutan and Kumaon.

L. nepalense var. *concolor* originates from Assam, is self-coloured, yellow, and without the purple throat.

In spite of repeated endeavours, breeders have had little success in crossing this lily with other funnel-shaped types. The only reports are from Tuffery of New Zealand, who has produced hybrids with *L. formosanum*, and from Palmer about Warburton hybrids arising from *L. regale* × *L. nepalense* × *L.* × *aurelianense*. (RHS-LYB 1951–52, 1954, 1956, 1962; International Lily Register)

L. nepalense var. *robustum*. A recently introduced form with pendulous, strongly reflexed, emerald flowers with purple-violet centres and of pleasing fragrance. It is said that this form is less susceptible to frost, and may even tolerate sub-zero temperatures. The stem runs underground before rising to the surface, and the first growing shoots do not appear until May. Flowers during July/August, requires deep, very well-drained yet damp soil.

L. nevadense   Eastwood 1933

Found in the Sierra Nevada from northern California to Mount Shasta and in Oregon, mostly on damp alluvial soils in meadows and along river banks. The bulbs are solitary, rhizomatous with triple-jointed scales. The stem is 2–3 feet high, occasionally higher, with broad lanceolate leaves arranged in whorls. Up to 25 small, speckled, scented flowers of orange-yellow with red tips. Should be planted 4–4½ inches deep in good draining leaf-mould mixed with peat and sand. Slow germination.

Successfully crossed with *L. parryi* (O. E. Wyatt).

L. nobilissimum   T. Makino 1914

Like *L. alexandrae*, with which it has for long been confused, it comes from only one of the Japanese Ryukyu Islands, namely Kuchi-no-shima; it grows on only the steepest cliffs, and can only be reached by mountaineers. Known locally as *Tamoto Yuri*. (44)

The stem is 20–24 inches high, and of particularly erect growing habit. It carries one to three erect, umbellately disposed flowers, funnel-shaped, 4–4½ inches long, pure-white inside, suffused with green on the outside, and strongly scented. The pollen is yellow, the stigma is of a light colour; the plant flowers during June/July, seeds germinate within 30–40 days. (RHS-LYB 1950, NALS-LYB 1952)

L. occidentale   Purdy 1897

One of the rarest lilies, growing along the north Californian coast to south Oregon and mostly in dry sphagnum bogs. The small bulbs grow on short rhizomes and the stem, bearing narrowly elliptic leaves in whorls, reaches 2–6 feet. The one to 15 small, pendulous, Turk's Cap flowers are green at their base, with brown-spotted, orange throat; the reflexed petals are tipped with crimson. Purple anthers, orange pollen, flowers during July, prefers lime-free loam soils with additions of leaf-mould and peat. Slow germination.

L. ocellatum   (Kell.) Beane 1955, ssp. *ocellatum* – ssp. *bloomerianum*

A native from Santa Barbara to San Diego. Both lilies were previously known by the names of *L. humboldtii* and *L. bloomerianum*, and belong to the land type, with jointed bulb-scales. The cadmium-orange, red-tipped, spherical, reflexed segments are marked with dark spots surrounded by a crimson halo; soft-green leaves arranged in more or less regular whorls. *Typicum ocellatum* is always stem-rooting; *ocellatum* grows to 4–6 feet and produces 30 or more flowers if situated in a favourable position; ssp. *bloomerianum* grows only 2–3 feet tall, with few flowers, favours dry, mountainous regions, and is not a stem-rooter. (RHS-LYB 1957)

L. oxypetalum   Baker 1874

West Nepal, Kumaon, Garhwal at altitudes of 9,500–13,000 feet. Grows only 8–10 inches high, single or double bell-shaped, pendulous, green-yellow flowers. (RHS-LYB 1951–52)

L. oxypetalum var. *insigne*. A purple form with green markings found in 1939 by Major Sherriff at Simla, Hill States. More vigorous in growth than the yellow type, but only gives of its best if grown on leaf-mould under light shade. Slow germination. (RHS-LYB 1962)

L. papilliferum   Franchet 1892

Although first discovered in 1888 by Delavay in north-western Yunnan, where it is to be found at an altitude of 10,000 feet among rocks and on stony mountain meadows, it was not introduced into cultivation until

46. *L. speciosum* var. *album* is, apart from *L. auratum*, one of the loveliest Asiatic lilies.
The many varieties of *L. speciosum* range from pink to deep-red. They produce their
best flowers when grown under glass

47. *L. szovitsianum* comes from the Caucasus and bears flowers ranging from the colour of straw to deep-gold-yellow

48. *L. tsingtauense* prefers damp situations; bulbs are rarely found in the trade and are therefore best raised from seed

49. *L. rubellum* from Japan, open trumpet flower, delicately flushed with pink

50. *Cardiocrinum giganteum* grows eight feet high if provided with damp soil rich in humus. Very strong-stemmed. Has white blooms marked in yellow and red. The variety *yunnanense* does not reach this height and produces bronze-brown leaves

51. *Cavalier* is a golden-yellow Dauricum-Maculatum-Davidii hybrid
52. Redbird hybrid
53. *Royal Sovereign*, golden-yellow and heavily spotted; a Jan de Graaff Mid-Century hybrid

54. *Roter Prinz*, a newly bred, terracotta-flowered lily with pyramid-shaped flower spikes. A tried and proved lily suitable as a garden plant and for cutting. Late-flowering and therefore fills a useful gap

55. *Sir Frederick Stern*, bred in England by Darby. An interesting lily. Heavily speckled yellow flowers inherited from Emsweller's Dark Princess. The petal margins are also spotted and give the plant a very individual character

56. Paisley hybrids from Jan de Graaff are Martagon hybrids in various shades of yellow, also red – all heavily spotted

57. Aurelian hybrids: *upper left, L. sargentiae; upper right, L. henryi.* The other varieties shown have been obtained from crosses of the above lilies

58. *Johannisblut*, a shiny, dark, blood-red hybrid from *L.* × *scottiae*
59. Parade hybrids, golden-yellow touched with orange. Originated from Jan de Graaff's *Parade* and Emsweller's *Cavalier*
60. *Sonnentiger*, a late-flowering Tiger hybrid, open, yellow blooms with orange centres

1946, and then by the plant collector Dr J. F. Rock. Soon afterwards it flowered in both England and the United States.

The bulb is about 1¼ inches high and has lanceolate scales; the stem, which first grows underground and eventually rises through the surface to a height of 2 feet, bears numerous linear leaves and carries one to three flowers. They are scented, of shiny dark-purple bordering on black, strongly reflexed – the inner petals more so – giving the appearance of a triangular outline. Brown stamens, orange pollen, flowers during August.

An interesting but apparently difficult lily to grow. Related to *L. davidii*. (RHS-LYB 1949)

L. paradoxum   Stearn 1956

Discovered at a height of 12,000 feet at the most northerly point of the Tsangpo river in south-eastern Tibet during 1947 by Ludlow, Sherriff and Elliot. A single-flowered lily, 8–10 inches tall, leaves arranged in whorls, erect-flowering, open, saucer-shaped, purple blooms of diameter 2–2¾ inches. Not in cultivation. (RHS-LYB 1958)

L. pardalinum   Kellogg 1859, Panther Lily

The Panther Lily of California is one of the easiest to grow, and certainly among the most beautiful, American wood lilies. Several bulbs with numerous yellowish, brittle and jointed scales grow from the thick and branching rhizomes. The stem reaches 4 feet–6 feet 6 inches, bears lanceolate leaves in whorls. The scentless Turk's Cap flowers, 2 inches in diameter, are borne on long, elegant, upward-spreading pedicels, and are of shiny orange-red with carmine tips and mottled in red-brown towards the centre; strongly reflexed. Nectary furrows are green, pollen is orange, the flowering period July, and the germination slow.

Only *L. harrisianum* (*L. pardalinum* var. *giganteum*) has a more brilliant colour. *L. pardalinum* requires damp, limefree soils, full sun, and protection from wind. This is a most variable species, and grows in northern California, southern Oregon and the coastal areas from Humboldt

County to San Diego County. Cross-fertilization with *L. parvum*, *L. parryi* and *L. humboldtii* is possible. (NALS-LYB 1952)

L. parryi   Watson 1878

This is perhaps the most beautiful of all American lilies. The stem, 2–6 feet high with leaves arranged in whorls, carries scented, funnel-shaped blooms on oblique, upward-slanting pedicels. The pale-yellow flowers, usually between one and 15, but occasionally up to 50 in number, are spotted brown, with the lower half of each segment incurved and reflexed. Usually found in southern California and Arizona at 6,000–10,000 feet, mostly on granite soils and in situations where the bulb is covered by ice and snow for half the year. Difficult to raise in cultivation; must have free-draining soil consisting preferably of two to three parts of leaf-mould and peat mixed with stone chippings and charcoal. Bulbs should not be planted too deeply, and preferably in situations where the base of the plant is not exposed to full sunlight. Water requirements are unusually heavy during growth but, as soon as flowering has ceased, bulbs should receive surface protection from rain until the onset of frosts.

L. parryi var. *kessleri* is from the San Gabriel Mountains in California, and is hardier than *typicum*. (NALS-LYB 1958)

Hybrid production especially with *L. pardalinum*, *L. kelloggii*, *L. humboldtii*, and *L. ocellatum* (Bellingham hybrids).

L. parvum   Kellogg 1862

An alpine lily growing at heights ranging from 5,000–10,000 feet from the Californian Sierra Nevada to the Cascade Mountains in southern Oregon; mostly along the banks of streams and in wet glacial meadows. From the small rhizomatous bulbs rises a stem 3–4 feet long which bears small, June/July-blooming, erect, bell-shaped, brown-spotted flowers of either yellow, orange or red (depending on altitude). Requires free-draining, sandy damp soil rich in humus, and multiplies without difficulty from both seeds and bulb-scales.

Capable of cross-pollination with *L. parryi* and *L. pardalinum*.

L. parvum var. *crocatum* has pure-orange-yellow, crimson-spotted, bell-shaped flowers without any red. (NALS-LYB 1952)

L. philadelphicum Linnaeus 1762

Named by Linnaeus, this lily grows throughout a vast area – from the eastern side of the Rocky Mountains to where the rivers Ohio and Mississippi join. Ovoid bulb on short stolons, lanceolate leaves, usually arranged in whorls around the stem, 1 foot 6 inches–3 feet long. One to five wide-open, erect, saucer-shaped flowers of bright orange-scarlet, turning orange towards the centre and mostly heavily speckled in brown. The claw-shaped segments are small, and resemble *L. catesbaei*. Mrs J. Norman Henry collected a great number of colour variants, ranging from pale lemon-yellow to orange and many shades of red and light-brown – both spotted and unspotted. Germinates slowly, requires sandy, free-draining loam enriched with leaf-mould and peat. Protection from winter rain and snow is essential.

L. philadelphicum var. *andinum* Ker-Gawler 1822. Found in the mountains along the Missouri river and as far as British Columbia – differentiated by its scattered linear leaves along the stem.

Dr F. L. Skinner raised hybrids from the North American and Asiatic saucer lilies *L. dauricum* and *L.* × *maculatum*.

L. philippinense Baker 1873

Occurs in the Philippine Islands on Luzon, where it grows on steep grass slopes at heights of 4,500–6,000 feet. The stem can be up to 3 feet long, and carries either one or two clear-white, long-tubed trumpet flowers during July and August.

Unfortunately not winter-hardy in central Europe, but as it is capable of reaching flowering stage within 18 months, it is ideal as a pot plant or for cutting. (NALS-LYB 1960)

L. pitkinense   Beane and Vollmer 1955

One of the *pardalinum* group; first discovered in 1952 and seemingly confined in nature to only one situation, the Pitkin Marsh in Sonoma County, California, where unfortunately it often falls victim to the grazing animals which roam the marshes of the region. Can grow as high as 6 feet from a stoloniferous rhizome, and resembles *L. pardalinum*. The July-flowering Turk's Cap blooms are reflexed, bright-vermilion to scarlet with yellow centres; slow germination.

Eric Mayell crossed this lily with *L. kelloggii*, and obtained delicate mauve-tinted, vigorous hybrids (Monterey hybrids). Hybrids with shiny vermilion to scarlet blooms were the result of a cross between *L.* × *burbankii* and *L. pitkinense*; they have rhizomes of such size and strength that they can only be parted with an axe! (NALS-LYB 1955, Vollmer; RHS-LYB 1966; RHS-LYB 1957; NALS-LYB 1960, Mayell)

L. polyphyllum   D. Don 1840

Comes from the Himalayas, where it grows at heights of 6,000–12,000 feet from Afghanistan to Kashmir and as far as Kumaon.

The long, small, white bulbs are deep-rooting, and grow at a depth of 1–2 feet below ground level. The stem mostly reaches a height of 16 inches–4 feet, occasionally even up to 8 feet, has linear or small lanceolate leaves and usually one to 10 blooms, but on occasions up to 40. The drooping flowers are bell-shaped, the lower halves of the petals are strongly reflexed, greenish-yellow within the funnel, cream on the outside, prettily spotted with lilac. The pollen is orange-red, germination is slow. A very difficult subject in cultivation which needs to be planted deeply, in half-shade, and protected from the wind; it must not be put in a south-facing position or be transplanted – in order to avoid damage to the long root system. Rapid germination. (RHS-LYB 1954)

L. pomponium   Linnaeus 1753

This European lily, described by Clusius in 1601 and by Parkinson in 1629, comes from the French Maritime Alps between Nice and

Ventimiglia, where it grows on limestone cliffs, in full sun, among grass and witch hazel on fairly dry ground.

The ovoid bulb has a diameter of $1\frac{1}{2}$–2 inches, and is cream in colour. The purple-flushed stem, 16–20 inches long, is thickly set with small, silver-margined, grass-like, linear leaves. Up to 10 pendulous, red-lead coloured, Turk's Cap flowers which are marked with small dark spots. Vermilion pollen, unpleasant smell, June-flowering, germinates slowly; multiplication by seeds and bulb-scales; should be planted in full sun on loam soil previously prepared with leaf-mould and limestone chippings.

L. ponticum   K. Koch 1849

Distributed along the south coast of the Black Sea, at Trabzon on the Zigana pass in Turkey and above Artvin, and at Batum in Russia. Grows at altitudes of 6,000–7,500 feet, usually on cliffs and grassy slopes and also above the tree-line.

The small conical bulbs, 1–3 inches in diameter, have few scales. One to three flowers, occasionally up to 12, on a stem 15–30 inches long with short but broad lanceolate leaves, ciliate at edges, giving the appearance of silver margins; hairy along veins on undersides of leaves.

The Martagon-type flowers, diameter $1\frac{1}{4}$–$1\frac{1}{2}$ inches, are similar to those of *L. pyrenaicum*, without hairs, and range from pale to deep-yellow and orange with heavily spotted throat which is often without markings and solely purple. The perianth has an outer flushing of purple, the pollen is orange, the smell is strong and unpleasant; freshly harvested seeds germinate immediately. (Illustrated in RHS-LYB 1964.)

There is yet another unnamed lily in the Trabzon region, first found by E. K. Balls in 1930 and which has been classified with *L. ponticum* and wrongly described as such in *Lilies of the World* by Woodcock and Stearn. Compared with *L. ponticum* it has very large lanceolate leaves, thickly covered with hair, and comparatively small flowers. (Marked as x on map, page 4.) (RHS-LYB 1964, 1966, Furse)

L. primulinum Baker 1892

The three varieties of this lily are from upper Burma, western Yunnan and Siam.

L. primulinum var. *burmaniacum* grows 4–8 feet high, has two to seven medium-large, greenish-yellow Turk's Cap flowers with purple-flecked throat. Winter-hardy in England, provided it is grown in a sheltered position.

L. primulinum var. *ochraceum* rises to a height of 4 feet, and has small, July-blooming, strongly reflexed wine-red flowers with green-ochre tips.

L. primulinum var. *primulinum* has self-coloured, primrose-yellow Turk's Cap blooms.

L. pumilum De Candolle 1812

This lovely and graceful lily, previously known as *L. tenuifolium*, is distributed over a wide area comprising northern Korea, Manchuria, eastern Siberia, Mongolia and northern China. Small, white, conical bulbs. Stem up to 18 inches high with numerous, grass-like, small leaves and one to 20 shiny red, nodding Turk's Cap blooms occasionally with lightly black-spotted throat. Scarlet pollen, flowers during June. *(43)*

Tolerates calcareous soils provided they are free-draining, likes full sun, is stem-rooting and should not be planted deeper than 4 inches; requires protection from rain. Should be propagated continuously from its rapid-germinating seeds, as plants in cultivation are short-lived. Highly suitable for use as cut flowers. Crossed with *L. martagon* var. *album* (*Golden Gleam*), *L. concolor*, *L. bulbiferum* var. *croceum*, *L. dauricum*, *L. philadelphicum*, *L. callosum*, *L. cernuum*, and *L. amabile*. (NALS-LYB 1968)

L. pyrenaicum Gouan 1773

The name indicates the Pyrenees origin of this relatively early known lily (1598), which flourishes in northern Spain, the eastern Pyrenees, and south-western France (Tarn) on wood margins, in meadows and on mountains (1,500–4,500 feet). It is even found growing wild in the hedgerows of England. The broad, round bulb of about 2¾ inches diameter has yellowish-white scales. Numerous linear-lanceolate leaves – too many in relation to the small blooms – grow on the 1–4 feet high stem. The unpleasant-smelling, pendulous, one to 12, strongly reflexed Turk's Cap flowers are greenish-yellow and marked with weak, black speckles. Dark-orange pollen, flowers early from the end of May until June, germinates slowly and is multiplied from either seeds, bulb-scales or by division. Grows well in heavy loam with high humus content; tolerates lime, full sun or half-shade. (*42*)

L. pyrenaicum var. *rubrum* is the more beautiful, with its orange red, brown-spotted flowers, and is considered as *typicum,* while the yellow-flowering form is the variant. Grows wild in the Burgos region of Spain.

L. regale   Wilson 1912, Regal Lily

Perhaps the most important of all E. H. Wilson's discoveries. Found in China in 1903, *L. regale* is confined to a small area, only part of a valley through which the River Min flows in northern Chengtu. The valley is desolate, uncultivated, excessively hot in summer, desperately cold in winter, and surrounded by the steeply rising cliffs of snow-covered mountains 18,000 feet high. But during June the valley changes into a veritable paradise full of the blossom and the sweet scent of the Regal Lily, which grows in hundreds of thousands on the rocky cliffs at about 5,000 feet above sea level. E. H. Wilson nearly lost his life and had his leg crushed by stones when he returned to this spot in 1910; but he collected between 6,000 and 7,000 bulbs which today still form the basic stock of *L. regale* in the Western world. (*10*)

The lanceolate scales of the round, 6-inch diameter bulbs turn purple if exposed to the light. The wiry, slightly arched stem reaches 2 feet 6 inches–4 feet, occasionally even higher, and has numerous one-veined linear leaves. There are one to eight (often more) highly fragrant, wide-open, trumpet-shaped flowers, arranged in a wheel-shaped umbel, with more or less strongly recurved, shiny, silk-like, white petals and yellow throat with an outer flushing of pink-purple, particularly along the centre rib. The anthers and pollen are yellow, the style and stigma green. Flowers during the first half of July.

It is a prolific seed producer, irrespective of whether self- or cross-pollinated; the only possible true cross is with *L. leucanthum* var. *centifolium*. When used as a pollen provider it has crossed with *L. sargentiae* (*L.* × *imperiale*), *L. sulphureum* (*L.* × *sulphurgale*). Good and quick germination. This stem-rooting lily should be planted in a sunny position in soils rich in humus, and must be protected from late frosts with heavy layers of mulch or a covering of straw. There is no other lily which is less demanding, more rewarding and more long-living than *L. regale*, and none so easily and cheaply raised from seed.

It is not certain whether the pure-gold-yellow *L. regale* (*Royal Gold*) is a hybrid or a mutation – but its beauty is beyond doubt.

L. rhodopeum   Delipavloff 1952

This recently discovered lily was found in the Smoljan district of the Bulgarian Rhodope Mountains at Sivino. Grows in meadows lying 4,000 feet above sea level, and is usually compared to *L. monadelphum*. It has one to two, but mostly three to five, nodding, unspotted blooms of

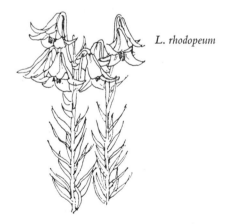

L. rhodopeum

diameter 3–6 inches with recurved orange perianth; umbellar. The pollen is scarlet, the bulb is white with numerous scales, the flowering period July, the stem 30–40 inches long and clothed with long linear leaves along its entire length. (RHS-LYB 1962)

L. rubellum   Baker 1898

An alpine lily mostly growing at heights from 3,000–6,000 feet among grass and thickets in the northern parts of the Japanese main island, Honshu, and known there as *Otome-Yuri*, the Maiden Lily. (*49*)

The bulb is very large, of long oval shape with ovate-lanceolate scales. The stem only reaches 1 foot in natural conditions, but rises to 20 inches under cultivation, The linear-lanceolate, short-petioled leaves are thicker on the upper part of the stem and are spirally arranged throughout its length. The fragrant horizontal trumpet flowers, one to three in number, $1\frac{3}{4}$ inches long and $2\frac{1}{2}$ inches wide, are at first a delicate pink, which darkens later to purple-pink. Yellow pollen, sphere-like seed capsules with triangular thin seeds which germinate within a few months.

The remarkable fact about this very delicately tinted lily is that it flowers about one month (mid-May to end of May) from the time it first produces shoots (mid-April). It achieves this, similar to a hyacinth, by building the flower within the bulb before winter breaks. There is undoubtedly a future for this plant and its hybrids for forcing purposes, as its quickly achieved maturity must lead to useful economies for horticulturists.

Its cultivation is not very simple, requiring a very acid soil, a great deal of water, protection from rain, and snow cover during the winter. K. Wada recommends that bulbs be planted in sphagnum-filled, free-draining pots which must be constantly kept damp and can be placed in a sunny position until flowering, after which half-shade prolongs the life of the blooms. (NALS-LYB 1951, Moto'o Shimizu)

The heavy water requirements of *L. rubellum* have been confirmed by Ralph Warner, who reports that he has successfully grown this lily on the banks of a stream with the roots at watertable height.

Crossed with *L. auratum, L. speciosum* and *L. japonicum*.

L. rubescens   Watson 1879

An American west coast lily growing from San Francisco Bay north-wards into Siskiyou County and usually found on northern faces of the

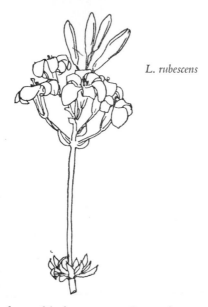

L. rubescens

redwood belt, on very dry soils up to 3,000 feet. White bulb with broad scales. Slim stem 2–6 feet high, often higher, carries several whorls of oblanceolate leaves, whorls decrease in size as they ascend the stem. The loose raceme inflorescence can carry up to 100, but as a rule three to 30 erect, trumpet-shaped flowers; the petals form a tube, but the last third of their length is strongly recurved. The flowers are at first white with fine-purple spots, but turn pink to wine-red later. Remarkable for its wonderful fragrance. June/July-flowering, requires damp loam and best possible drainage. Germinates slowly. Crossed with *L. columbianum*. (RHS-LYB 1934, NALS-LYB 1952)

L. sargentiae   Wilson 1912

Another significant discovery by E. H. Wilson, who first collected *L. sargentiae* in 1903 in the Tung valley in Szechwan, where it grows between rocks on shale and among grass and scrub. The climate in this region is well known for its hot summers and long, cold winters. (57)

The round bulb, 6 inches in diameter, has broad, red-purple scales. The stem, too, is purple, and grows 4–5 feet tall; it bears many dark-green, closely spaced, lanceolate leaves – broader than those of *L. regale* – with bulbils in their axils. The large, funnel-shaped flowers are pure-white within, have a yellow throat, and are shaded in either purple-pink, brown or green on the outside. The rose tints on the outside of the petals are remarkable in so far as they even spread to the inside, and breeders have succeeded in emphasizing this characteristic in the Pink Trumpets. The plant carries up to 18 elegantly recurved and deliciously fragrant blooms, which appear two weeks later than those of *L. regale*. Purple anthers, brown pollen, purple style and stigma. Multiplication by axil bulbils and seeds; seeds germinate immediately; more delicate than *L. regale*; requires good drainage, a warm location or a cool greenhouse, and rich soil.

Crosses with *L. regale* (*L.* × *imperiale*), with *L. henryi* (*L.* × *aurelian-ense*).

L. sempervivoideum   Léveillé 1915

A Chinese lily from Yunnan, which only grows 6 inches tall, has fine, grass-like leaves, and up to three small, white, pendulous, finely purple-spotted flowers. Grows on stony ground at heights of about 8,000 feet. The shape of its bulb gave rise to the name *sempervivoideum*. Not in cultivation.

L. shastense   (Eastw.) Beane 1955

Native to the American counties of Plumas, Shasta and Siskiyou; named after Mount Shasta in Siskiyou County, where it grows in rich profusion. Looks like a diminutive *L. harrisianum*. *L. shastense* has strongly reflexed, cadmium-yellow flower petals with cadmium-red to sienna-brown tips – but these darker colours spread over the whole bloom as it matures; ochre-yellow pollen. One or more stems, bearing linear to lanceolate leaves arranged in whorls, rise from scale-covered rhizomes. (RHS-LYB 1957)

L. sherriffiae   Stearn 1950

First found in 1949 by Mrs and Major Sherriff in the Himalayas (Bhutan) at an altitude of 9,000 feet. Delicate, 2 feet tall; winter-hardy in both England and Scotland; one to three bell-shaped flowers of light and dark purple; tessellated like a *fritillaria*. Seeds germinate immediately. (RHS-LYB 1951–52, 1957, 1962, 1965)

L. souliei

This alpine lily was until recently considered as *Nomocharis*, but is now included in the genus *Lilium*. It grows from a small bulb with lanceolate scales to a height of about 6 inches, and has saucer-shaped, pendulous, deep carmine-brown flowers. Its native habitat is at an altitude of 10,000–14,000 feet in south-western Yunnan, south-eastern Tibet, and northern Assam. Named after the French missionary Soulié, who first discovered it, and who was murdered in 1905 by Tibetan monks. Not found in cultivation. (RHS-LYB 1951–52)

L. speciosum   Thunberg 1794

Next in beauty to the Golden-Rayed Lily of Japan, this magnificent species comes from the southern Japanese islands of Shikoku and Kyushu, but grows also on the island of Formosa and in the central Chinese provinces of Kiangsi and Anhwei. (46)

The yellow to purple-brown bulb is round. The stem is 3–4 feet high, wiry and clothed with scattered, leather-textured, broad, green, lanceolate leaves. The large, fragrant, nodding blooms, four to 10 in number, are carried during August and September on somewhat stiff pedicels; the blooms are strongly reflexed and of a delicate pink with wavy white margins, while the lower parts of the petals are spotted with crimson papillae; prominently protruding anthers and stigma, chocolate to purple-brown pollen.

If grown in the open, botrytis and autumn rains often spoil the magnificent blooms of this rather late-flowering lily, which only shows its full perfection if cultivated as a pot plant or if grown in a cool greenhouse. The seeds, slow germinators in any circumstances, seldom ripen on plants grown outdoors, although multiplication is possible by means of the numerous bulblets this stem-rooter provides. If it must be grown in an open garden, a well-sheltered place with good soil liberally enriched with peat and leaf-mould is essential: the chosen site should also afford ground shade. Wonderful lilies have resulted from a cross with *L. auratum*; other existing crosses are with *L. nobilissimum*, *L. henryi* and *L. nepalense*.

L. speciosum appears in many forms in nature, and selections have in addition given a host of different colour shades, of which the most important are:

L. speciosum var. *album* and *L. speciosum* var. *album-novum*; both are white-flowering, but the last-named is the more vigorous.

L. speciosum var. *gloriosoides*. A fine, rare, but susceptible form, which takes the place of *L. speciosum* in both China and Formosa. Strongly reflexed, waved perianth, deep-scarlet with the colour concentrated in the bottom quarter of the petals.

L. speciosum var. *kraetzeri*. Pure-white with a green stripe along the petal centres. Used for forcing.

L. speciosum var. *rubrum*. Dark-purple stem and carmine flowers.

L. speciosum Gilrey. A selection of ruby-red blooms made by Gilbert Errey of Australia. (NALS-LYB 1962)

L. stewartianum   Balfour 1925

Forrest first found this lily growing in stony alpine meadows on limestone cliffs in Yunnan during 1913 at a height of 10,000–11,000 feet. The plant collector Dr Rock saw it again in Yunnan in 1949, but only at one single site, and again on the snow-line. A fine, delicate plant with grass-like leaves and small, cylindrical-shaped, drooping blooms strongly recurved from the lower third of the perianth segments. Fragrant, deep greenish-olive-yellow, finely spotted with chestnut-brown. Although it flowered in England in 1952, it is not now in cultivation.

L. sulphureum   Baker 1891 (*L. myriophyllum* Franchet)

Described in lily literature for some time as *L. myriophyllum* Franchet, and discovered by the French missionary Delavay at Lankong in north-western Yunnan. Its home country extends from south to north Yunnan (Tali Mountains) into the Shan States of upper Burma, growing at heights of 4,000–5,000 feet on stony, red loam.

Thick, fleshy, purple scales form the bulb, which is approximately 4 inches in diameter. The erect stem rises 3–6 feet high, and is clothed with numerous, spreading, linear-lanceolate leaves, and a seemingly equally high number of axil bulbils. Bears up to 15 narrow, drooping, trumpet-shaped blooms (6–8 inches long) which are fragrant and have a deep-yellow throat changing to ivory-yellow on the petal tips; flushed pink on the outside. Brown anthers, yellow pollen, poor seed production.

Although it can be grown in the open in Europe, it is unfortunately not very long-living. Perfect drainage with a gravel and rubble base are a must, and so is a southerly position and shelter from cold winds. The bulb should be planted 10–12 inches deep, preferably in good loam fortified with leaf-mould, sand, and some bonemeal. Alkaline soils are to be avoided; surface protection during winter months is advisable. This is a late plant, and shows no top growth until mid or late May, when some other lilies are perhaps already 20 inches tall; it flowers at the end of August or early September.

L. sulphureum is used a great deal for breeding. The hybrid *L.* × *sulphurgale* which first flowered during 1915 was bred by Professor Scheubel, Oberlahnstein, Germany, from *L. sulphureum* × *L. regale*. The Crows hybrids are the result of *L.* × *sulphurgale* × *L. imperiale*. *T.A.*

Havemeyer is of *L. sulphureum* × *L. henryi* parentage. Other existing hybrids have been produced from crosses with *L. centifolium* and *L. sargentiae*. (RHS-LYB 1950)

L. superbum   Linnaeus 1762

From the eastern United States, already known in London in 1738, and included in *Species Plantarum* by Linnaeus in 1762. It ranges from Massachusetts in the east and Indiana in the midwest to Alabama and Florida in the south, and is especially numerous on the Atlantic coast, where it is found in rich and damp humus on grassy slopes, acid meadows and marshes. (40)

The round, pointed, white bulb is mounted on strong stolons. Lanceolate leaves, in whorls, clothe the purple stem, which in cultivation rises to almost 10 feet and carries a pyramid-shaped head of up to 40 long-petioled, large, nodding, Turk's Cap blooms of orange-yellow with carmine petal tips; speckled-brown throat, green star at base of flower. The colour of the flowers is variable, and many yellow-shaded forms have been observed, as well as pure-red, collected by Mrs J. Norman Henry. Flowers during July/August; slow germination; susceptible to virus. It does well if grown in the open, provided it is planted 6–8 inches deep, on a gravel base and in damp, lime-free soil – preferably among low-growing shrubs but with the stem exposed to the full sun.

Crossed with *L. canadense* and *L. michauxii*.

L. szovitsianum   Fisch. and Lall. 1840

Found in woods, wood clearings and margins, and on the rocky slopes in the subalpine zones of western and southern Transcaucasia, as well as on the south shore of the Black Sea from Batum to Trabzon at heights of 2,000–5,000 feet. (47)

Equally as beautiful as the similar *L. monadelphum*. Small-scaled, large bulbs $2\frac{3}{4}$–$4\frac{1}{2}$ inches. Two to eight flowers, sometimes as many as 20, on stems 3 feet 3 inches–5 feet long, lanceolate leaves.

The strongly scented, Martagon-type flowers of 2¾–3 inches diameter have recurved, light-yellow segments, brown pollen. Flourishes in cultivation, but, like *L. monadelphum*, requires heavy soil, and being a stem-rooter should only be transplanted during the autumn. Autumn-sown seeds germinate during the following spring, and should be left in the seedbed for up to two to three years before being transplanted to their permanent quarters – preferably during the autumn. Free-draining loam and a planting depth of 4–6 inches suits them well. Covering with either leaves or wood shavings is recommended in winter.

Crossed with *L. maculatum* hybrids (Mitchurin 1914, Orekhov 1960). (RHS-LYB 1964, 1966, Eremin, Saliwski)

L. taliense   Franchet 1892

Named after the Tali Range in north-eastern Yunnan. Resembles *L. duchartrei* both in shape and in the colour of its nodding, white, purple-speckled, Turk's Cap flowers. It is equally strongly scented, but differs from *L. duchartrei* in two respects: its racemose inflorescence; and the dark-purple nectary furrows in the centre of each petal.

Multiplied on a large scale from seed by Jan de Graaff. Appears to be suitable for breeding, particularly with the Harlequin hybrids (*L. cernuum* × Midcentury hybrids).

L. tigrinum   Ker-Gawler 1810, Tiger Lily

Japan, Korea, eastern China and Manchuria are the home of this lily. Like potatoes, the bulb contains starch, and it is cultivated, cooked and eaten in both Japan and China; in fact, it resembles the taste of mashed potatoes. The Japanese name for this triploid lily (three sets of chromosomes) is *Oni-Yuri*.

The bulb is white, the scales are thick, fleshy and broad. The stiff stem rises 3 feet 3 inches–4 feet high, and bears leaves arranged in a regular pattern. The round, black-brown axil bulbils develop from June onwards and when fully ripe drop on to the ground during autumn. The

racemosely arranged blooms open during late August or early September
to expose strongly recurved petals of orange-vermilion red bearing
numerous chocolate-brown spots; red-brown pollen. *L. tigrinum* is self-

L. tigrinum

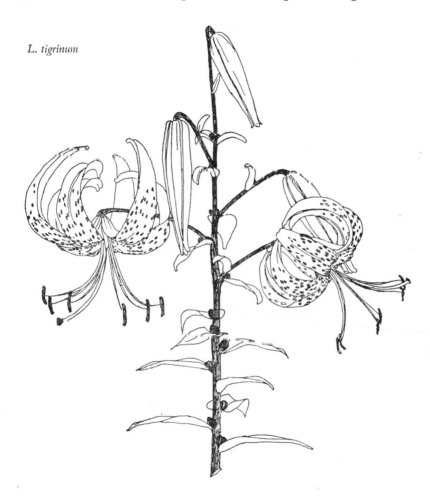

sterile, but seed formation (most seeds are not viable and resulting seedlings short-lived) is possible if it is crossed with carotenoid-containing
lilies (e.g. *L. maculatum, L. bulbiferum, L. × umbellatum, L. amabile, L.
davidii, L. leichtlinii* var. *maximowiczii*). *L. tigrinum* var. *splendens* has the

largest distribution of all the triploids. The variety *fortunei* has salmon-orange blooms with densely woolly stem and flower buds, while var. *flore-pleno* is less attractive, and unimportant. (NALS-LYB 1954)

L. tigrinum var. *diploid* is self-fertile, has the normal number of chromosomes (2n = 24) and is also capable of being crossed with the carotenoid-containing lilies listed above. Its distribution area is small, and it is only found in the island of Tsushima and on the opposite Kyushu coast. Jan de Graaff has used this small-flowering plant, which is weaker than the triploid, in many of his crosses.

L. tigrinum var. *flaviflorum* Makino 1933. A yellow-flowered diploid of weak growth, with 2n = 24 chromosomes, which plays a large part in the breeding of yellow-flowering Tiger hybrids.

Crosses with *L. tigrinum* have been made with the following lilies: *L. amabile* (*Cardinal*); *L. bulbiferum* var. *croceum* (*L.* × *manglesii*); *L. leichtlinii* var. *maximowiczii* (*Tigrimax*); *L.* × *maculatum* (*Margaret Johnson*, *L.* × *umbtig*).

L. tsingtauense   Gilg 1904

From the Chinese province of Shantung and the Korean Diamond Mountains. Although already known since 1863 and often confused with *L. medeoloides* in the past, it was not given its present name until 1904, when Gilg collected it at Tsingtau. (*48*)

The 1-inch white bulbs are oval. Some scattered and lightly marbled leaves, but most of them in whorls, clothe the 16–36 inch high stem. This carries one to six erect, star-shaped, reddish-spotted flowers with irregularly arranged, shiny orange-red segments; light, unpleasant smell. Orange pollen, slightly winged, short, stubby seed capsules, large wingless seeds, slow germination, flowers at end of June. This interesting lily, with varying characteristics, is easily raised from seed, but needs light shade (from ground cover) and conditions damper than normal.

Crosses with Marhan hybrids are said to be possible.

L. tsingtauense var. *flavum*. A yellow-flowered variety.

L. vollmeri   Eastwood 1948 (*L. roezlii* Purdy)

Occurs in Del Norte County, California, and Josephine County, Oregon. A so-called bog lily, with yellow, horizontal-creeping rhizomes covered with yellow-jointed scales, found in wet but nevertheless well-drained soils. Pale-green leaves, either scattered or in whorls, clothe the stem, 2 feet 6 inches–3 feet long, bearing one to three (and occasionally more) long-petioled flowers. They are orange, marked with dark-red to almost black flecks on the inside, of Turk's Cap type and with reflexed petals. Named after Dr Albert Michael Vollmer of San Francisco, who not only wrote about the Pacific coast lilies but also made numerous excursions in search of them. Damp, free-draining soil is necessary for successful cultivation.

L. wallichianum   Schultes 1830

A white Himalayan trumpet lily found at heights of 3,000–4,500 feet and over a wide area from Kumaon to Nepal, Sikkim, Bhutan, and Assam.

L. wallichianum

Small colonies of it grow among the limestone ridges in conifer woods, as well as among scrub and grass. Its purple-coloured bulb usually lies 8–10 inches below ground level. The stem first wanders underground and builds bulblets on the internodes before rising through the soil surface to a height of 3–6 feet. It carries numerous dark-green, grass-like leaves, and one or more cream-white flowers with an outer flushing of green. The narrow-tubed bloom, 7–8½ inches long, widens, trumpet-like, to a width of 6–8 inches; yellow pollen. This handsome lily, perhaps the latest of all to burst into growth – often not until July – is unfortunately not winter-hardy in Europe, but can be raised from seed and bulblets as either a pot or cool greenhouse plant. It is named after the Danish botanist Wallich (1786–1854), who first described it. (RHS-LYB 1951–52, F. Kingdon Ward)

L. wardii Stapf 1932

Native in south-eastern Tibet, where it grows in the Tsangpo valley (continuation of the Brahmaputra valley), and in the Lohit valley north-west and north-east of Sadiya, Assam; also near the source of the River Lohit near Rima, at heights of 5,000–10,000 feet among thickets, conifers and on rocky cliffs in dry situations. It grows so profusely in this region that the air is filled with its scent. First discovered in 1924 by Frank Kingdon Ward, after whom it is named.

The 2-inch diameter bulb is in the form of a flat sphere and finely spotted with red. The underground stem forms bulblets on the internodes before rising through the surface to a height of 5 feet and exposing its purple exterior and numerous scattered, lanceolate leaves, dark-green in colour, oblong-elliptic in shape, 3-veined, and about 2¾ inches long. There are up to 40 Martagon-type, deep-pink flowers, spotted with dull carmine, and carried in racemose inflorescence. This lily grows well in England, particularly if placed in half-shade in loam soils enriched in leaf-mould. Reports from Transvaal maintain that it only flourishes if planted under conifers and where it automatically obtains the surface cover of fir-tree needles so essential to its well-being. (RHS-LYB 1951–52, 1963)

L. washingtonianum Kellogg 1859

Named after Martha Washington, wife of George Washington. A Californian lily from the Sierra Nevada, growing northwards from

Yosemite Valley to Mount Shasta, and even further to the Cascade Mountains.

From the white, rhizomatous-like bulbs rises a stem 4 feet (often up to 6 feet 6 inches) long, with light-green, oblanceolate leaves. A deliciously fragrant lily carrying two to 20 horizontal, trumpet-shaped flowers during June/July with slightly recurved segments of pure white with purple spots which later turn to purple-lilac in the throat. Difficult to grow, as it can tolerate neither excessive dampness nor cold. Slow to germinate.

L. washingtonianum var. *minor*. Smaller than the type, and often called Shasta lily because it grows at the foot of Mount Shasta.

L. washingtonianum var. *purpurascens* is easier to grow than the type. Unlike it, it has a larger, nonrhizomatous bulb, more leaves, smaller white or wine-red flowers which soon turn purple-lilac, is scented and found in great numbers in the Mount Hood area. Difficult to transport, as the bulbs rapidly deteriorate when exposed to the air. Should be planted 6–7 inches deep.

L. wigginsii Beane and Vollmer 1955

Formerly known as *L. roezlii*; received its present name in 1955. It inhabits only a small area in southern Oregon, California, and the Siskiyou Mountains. Thick, scale-covered rhizomes serve as a bulb. The leaves are borne in two to four whorls on a 4-feet tall stem; the horizontal or nodding, pure-yellow, Turk's Cap flowers are purple-spotted and supported by pedicels 6–12 inches long; stem-rooter; yellow pollen. (RHS-LYB 1957)

L. wilsonii Leichtlin 1868

The first bulb of this lily arrived in a consignment of Golden-Rayed Lilies from Japan; its origin – if it is even a genuine variety – is often disputed.

The bulb is white and spherical. The stem is 3 feet long, and bears scattered, lanceolate leaves and erect, saucer-shaped blooms 5 inches in diameter. The August-flowering, recurved, heavily brown-spotted segments are small at the base and red-orange with an apricot band along their centre. Best planted 4–6 inches deep in sunny or partially shaded positions.

L. wilsonii var. *flavum* carries six to 10 primrose-yellow, red-purple speckled flowers on a stem 2 feet–2 feet 6 inches long. Brought into commerce under the name *Marlyn Ross*. (RHS-LYB 1962)

Cardiocrinum   Lindley

The genus *Cardiocrinum* is considered here because its members are mostly cultivated like a lily and often planted with them. The heart-shaped leaves of *Cardiocrinum* have given rise to the name of this genus.

C. cathayanum   Stearn 1948

Found in large numbers on the river banks of eastern and central China; Kiangsi, Hupeh, Hunan, Anhwei, and Kiangsu.

Long-stemmed, heart-shaped leaves in one whorl on the 1–4 feet main stem. One to four horizontal, $4\frac{1}{2}$-inch long trumpet flowers, green-white on the outside, cream with few purple spots on the inside; yellow pollen. The smallest and least beautiful *Cardiocrinum* variety.

C. cordatum   Makino 1913

Widely distributed throughout the three main Japanese islands, and also in Sakhalin and the Kuril Islands.

The stem, 4–8 feet tall, bears a whorl of long-petioled, heart-shaped leaves just below mid-height. The first young shoots are red-bronze, but those of later growth are usually green flushed with bronze. The four to 10 trumpet-shaped, cream-white flowers are about 6 inches long, the three lower petals are marked with deep yellow stripes, throat lightly spotted in brown-red. Yellow pollen. Starts growth during early spring and therefore requires protection from night frosts. The inhabitants of the island of Hokkaido cultivate the bulbs for food. New plants always grow from the daughter bulb, as the main bulb dies after flowering.

C. giganteum   Makino 1913

Himalayas: Simla, Nepal, Sikkim, Bhutan, upper Assam, northern Burma, south-eastern Tibet. This large, majestic lily has a strong, hollow stem 6–12 feet long, and is mostly found growing in very wet woodland glades. The broad, green, heart-shaped basal leaves form a rosette, and the others, scattered along the stem, are supported by long horizontal petioles. The scented, regularly funnel-shaped, 6-inch long flowers, also borne horizontally, are greenish-white on the outside and red-purple spotted with white on the inside. The large, reddish bulb

Cardiocrinum giganteum

requires shallow planting; as it dies after flowering it leaves small, offset bulbs on the base of the dying bulb. Should be planted in very damp, deep soil rich in plant nutrients. The planting hole, 24 × 24 × 20 inches in size, should first receive a layer of brushwood and be filled with leaf-mould and topped with well-rotted manure. Winter protection with leaves, wooden boxes or wicker baskets. Three bulbs should be planted to ensure continuous yearly flowering. Seed capsules reveal their fibrous teeth on opening, and release a rich harvest of light seeds. Germinates after one year, seedlings flower mostly after seven years. (*50*)

C. giganteum var. *yunnanense* Stearn 1948. Western and central China (Yunnan, Szechwan, Hupeh). Height 5 feet–6 feet 6 inches, first shoots are bronze-coloured. Pure-white to yellow-green flowers with wine-red markings on the inside.

9. The new lilies – hybrids

Plant breeders have only been able to give us the beautiful new, exotic lily hybrids during comparatively recent years. The reasons for the delay in development are many, chief among them that wild lilies suitable for breeding purposes were not found until the beginning of the present century, and that it took many more years before they could be developed and achieve worthwhile distribution. Two World Wars further disrupted advances in breeding, multiplication, and distribution. Another reason was the unreliable reputation the genus received, due to the slow, cumbersome and inefficient transport methods which were the only available means during the early part of the present century of bringing bulbs from the Far East and Middle East for European and American distribution. The lengthy and laborious collection of bulbs was followed by extremely long caravan journeys along the interior land tracks to the nearest port; next came a sea voyage of many months to the port of destination, and still further transportation by rail before final delivery to the purchaser – this in many cases was a dealer who still had to get the bulbs to the user. No wonder, therefore, that a big percentage of imported bulbs were spoiled and rotten – they had travelled for many months through tropical heat and sometimes in sub-zero temperatures in unventilated, tightly packed wooden boxes. The situation is radically different today, and perishable bulbs and plants reach their destinations – however vast the distances involved – within a short time and in perfect condition. The many diseases to which lilies are prone proved another obstacle to their popularization. Diseases were either not recognized or wrongly diagnosed, and the chemical preparations we now use to prevent or cure these troubles were not available. Thousands of boxes of *L. auratum* and *L. speciosum* bulbs, exported from Japan to Europe and North America every year, completely disappeared from the soil after only a short time. This happened year after year, and it is now clear that only fusarium and virus diseases could have been responsible for such wholesale destruction of bulbs. The origin and cause of diseases, and the means of preventing, or at least restraining them, only became known when scientists began their investigations into the biological factors involved. Industry was not slow in using the knowledge gained by these researches, and now produces ever more effective fungicides and insecticides to prevent, fight and control the spread of disease and pest attacks. The unusual combination of transport development (particularly aviation), the scientists, and the chemical industry has made the ever-increasing popularity of the lily possible, and ensures its safe and certain future.

Easily multiplied and disease-resistant, the new hybrids offer none of the problems that even long-experienced growers find with certain lily species, which are notoriously difficult to raise and maintain for any length of time. Taking the beauty and rich flower potential of hybrids for granted, even if only for a moment, their main advantages are health, adaptability to all kinds of soil, easy management and prolific multiplication potential.

Today's lily hybrids are just as easy to grow as tulips and hyacinths. They flourish in any good garden soil, have no particular or difficult soil preferences, are able to overwinter in the open garden, and demand no special care or attention of any kind. No gardener who has once grown them will ever wish to be without them.

No wonder that the number of lily hybrids increases annually, and the total is certainly too high for each one to be individually detailed in this book. There are at present over 1,500 names given in the International Lily Register of the Royal Horticultural Society, London, and additions are made annually. The best overall appreciation of hybrids is obtained by classifying them into groups according to their origin. We already know that only related species are able to cross with one another, and that crosses between distantly related species are mostly unproductive.

If such an exceptional cross does occur, even if only very rarely, the new hybrid could represent a most interesting and very valuable combination of chromosomes for further breeding.

Hybrid lilies have accordingly been classified into eight categories for gardening purposes, both in England and America. They are perhaps best referred to as breeding categories, and are:

1. Asiatic hybrids
2. Turk's Cap (Martagon) hybrids
3. Candidum hybrids
4. American hybrids
5. Longiflorum hybrids
6. Trumpet hybrids
7. Oriental (Japanese) hybrids
8. Hybrids of various other origins which do not fit into the above categories

Asiatic hybrids

These include all hybrids – the number of those registered is already in the hundreds – resulting from crosses of *L. bulbiferum*, *L. dauricum*, *L. wilsonii*, *L. concolor*, *L.* × *maculatum*, *L.* × *hollandicum*, *L. philadelphicum*, *L. pumilum*, *L. amabile*, *L. davidii*, *L. leichtlinii* var. *maximowiczii*, *L. tigrinum*, *L. cernuum*, and *L. callosum*.

The number of possible genetical combinations within this breeding category is almost countless. With the exceptions of the European *L. bulbiferum* and the American saucer-shaped *L. philadelphicum*, they consist entirely of lilies of Asiatic origin, with either Turk's Cap or saucer-shaped flowers. Apart from *L. cernuum*, the blooms of all these lilies contain carotenoids.

The first in the field of lily hybridizing, about 250 years ago, may have been the Japanese gardeners, with *L.* × *elegans* hybrids (*L.* × *maculatum*), of which there are 150 cultivars. Cytological examination has established the wild *L. dauricum* and *L. maculatum* as parents (Shimizu, NALS-LYB

1960). At the same time, Fritz Berckmüller of Hamburg (1927) suspected, and also tried to prove experimentally, that *L. maculatum* is a hybrid of *L. concolor* and *L. dauricum.*

At the time of writing, the following *L. maculatum* forms and clones are in commerce:

L. × maculatum Alice Wilson: pure lemon-yellow with dark-red speckles, 1877

L. × maculatum Alutaceum: a dwarf type with large, apricot-coloured flowers, known as *Kikak*

L. × maculatum Atrosanguineum: dark-red and black-spotted

L. × maculatum Aureum: black-spotted, orange-yellow flowers

L. × maculatum Auranticum: unspotted, deep-orange flowers

L. × maculatum Batemanniae: unspotted, apricot-coloured blooms with stem up to 3 feet 3 inches high

L. × maculatum Bicolor: shiny orange flowers with fire-red petal margins

L. × maculatum Diadem: also known as *Leonard Joerg*, apricot with yellow median band, late-flowering, used by Jan de Graaff in the breeding of Midcentury hyrids

L. × maculatum Mahogany: very broad flower petals, deep red-brown to mahogany-red; progeny inherits dark colour easily

L. × maculatum Sanguineum: black-spotted, deep-red blooms

L. × maculatum Venustum: pure apricot without spotting

L. × maculatum Wallacei: imported in 1876 from Japan, apricot-pink, rises up to 27 inches, flowers in August; should be planted in sandy soils and well watered

Siebold imported several kinds of Japanese lilies into Holland around 1830. The London gardener Henry Groom is probably responsible for *L. × hollandicum*, for he obtained many dark flower colours from crosses he made from 1840 to 1853 between *L. bulbiferum* and *L. atrosanguineum* (*L. × maculatum Atrosanguineum*).

The best-known of the many *L. × hollandicum* varieties now available are:

Apricot: with delicate apricot-coloured flowers, umbellar
Darkest of All: dark-red, mahogany-red with broad flower petals

Erectum: carmine-scarlet with some orange, 2 feet tall
Golden Fleece: very strong, light apricot-yellow, large blooms
Invincible: large, dark-orange coloured flowers with scarlet tips, 2–3 feet tall
Orange King: large umbellate inflorescence, orange centres, dark-orange petal margins
Refulgence: orange-scarlet, 27 inches long
Splendid: cinnabar with orange, without spots, 27 inches tall
Vermilion Brilliant: carmine-blood-red, umbellar, vigorous, 16 inches
Coolhurst hybrids: glowing orange-red, bred in England in 1932

Jan de Graaff's Rainbow hybrids must also be included in this category, as must the Golden Chalice hybrids which were selected from them.

Miss Isabella Preston, of Ottawa, must be given a great deal of credit for first working with this group of lilies during the 1920s and 1930s and for first bringing *L. davidii* var. *willmottiae* into the field of hybridization. She created the well-known varieties *Lillian Cummings* and *Brenda Watts* – two of her famous Stenographer lilies of (*L.* × *dauricum* × *L.* × *maculatum*) × *L. davidii* var. *willmottiae* parentage. They are pretty, saucer-shaped blooms arranged in rich racemose inflorescence; part nodding, part outward-facing; some more, others less recurved; and shaded from orange-red to scarlet.

The Fighter lilies came into being during the Second World War and were named after various famous aircraft – *Spitfire, Hurricane, Mosquito,* etc. These erect-flowering saucer lilies, in a wide variety of red shades, aroused considerable interest and discussion at the time, as did the yellow-flowered *Coronation* and *Sovereign*.

F. L. Skinner introduced *L.* × *scottiae* in 1931, produced from *L. davidii* var. *willmottiae* × *L.* × *maculatum Mahogany*. It is an orange-yellow, outward-facing saucer lily much used as a parent because of its ability to pass the mahogany-red colour of Mahogany to its progeny.

The first diploid Tigrinum hybrids unlike the crosses with the triploid Tigrinum, were fertile, and originated at the Boyce Thomson Institute, New York, during 1940. The parentage of these saucer-shaped, recurved hybrids, called *Umbtig*, is *L. tigrinum* var. *diploid* and *L.* × *hollandicum*.

The year 1934 saw the foundation of the Jan de Graaff Oregon bulb farms, an offshoot from the Dutch parent company which at the time was solely interested in the production of tulips, narcissi, and bulbous irises. Jan de Graaff was, however, fascinated by lilies; not satisfied with just collecting them, he started to breed and select. The instinct of the sure and born breeder drove him on to develop a large, comprehensive and successful breeding programme which now, consolidated with American farming techniques, provides 2¼ million bulbs annually – or, in other words, 80 per cent of the world's lily production.

Jan de Graaff selected his excellently shaped, multi-coloured, erect-flowering, saucer-shaped Rainbow hybrids from a rich supply of erect-flowering crosses obtained brom *L.* × *maculatum*, *L.* × *hollandicum*, and *L. dauricum*. The Rainbow hybrids come in every colour tone from yellow to orange and red. A further selection of the golden-yellow types led to the sparsely spotted Golden Chalice hybrids. All these lilies are particularly suitable for borders, forcing, and cutting.

Jan de Graaff produced the Fiesta hybrids from crosses first made by Dr Abel, of New York, between *L. davidii* × *L. leichtlinii* hybrids, and crossing *L. amabile* and the yellow-flowering *L. amabile* var. *luteum* into it.

The Fiesta hybrids combine the strong, erect growing habit of *L. davidii* with gay colours ranging from golden-yellow to orange, red, and chestnut-brown. The pure-yellow Citronella, ruby-red Burgundy and bronze Bronzino strains have all been selected from Fiesta hybrids. *Amber Gold*, with good inflorescence; *Ebony*, with large, dark copper-bronze flowers; *Fury*, with startlingly red blooms – all are clones and all commercially available.

Jan de Graaff introduced more than a dozen named clones as Mid-century hybrids during 1949; although they originate essentially from saucer-shaped lilies and *L. tigrinum*, their breeding is involved and follows these lines:

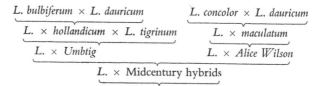

$$L. \text{ bulbiferum} \times L. \text{ dauricum} \qquad\qquad L. \text{ concolor} \times L. \text{ dauricum}$$
$$L. \times \text{ hollandicum} \times L. \text{ tigrinum} \qquad\qquad L. \times \text{ maculatum}$$
$$L. \times \text{ Umbtig} \qquad\qquad L. \times \text{ Alice Wilson}$$
$$L. \times \text{ Midcentury hybrids}$$

The exceptionally strong, nearly table-high Midcentury hybrids have umbellate to racemose inflorescences with wide-open, erect or outward-facing, saucer-shaped flowers in a range of colours from pale-yellow to dark-red. *Enchantment* was introduced first, and is perhaps the best-known, because of its almost luminous nasturtium-red colour, but *Harmony*, *Joan Evans*, and *Valencia* soon followed; later came the pure-yellow varieties such as *Croesus*, *Destiny*, *Prosperity*, and the red to dark-red *Cinnabar*, *Sunspot*, *Sunstar*, *Tabasco* and *Paprika*. These strongly coloured, prolifically flowering lilies add interest to even the most magnificent gardens, thrive in every type of soil and in any temperate climate, and multiply well – some produce new bulbs by division, others produce axil bulbils.

Other North American and Canadian breeders have worked in a similar direction. F. L. Skinner, of Dropmore, Manitoba, crossed the North American saucer lily *L. philadelphicum* with the Asiatic *L. dauricum* and proved that a relationship existed between the two varieties, although they were parted by an ocean. Saffron-yellow *The Duchess* is a *L. amabile* × *L.* × *maculatum* cross, blood-red *Dunkirk* a Davidii cross, and *Lemon Lady* a lemon-yellow Davidii cross. *Evening Star* has a remarkable parentage – *L. concolor* × *L. callosum* – a cross very seldom made.

The three very good, dark-red hybrids – *Byam's Red Giant*, *Byam's Ruby* and *Dark Eyes* – bred by Percy Byam, of Toronto, are in the same class.

Professor Taylor, of Guelph, Ontario, is known for his early introduction of *Cardinal*, a *L. tigrinum* × *L. amabile* cross, in addition to the golden-yellow *Goldcrest*, *L. philadelphicum* × *L. pumilum*.

Skyrocket was introduced by Dr E. F. Palmer, of Vineland Station, Ontario, in 1945 – a vigorous, tall-growing cross between *L. davidii* and *Lillian Cummings*. Equally vigorous and of the same good parent material are his *Redbird* and *Valiant*, obtained from *L. bulbiferum* var. *croceum* × *L.* × *maculatum* *Mahogany* × *L. tigrinum*. All three are medium-red and heavily spotted. Other well-known Palmer hybrids are red-flowered *Samarkand*, and *King William*.

The Stones' Lemon Yellow hybrids originate from *L. tigrinum* var. *flaviflorum* and are the result of Ralph Warner's work, which the

American lily enthusiast David Stone is continuing. He has produced two clones: the self-coloured, orange-red, unspotted *Connecticut Yankee*; and the related lemon-yellow *Nutmegger*. Both are absolutely hardy, vigorous Tigrinum hybrids with a rich stand of flowers.

The saucer lily *Nubian* is remarkable for its black-red colour; it came from the Preston seedling *Edna Kean*, which was first introduced in 1950 by Percy Wright, of Saskatoon, Canada.

Dr S. M. Emsweller, of the Plant Industry Station, Beltsville, obtained several vigorous saucer lilies from a cross between *Brenda Watts* and a yellow Hollandicum seedling – yellowish, cognac-coloured *Brandywine*; golden-yellow and tall-growing *Cavalier*; somewhat weaker canary-yellow *Mega*; pepper-red *Mountaineer*. More vigorous and larger-bloomed lilies were later bred from *Brandywine*, *Mega*, and *Mountaineer* as a result of doubling the chromosome numbers.

L. B. Tuffery of New Zealand – which has the advantage of a good climate for lilies – had bred a number of lily varieties in this class.

Other new varieties in the present group have been bred by A. J. Porter, of Parkside, Saskatchewan, Canada. The best-known are: *Rosabelle* – a strong, pink, saucer type, 2 feet 6 inches tall; *Firebright* – outward-facing, red, saucer-shaped, scented; and also late July/August-flowering *Delicious* – scented and bred from Isabella Preston's *Edna Kean*.

The late Professor C. F. Patterson of Saskatchewan University was successful in crossing the weak, lilac *L. cernuum* into this lily complex, and so introduced lilac into the hybrids which has given rise to hybrids with pastel shades. His earlier successes, all of them winter-hardy in the cold climate of the Canadian prairie, are: *White Gold* and *White Princess* – cream-coloured blooms; *Pink Charm* and *Edith Cecilia* – pink-flowered; *Rose Dawn* and *Rose Queen* – dark pink; and *Burnished Rose* – apricot. *Rosalind*, a Tigrinum hybrid, and two Cernuum hybrids, *Fuchsia Queen* and *Orchid Queen*, were introduced in 1960.

It is curious that some of the Patterson Cernuum hybrids are sterile, while others have more than the normal 24 chromosomes of diploid varieties. Chromosome numbers in brackets are: *Burnished Rose* (45), *Crimson Queen* (46), *Fuchsia Queen* (42), *Jasper* (36), *Pink Charm* (38),

61. Backhouse hybrids. Particularly strong Martagon hybrids raised in England
62. *Oliver Wyatt*, raised by the breeder of the same name. Cadmium-orange, excellent flower shape
63. *Nora Darby*, a hybrid produced by Darby. Slightly recurved, purple-spotted, delicate-orange flowers

64. *Honeydew*, an Aurelian hybrid produced by de Graaff. Green-yellow, beautifully formed trumpets in the shape of a pyramid. Similar Aurelian hybrids are the intense golden-yellow *Life*; *Limelight*, canary-yellow with red suffused back; and *Helios*, self-coloured, pure soft yellow

65. Olympic hybrids – a selection from a cross between trumpet lilies made 20 years ago and still well worth growing

66. *Pink Perfection*. A selection of dark, carmine-red trumpets of Centifolium-Sargentiae origin. Its colour deepens during cool weather and in the shade

67. *Saffronbelle*. From the English breeder Foxwell, one of his exquisitely beautiful range of Aurelian hybrids. The flower shape can only be described as classical. Other Foxwell hybrids are chrome-yellow *Aureolinbelle*, canary-yellow *Canarybelle*, and sulphur-yellow *Sulphurbelle*

68. The American lily-breeder Jan de Graaff with his most beautiful lilies, *Imperial Silver* and *Imperial Crimson*. Only expert breeding knowledge can produce such colourful, marvellously shaped, large-flowered plants. Because of their expense, are best grown in pots

69. Aurelian hybrids with splendid inflorescence, lemon-yellow flowers
70. Aurelian hybrids from Yerex, canary-yellow, star-shaped flowers
71. *Golden Sunburst*, an elegant Jan de Graaff Aurelian hybrid distinguished by papillae in the inner part of the flower – these are inherited from *L. henryi*

72. Madonna Lily. A painting of this lily, completely true to nature, by Matthias Grünewald and now in Stuppacher Church. Since Grecian and Roman times, the white lily
has traditionally been the attribute of the Gods

Von Goltwurtz/ Heidnischblümen/
Cap. lxxxiij.

Je Goltwurtzel ist fast ein geele zwibel mit vilen fachen / welche jär-
lichs vil junger stößt / gleich wie die zamen Saffran zwibel / aller ding
den weissen Gilgen zwibeln gleich mit der gestalt. Gegen dem Meyen stößt
das gewechs sein runde stengel / zü rings vmbher mit blettern besetzt einem
redlin gleich / jedes blat / so es sunderlich ist / vergleicht es sich dem breiten
Wegerich / aber grüner vnnd satter on scharten / aller ding wie das kraut
Vue Lupine anzüsehen. Die blümen komen in der Ernd / seind leibfarb rot

Goltwurtz.

Martagum

mit seer kleinen braunē düpf-
felen gemalet / etwas kleiner
dann die gemeinen Lilgen /
die bletlin seind rumbher ge-
bogen / gemeinlich vj. an je-
der Gilgen / des gleichen in je-
der vj. brauner zepfflin / eins
lieblichen geruchs. Nach der
blüet sicht man lange Mag-
samen köpfflin mit breittem
gelē samē vßgefüllet. Solche
blümen zielt man für ein wol-
lust wie andere blümen vnnd
Gilgen in den gärten / sunst
wachsen sie in den hohen wel-
dē / als im schwartz waldt / in
der Eydgnoschafft / vnd vff
dem Dürst berg gegen dem
Waßgaw.

Von den namen.

Ich hab erstmals ge-
meint / diß gewechs sei
Asphodelus od Hastula Re-
gia Dioscoridis lib. ij. capite
clit. nach dem ich die beschrei-
bung aber der alten besihe /
so wil sich diß gewechs mit zü
Asphodelo schicken / möcht
villeicht bald kantbar wer-
den. Aber dise gegenwürtige
zwibel / mit den besprengten
Lilien halt ich nun mit Marco Platea. aus Flandern / für dz Hyacinctū d
Poeten von welchē der Ver. vn der Out. also schreibē. *Die quibus in terris inscripta*
nomina regum, Nascuntur flores. Verg. æclo. 3. & in Ouidio lib. ij. Metamor. Ipse suos gemitus folijs in-
scribit & æ, Flos habet inscriptum funestaq; litera du ix est. Vnd weither stehet geschriben /
Litera communis medijs pueroq; uiroq;, Inscripta est filijs hæc nominis illa querela. Die Fabel Hya-
cincti wie er zür blümen woxde / melt der alt Nicander in Theriaca. So ist
mir nun kein blüm bekant / die sich baß mit jren blüts dröpffelin zům Hya-
cincto oder Poeten reime / als eben der Goltwurtz / die andern Hyacineten
seind droben beschriben.

Von der krafft vnd würckung.

Je würckung Hyacineti seind auch droben angezeigt / doch so ist die
Goltwurtz auch nutz vnd erfaren in der artznei.

Innerlich.

---

73. Goldroot. The old herbals, complete with wood-block illustrations and
verbose descriptions, listed most worthwhile plants of their day and dealt exhaust-
ively with all known facts gathered from a variety of sources

Rosalind (46), *Rose Queen* (38), *White Gold* (38), *White Princess* (42). Unfortunately, Patterson did not make it clear in his records if the increase in chromosome numbers is due to the triploid *L. tigrinum* cross, or to colchicine treatment.

Jan de Graaff also markets the *L. cernuum* hybrids under the name of Harlequin hybrids. Another particularly striking selection is offered as clones: *Corsage* – outward-facing, wide-open blooms in ivory and pink; *Adagio* – deep-red; *Fuga* – black-spotted orange; and *Tarantella* – heavily black-spotted, saffron-yellow, Turk's Cap flowers suffused with pink. All of them grow 3 feet 3 inches–5 feet tall, and produce 15 flowers during June and July.

Royall W. Bemis, of Blackthorne Gardens, United States, introduced the Cernuum hybrids into the trade under the name of Rosette strain.

The English lily-breeder, the late G. W. Darby, bred a number of very beautiful and valuable Asiatic hybrids. His parents were: *L. davidii Maxwill, Edna Kean, Dark Princess*; *L. tigrinum* var. *flaviflorum*; and *L. dauricum* var. *flavum*. His best hybrids are: *Walter Bentley* – yellow-orange with nodding flowers; *Lady Bowes-Lyon* – copper-red; *Joseph Fletcher* – dark canary-yellow; *Walter Darby* – strong, dark-red, outward-facing flowers; *David Bowes-Lyon* – light yellow; *Frederick Stern* – golden-yellow and heavily spotted, an inheritance from Dr S. L. Emsweller's *Dark Princess*. The breeding of the lily *Sir Frederick Stern* is made clear in the International Lily Register as per the following extract: (55, 63)

PRESTON 1939	EMSWELLER 1945
L. dauricum × *L. maculatum* hybrids × *L. davidii* var. *willmottiae*	*L.* × *mac. Wallacei* × *L. mac.* *Batemanniae* × *L. tigrinum* diploid

DARBY   *L. davidii Maxwill* × *Edna Kean* × *Dark Princess*

DARBY 1958 *Pygmalion* × *tigrinum* var. *flaviflorum*

DARBY 1963 *Progenitor* × *tigrinum* var. *flaviflorum* × *Marlyn Ross*

DARBY 1965 *Sir Frederick Stern*   (*Marlyn Ross* =
                                              L. wilsonii var. *flavum*

Following is a summary of the worthwhile and commercially available Asiatic hybrids, listed under the names of their breeders:

ISABELLA PRESTON, of Ottawa, Canada
Brenda Watts: fire-red
Grace Marshall: orange-red
Hurricane: strong red, erect saucers
Mosquito: delicate orange, pendant blooms
Addington: yellow, erect
Coronation: yellow, pendant blooms

JAN DE GRAAFF, of Gresham, Oregon
Cinnabar: red, erect saucers
Croesus: golden-yellow, erect
Destiny: lemon-yellow, erect (*3*)
Enchantment: nasturtium-red, outward-facing (*1*)
Golden Chalice hybrids: erect, saucer-shaped, golden-yellow
Harmony: orange-yellow, erect saucers, large (*8*)
Joan Evans: golden-yellow, large erect saucers
Midcentury hybrids, various forms: yellow, orange, red-orange, red
Rainbow hybrids: erect saucers, golden-yellow, orange-red, mahogany-red
Tabasco: chestnut-red, erect
Corsage: Cernuum hybrid, with ivory and pink Martagon blooms
Paprika: blood-red, sideways-facing blooms
Prosperity: chrome-yellow, sideways-facing
Queen of Hearts: erect saucers, scarlet, 3 feet
Sunspot: erect, blood-red saucers, 16–24 inches
Talisman: red-orange, spotted, Martagon-type flowers, axil bulbils
Amber Gold: butter-yellow, pendant Martagon type
Royal Sovereign: lemon-yellow, heavily spotted
Panamint strain: Harlequin hybrids with large cream-yellow, strongly reflexed flowers
Prince Charming: erect flowers, lilac-red with ivory centre
Bronzino strain: Fiesta hybrids; dark-amber to brown

Burgundy strain: Fiesta hybrids; wine-red, Martagon-type flowers
Citronella strain: Fiesta hybrids; lemon-yellow, Martagon-type flowers
Mercury strain: flowers from true lilac to magenta and old rose, spotted
Fiesta hybrids: Martagon-flowered; wide variety of colours (*15*)
Harlequin hybrids: delicate pastel shades, yellowish, pink (*9, 16*)

DR EMSWELLER, of Beltsville, Maryland
Brandywine: light-yellow, cognac-coloured, outward-facing
Cavalier: golden-yellow, erect saucers, 3 feet (*51*)
Mega: canary-yellow, erect saucers, 2 feet
Mountaineer: lovely red, erect saucers, 3 feet

DR F. SKINNER, of Dropmore, Canada
Dunkirk: shiny red, outward-facing
Lemon Lady: lemon-yellow, erect with Martagon flowers
L. × scottiae: orange-red
Amaryllis: wide-open, delicate pink flowers
Azalia: cup-shaped, azalea-pink
The Duchess: saffron-yellow, wide-open

PERCY BYAM, of Toronto, Canada
Dark Eyes: deep red, outward-facing flowers
Ruby: ruby-red, erect saucers, 2 feet 6 inches

DR E. F. PALMER, of Ontario, Canada
Redbird: red-spotted Martagon flowers (*52*)
Valiant: red, erect flowers

J. C. TAYLOR, of Guelph, Ontario, Canada
Cardinal: fire-red
Waxwing: orange-yellow, outward-facing

DAVID STONE, of Wolcott, Connecticut
Nutmegger: lemon-yellow, spotted black
Connecticut Yankee: salmon-orange, Martagon flowers

A. J. PORTER, of Canada
Rosabelle: pink-red, erect flowers
Firebright: redcurrant-red, unspotted, outward-facing
Delicious: golden-yellow, late, scented

Professor PATTERSON, of Saskatoon, Canada
Apricot Glow: apricot-pink
Bronze Queen: nodding Martagon flowers, bronze-yellow
Rosalind: pink, reflexed
Rose Queen: rose-lilac, outward-facing, 6 feet
Edith Cecilia: cream and pink, Martagon-flowered, nodding
Lemon Queen: lemon, Martagon-flowered
White Gold: apricot-pink to white, sideways-facing, 2 feet 6 inches
White Princess: apricot to cream, sideways-facing, 4 feet
Red Torch: red, sideways-facing, 4 feet
Jasper: pink, nodding, bell-shaped

DR R. C. PALMER, of British Columbia
Samarkand: dark-red, nodding, reflexed
Skyrocket: red, nodding, Martagon flowers, Davidii type

PERCY WRIGHT, of Saskatoon, Canada
Nubian: black-red, Martagon flowers

C. FELDMAIER, of Pfarrkirchen, Germany
Leuchtfeuer: Davidii-Maculatum hybrid with fiery cinnabar-red, slightly recurved, sideways-facing, saucer-shaped flowers; good inflorescence; 4 feet 3 inches; flowers early July
Ralph: redcurrant-red, erect, star-shaped; 4 feet 3 inches–4 feet 6 inches; late July (*20*)
Roter Prinz: Davidii-Maculatum hybrid with brick-red, slightly recurved, half-erect, saucer-shaped blooms in racemose inflorescence; 5 feet; July (*54*)
Sonnentiger: very flat, broad-petalled, Aurelian-yellow flowers; 4 feet; July (*60*)

Turk's Cap (Martagon) hybrids

This group comprises the hybrids of the genuine Martagon lilies – *L. martagon* and its varieties *album* and *cattaniae*, the Korean yellow Turk's Cap *L. hansonii*, and orange-flowered *L. medeoloides* of Japanese origin. The rich colour spectrum of the Martagon hybrids is due to the introduction of the yellow flower colour of *L. hansonii* and the pink to lilac and dark wine-red shades of *L. martagon* and *L. martagon* var. *cattaniae*, as well as the white of var. *album*. C. Baden-Powell, of Southborough, England, produced the first hybrid of this group and named it *L. × dalhansonii*, a racemose plant with reddish, chestnut-brown flowers and orange centres. The first syllable of the name *dalhansonii* was taken from *L. martagon* var. *dalmaticum* – a synonym for *L. martagon* var. *cattaniae*.

L. martagon var. *album* was the mother plant of Van Tubergen's thick-fleshed, mostly orange or yellow-tinted Marhan hybrids, which followed in 1886. The Backhouse hybrids, bred by the family R. O. Backhouse, are similarly coloured. (*61*)

More recent is E. L. Kline's introduction of the Painted Lady hybrids – Turk's Cap lilies ranging from oxblood-red to orange, chrome and lemon-yellow to pearl-white, with glossy red, dark-red, brown and lilac markings and spots. Jan de Graaff's Paisley strain (*56*) is similar. Dr Norma Pfeiffer developed the vigorous Terrace City hybrids, a long-living strain if grown under suitable conditions. *L. martagon* has also been crossed with *L. medeoloides* (*L. × Marmed*) and with *L. kelloggii* (*Kelmarsh*).

Candidum hybrids

A chance cross between the white Madonna Lily *L. candidum* and the red, Martagon-flowering *L. chalcedonicum* from Greece produced the first ever known hybrid – *L. × testaceum*, called Isabell or Nanking Lily. First found by Franz Anton Haage, of Erfurt, Germany, in a Dutch consignment of lily bulbs in 1836, this strong-growing plant, with delicate yellow flowers tending a little towards brown, still does well in spite of its age! It resembles the Madonna Lily in its preference for calcareous soils, warm situations, and humidity. *L. candidum* × *L. chalcedonicum* were crossed, crossed in reverse, and back-crossed several times with the parents (Wyatt, England; Jan de Graaff.) Professor Scheubel, of Oberlahnstein, Germany, successfully bred the beautiful *White Knight* from a back-cross between *L. testaceum* and *L. candidum*. It is thought that a cross between *L.* × *testaceum* and *L. szovitsianum* should be possible; and it may even be feasible to cross *L. candidum* with other lilies – always provided that pollination takes place in a suitable climate.

The Madonna Lily's failure to set seed in Germany – in contrast to France, Italy and its native countries – may be due to the climate, or the fact that there it is a self-sterile clone. Jan de Graaff's Cascade strain is a selection of seed-bearing *L. candidum*, collected in France by E. Debras.

L. candidum crosses with *L.* × *testaceum*, and *L.* × *testaceum* with *L. chalcedonicum*. De Graaff obtained his Candidum-type lilies from this source – however, they have orange-red pollen.

Ares, *Artemis* and *Zeus* are orange-red, pink and brick-red hybrids from O. E. Wyatt's work in England with *L.* × *testaceum* × *L. chalcedonicum*.

American hybrids

These are divided into three groups, according to parents' place of origin:

1. The lilies from eastern America – *L. canadense, L. michiganense, L. philadelphicum, L. michauxii, L. grayi, L. catesbaei, L. iridollae*
2. The land-type lilies from western America – *L. washingtonianum, L. rubescens, L. kelloggii, L. columbianum, L. humboldtii, L. ocellatum, L. bolanderi, L. parryi*
3. The bog-type lilies – *L. pardalinum, L. vollmeri, L. occidentale, L. maritimum, L. nevadense, L. wigginsii, L. harrisianum, L. pitkinense, L. kelleyanum*

Luther Burbank had already crossed various American wild lilies, but the only result of his large-scale work still left today is *L.* × *burbankii* (*L. parryi* × *L. pardalinum*), which entered commerce in 1901, followed by *L.* × *pardaboldtii* in 1907.

The first big step forward in bringing American lily hybrids onto the market was made with the introduction of the Bellingham hybrids. The seed originated from Robert Kessler, of Los Angeles, who crossed *L. humboldtii* var. *ocellatum*, *L. pardalinum*, and *L. parryi* with one another. David Griffiths, of the Plant Industry Station, Bellingham, Washington, raised 3,000 plants from them before selecting just 10 clones for commercial release in 1924. Three of the 10 hybrids with *L. parryi* blood soon disappeared. Of the remaining seven arising from *L. pardalinum* × *L. humboldtii* only *Shuksan* is still with us today; the remainder – mixed and further selected – form the basis of today's Bellingham hybrids. Jan de Graaff also markets the hybrids *Afterglow* and *Buttercup*. All these lilies are strong growers, reach a height of 5 feet, bear fresh green leaves in whorls, are racemose, and have strongly recurved, nodding, Turk's Cap flowers supported by elegant, erect pedicels. If *L. parryi* is in the cross, the basic colour is usually strong yellow or orange, or heavily brown-spotted, sharp lemon-yellow. Some varieties have only their petal tips tinted with carmine, in others the carmine spreads over more than half the segment area. They are vigorous lilies, lime-haters, prefer damp situations in half-shade, multiply well, and flower profusely. (*6, 8*)

Eric Mayell bred the thriving, delicately coloured, red, pink and mauve-shaded Monterey hybrids from *L. pitkinense* (discovered less than 20 years ago) and *L. kelloggii*. The Pitkinense hybrids bred by A. D. Rothman, of Rhinebeck, New York, with rhizomes of such giant proportions that only an axe will divide them, arose from a cross between a scarlet-flowering *L.* × *burbankii* hybrid and *L. pitkinense*. Pendulous, slightly recurved flowers of a rare magenta shade are the result of a *L. pardalinum* × *L. bolanderi* cross – the best of these hybrids is *Henry Bolander* (RHS-LYB 1960, p. 149).

O. E. P. Wyatt, formerly of Maidwell Hall, Northampton, England, has devoted himself to the cross-fertilization of North American lilies, and has bred the densely yellow *L. nevadense* × *L. parryi* hybrids

Yellow Maid and *Bridesmaid*, and another *L. parryi* hybrid, *Sir Lancelot*. Further work with *L. parryi* crosses gave a particularly good-looking and graceful yellow lily with flat, wide-open, nodding flowers which H. R. Baar named after Oliver Wyatt. (*62*)

The pale-yellow *Index*, *Comtance* and *Elinor* hybrids from S. L. Shride, of Seattle, Washington, can certainly not belie their *L. parryi* origin – they were bred after the Second World War and only after several crosses between *L. Shuksan* and *L. parryi*.

Wade Sturgeon, of Sebastopol, Oregon, raised several hybrids from a *L. rubescens* × *L. columbianum* cross.

Dr A. M. Showalter, of Harrisonburg, Virginia, collected American lilies and bred many varieties from them. He raised two hybrids by crossing *L. canadense* with *L. michiganense* and *L. michauxii*, which produced *Carolina Bells*. A cross between *Carolina Bells* and *L. harrisianum* can lead to further useful hybrids, but crosses of *L. michauxii* with *L. michiganense* or with *L. superbum* gave only weak and poor-looking plants. The *L.* × *harrichauxii* hybrids, bred by Ralph Warner from *L. harrisianum* × *L. michauxii*, are fertile, and set seed if cross-pollinated with *L. michauxii*, *L. harrisianum*, *L. canadense*, and other hybrids from this group. *L. canadense* also proves fertile with *L. davidii* var. *willmottiae* pollen, and produces seedlings which clearly indicate the *L. davidii* var. *willmottiae* parentage; the seedlings can also be back-crossed with *L. davidii* var. *willmottiae* (NALS-LYB 1960, 1961, 1964, RHS-LYB 1965).

Not to be forgotten are the results which F. L. Skinner, of Dropmore, Canada, achieved in the 1920s with *L. philadelphicum* and *L. dauricum*, two lilies with cup-shaped flowers, the one from North America, the other from Siberia and East Asia; nor his umbellate, saucer-shaped lilies – orange, *Skinner's Orange*; red and gold, *L.* × *phildauricum*; and shiny red *Philada*. This last lily is apparently no longer available.

Longiflorum hybrids

All hybrids arising from *L. longiflorum*, *L. formosanum*, *L. wallichianum*, and *L. neilgherrense* are included in this group.

Few crosses have been successful, or have even been tried, between the trumpet lilies of southern Asia and Japan which also belong to this group. The few successful crosses are from Japan and New Zealand, which would seem to indicate that warm weather is essential to further progress.

The white trumpet hybrids *Formobel*, *Florosanum*, and *L. × formolongi* are all derived from *L. formosanum* and *L. longiflorum*.

L. formosanum Welwyn is a tetraploid, and *Tetrabell* a tetraploid *longiflorum* type with large, substantial flowers. Tuffery of New Zealand reports 'Formolense' hybrids – a cross between *L. formosanum* and *L. nepalense*.

Trumpet hybrids

The number of commercially available hybrids produced from Chinese lilies in this group is almost immeasurably high. They have arisen from *L. regale*, *L. sargentiae*, *L. leucanthum* var. *centifolium*, *L. brownii*, *L. sulphureum*, and *L. henryi* – the last is the only exception in so far as it is not a trumpet lily, but bears orange Turk's Cap flowers.

This group is divided into four sections for classification and exhibition purposes:

(a) *Chinese Trumpets.* All genuine trumpet lilies and their hybrids of true funnel form, with the exception of those derived from *L. longiflorum*, *L. formosanum*, *L. wallichianum*, *L. philippinense* and *L. neilgherrense*. The types are *Limelight*, *Damson*, and the Olympic hybrids

(b) *Bowl-shaped lilies*. This category includes all hybrids descending from those mentioned above with either erect or outward-facing flowers of wide-open, bowl shape, e.g., *Heart's Desire* and *New Era*

(c) *Pendant type*. All hybrids of above descent with nodding, mostly wide-open flowers, e.g., *Golden Showers*

(d) *Sunburst type*. This group comprises the hybrids of above descent with flat, star-shaped, wide-open blooms, like the Sunburst hybrids *Bright Star* and *Good Hope*

The various Chinese trumpet lilies cross-pollinate comparatively easily with one another, and so do their progeny. Because these hybrids produce sumptuous, profusely flowering inflorescences, because the flowers are among the largest and most striking that the plant world has to offer, and because these lilies belong to the healthiest and most long-living plants of the genus, they are becoming more and more popular. They look particularly effective if planted against a leafy background – this helps to highlight their white and yellowish colours. Their sweet fragrance spreads far into other gardens. These lilies are plants which can be wholeheartedly recommended for the landscape gardener.

The trumpet lilies only appeared in our gardens after E. H. Wilson had discovered *L. regale*, the Regal Lily, and the similar *L. sargentiae* in the Chinese province of Szechwan in 1903. But it took another seven years before bulbs were imported in large enough quantities for nurseries to be able to take a commercial interest. A chance cross between the adjacent growing varieties *L. regale* and *L. sargentiae* occurred in the Farquhar Nurseries, Roslindale, Massachusetts, in 1916 and resulted in *L. imperiale* – a hybrid with a rather wider funnel than its parents, but similar to them in other respects. This often repeated cross was, among others, also tried by Miss Isabella Preston while she worked at Guelph, Ontario; her best seedling was a tall-growing plant, bearing open, white trumpets, known as *L.* × *imperiale George C. Creelman*.

L. sulphurgale was commercially introduced in England from a cross made in 1913 by Professor F. Scheubel, of Oberlahnstein, Germany, with *L. sulphureum* and pollen from *L. regale*. *L. sulphurgale* resembles *L. regale* but blooms two weeks later and very often with a greenish-coloured throat. The Crow's hybrids, later brought into the trade as *L.* × *Gloriosum*, are due to the work of Professor J. W. Crow, of Ontario, who crossed *L.* × *sulphurgale* with *L.* × *imperiale George C. Creelman*. Again, they were very vigorous, had a greenish throat and often ivory rather than white trumpets. *L. leucanthum* var. *centifolium* was crossed with *L. regale* at Kew in 1920, and also with forms of *L. imperiale* in the United States, where it produced hybrids 5–9 feet tall with up to 20 large, spectacularly coloured, chocolate-brown backed flowers marked with pink transparent veins on the inside.

The cross between *L. sargentiae* and *L. henryi* which E. Debras, of Orléans, France, carried out proved of especial significance in the development of new hybrids. The new hybrid, called *L.* × *aurelianense*

Aurelian hybrid

after the Roman name for the city of Orléans, first flowered in 1928, and combined a white trumpet lily with an orange-yellow Martagon type. Leopold Frietsch Rastatt, Germany, worked on the same cross independently, and called his hybrid *L. frietschii* after it first flowered in 1931. The original racemose plant, now lost, was strong, up to 6 feet high, and bore wide-open, pendulous, star-shaped, orange-suffused, yellow blooms. It is almost impossible to list and describe the plethora of forms and colours of varieties produced by breeders, partly through a series of back-crosses with parents but also by crossing the Aurelian hybrids with other trumpet lilies like *L. leucanthum* var. *centifolium*, *L. regale*, and *L. sulphureum*. All Aurelianense, or Aurelian hybrids as they are called nowadays, are exceptionally healthy, hardly ever suffer from disease, withstand cold and frost and thrive in most soils. A foolproof lily! Mention must also be made of the *L. sulphureum* and *L. henryi* cross made in 1937 by Tom Barry, of Lambertsville, New York. The hybrid was named *T. A. Havemeyer*, and although the original plant is now probably lost, it was a counterpart to *L.* × *aurelianense*, grew over 6 feet tall and had brownish-orange, wide-open flowers marked with a green median band. It was also crossed with *L. aurelianense.*

Two further crosses served to increase the popularity of the new 'man-made' lilies – one a pink trumpet and the other a pure-yellow regal type. L. N. Freimann, of Bellingham, Washington, noticed one *L. leucanthum* var. *centifolium* hybrid seedling with the margins of the tepals suffused with pink; this he continued to cross for some generations with the plants which showed this characteristic most prominently, until he obtained a plant with entirely fuchsia-pink petals – although it was weak through continual inbreeding. He corrected this by back-crossing with *L. regale,* which gave him a 100 per cent fuchsia-pink progeny. But it took 15 years of hard work before these pink trumpets were ready to be distributed through normal trade channels.

Freimann also bred the pure-yellow Regal Lily, but this time took only five years; this clear to deep-yellow lily – yellow both inside and outside from throat to segment tips – was ready for release in 1946. He sowed a packet of Gloriosum hybrids of *L. regale, L. sargentiae* and *L. sulphureum* parentage in 1941. One of the seedlings produced cream-coloured flowers and was crossed with *L. regale,* another particularly good seedling was crossed with the regal seedling *Lesterina,* the seed of which also came from a Regal Lily, and which the plant breeder Luther Burbank had (to use his own words) 'worked on' – i.e., pollinated by one means or another. Ten per cent of the resulting seedlings were cream-coloured, and repeated crossing of the best and truest colours led to the fulfilment of the original aim.

Later, Jan de Graaff produced yellow Regal Lilies from *L. regale, L. sulphureum* and *L. leucanthum,* known as *Royal Gold.* E. C. Butterfield bred and gave his name to the *L. regale* yellow clone first marketed in 1953.

Before Jan de Graaff first started to work with lilies, he collected all the trumpet types it was possible to obtain from wherever he could get them – the United States, England, China, and Japan. The best of these lilies provided the foundation of his work, and the Green Mountain hybrids, up to 6 feet high, with pyramid flower-heads and with long,

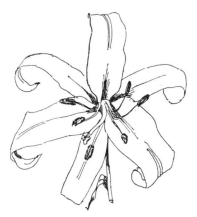

Aurelian hybrid, Sunburst type

Aurelian hybrid, Sunburst type

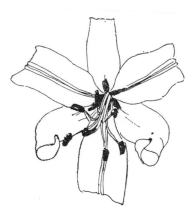

Aurelian hybrid

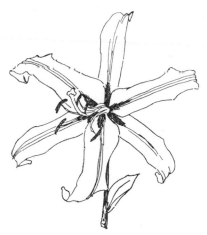

Aurelian hybrid, Sunburst type

often greenish trumpets and chocolate-brown stamens, were essentially the product of *L. leucanthum* var. *centifolium.*

The Olympic hybrids originated from breeding work with *L. centifolium*, *L. sargentiae*, and *L. regale*. The selection process for the best types of each generation, their subsequent pollination, reselection, and further crossing was repeatedly carried out, and new generations of always-improved Olympic hybrids were continuously brought onto the market. Their 5–6 feet stems carry large white trumpets arranged in a beautiful racemose inflorescence, while the umbellate flower arrangement of *L. regale* is, by contrast, less pleasing. Further selections for other characteristics by Jan de Graaff produced more strains and clones:

Black Dragon: clone; classically beautiful; wide-open blooms, white inside, purple-brown outside, 6 feet high, up to 12 flowers; derives in the main from *L. leucanthum* var. *centifolium*

Black Magic: *Black Dragon* multiplied as a strain

Carrara: strain, pure-white trumpet lily with pale-yellow throat both inside and outside; 3–5 feet

Green Dragon: clone, wide-open flowers, colour of Chartreuse, green suffused on outside: another *L. leucanthum* progeny

Green Magic: strain, like the above clone but multiplied from seed; green throat

Pink Perfection: strain; tall; pyramid-shaped flower-head of fuchsia-pink suffused, trumpet-shaped blooms; requires broken shade if its colour is to be preserved

Damson: clone; a particularly dark form of Pink Perfection

Royal Gold: strain; the already previously mentioned pure golden-yellow Regal Lily; 3–5 feet

Sentinel: strain; pure-white, open trumpets with yellow throat, brown pollen; very elegant and loose inflorescence

The Temple, or Centifolium, hybrids, selected for a variety of different characteristics, were introduced by John M. Shaver, of Newburg. Their names are: *Pearl Temple* – shiny mother-of-pearl; *Amethyst Temple* – deep amethyst-red; *Marble Temple* – white-ivory, bronze and purple on outside, green throat; *Jade Temple* – pale-green and ivory, green and brown outside.

Crosses with Aurelian hybrids are *Topaz Temple*, *Sun Temple*, and *Golden Temple*, all of which show varying shades of yellow. Shaver's Shellrosa hybrids are predominantly pink.

E. F. Palmer, of Vineland Station, Ontario, Canada, has been equally successful in the breeding of yellow trumpet lilies. *Galahad*, with long, greenish, sulphur-coloured funnels, is his best, and originated from the Sulphureum hybrids.

The Shelburne hybrid strain introduced in 1930, and *Shellman*, which came a little later, were introduced by Fred Abbey, of Shelburne, Vermont; both are *L. sargentiae* × *regale* hybrids. The shell-pink *L. leucanthum* var. *chloraster* hybrids were named Shellrose hybrids. *Winter Sunset* is a very good pink trumpet lily of Regale character; more recent is the vigorous, pink *Cherry Glow*.

Aurelian hybrids are universally popular with breeders, for a variety of good reasons: they are robust, undemanding in their soil and climatic requirements, healthy, and provide an almost inexhaustible number of colour and shape variations.

Jan de Graaff's first Aurelian hybrids consisted of three strains selected for reasons of shape. Yellow, lemon and gold trumpets comprise the Golden Clarion strain. The flower shape of the Heart's Desire strain lies between the trumpet shape and the wide-open Henryi type, and is in the form of flat saucers, white, cream or yellow-orange in colour. The Sunburst strain has wide-open, star-shaped, often strongly recurved blooms resembling *L. henryi* and in many cases complete with the papillae so characteristic of this lily; they are white, gold, and orange, and many have orange-coloured centres. A number of particularly good Aurelian hybrid selections were only made available as either strains or clones. They are: African Queen, a strain of orange trumpets; Copper King, strain, a very impressive lily with wide-open orange trumpets with dark-red outer colouring; Emerald, strain, translucent yellowish-green trumpets or pyramidal flower-heads; *Honeydew* – a lily of classic beauty and inflorescence, long, yellowish-green trumpets with green back and gold-brown pollen; *Limelight* – excellently shaped sulphur to

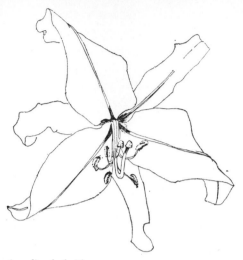

Aurelian hybrid

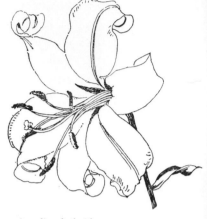

Aurelian hybrid

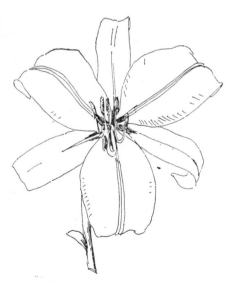

Aurelian hybrid, Sunburst strain

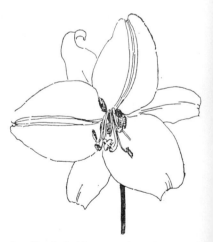

Aurelian hybrid, saucer-shaped

Chartreuse trumpets; Red Gold, strain – a lily with a future, golden trumpets with pink margins and veins; *Verona*, strongly pink-lilac coloured trumpets. The ivory *New Era* is very beautifully shaped and perhaps the best of the saucer-shaped types. Lilies with star-shaped, flat-open and partly sideways-facing blooms are numerous, and include: *Bright Star* – silver-brushed white with orange centres; *Stardust* – large flowers with orange centres and green star; *Thunderbolt* – wide-open, melon-orange blooms and giant-sized inflorescence.

Aurelian hybrid, saucer-shaped   Aurelian hybrid, trumpet-shaped

Carleton Yerex, of Sherwood, Oregon, has produced extraordinary well-shaped and beautiful Aurelian hybrids which came into commerce under a variety of names: Aurelian Apricot Trumpets, Aurelian Golden Trumpets, Aurelian Green Gold Trumpets, Corona Aurelians, Aurelian Flares, Green Knight Flares, Sunshine Flares, Superba Flares. His latest introductions are: *Citrolirion, Eventide, Greensprite, Whirlybird, Ta Ming, Pagoda Bells, Carnival Queen, Shenandoah, Wahlula.*

Douglas Foxwell, of Balcombe, Sussex, England continued to work on the Yerex hybrids and produced a number of selections which have been reported for inclusion in the International Lily Register. They are: *Amberflare, Aureolinbelle, Broombelle, Canarybelle, Canaryflare, Chineseflare, Muskbelle, Saffronbelle, Starbelle, Strawbelle,* and *Sulphurbelle.*

The Aurelian hybrids from R. W. Bemis, of Blackthorne Gardens, Holbrook, Massachusetts, are known under the name of 'Royal Coronas', and range in colour from white to cream, lemon, gold and apricot.

The spectacular, wide-open, pale yellow with green flowers of *Sundance, Moonbeam,* and *Starlite* provide a contrast for their chocolate-brown stamens. They were raised by E. F. Palmer, of Vineland Station, Canada, from his Sulphur hybrids and *L.* × *aurelianense.*

Mrs Joan Ericksen, of Wauchope, Canada, recently registered two types of hybrids: the white and lemon Saskaleen hybrids with wide-open flowers, of Centifolium-Aurelian parentage; and also the white to apricot Saskawin hybrids.

Ever more Aurelian hybrids are being bred and offered to the public, because they are very adaptable, easy to grow, healthy, and offer a rich variety of shape and colour.

Trumpet lily hybrids in commerce:

JAN DE GRAAFF, of Gresham, Oregon
African Queen: strain, apricot trumpets
Aida: clone from African Queen strain with apricot trumpets
Black Dragon: large white trumpets, purple-brown on outside
Black Magic: strain, developed from *Black Dragon*
Carrara: strain, pure-white trumpets
Copper King: strain, wide-open, orange Aurelians, rust-brown on outside
Damson: clone, very dark, fuchsia-red trumpets
Emerald Isle: wide-open, pure-white trumpets, emerald-green on outside
Golden Clarion: strain, lemon-yellow Aurelians; trumpet-shaped
Golden Splendor: strain, deep-gold trumpets with reddish back
Green Dragon: clone, wide-open, greenish-yellow trumpets with green buds

Green Magic: strain, white and green
Helios: clone, delicate yellow-shaded green; flowers profusely
Honeydew: clone, greenish-yellow trumpets, green outside; flowers
  profusely
Life: clone, golden-yellow with bronze outside: wide-open
Limelight: Chartreuse-yellow, green back; flowers profusely; large
  inflorescence
Luna: clone, delicate cream-yellow; flowers carried in garland
Moonlight: strain, Chartreuse-yellow; strong and vigorous; wide-
  open
Olympic hybrids: strain, very thriving white trumpets
Pink Perfection: strain, pink trumpets; good inflorescence
Royal Gold: strain, golden-yellow Regale
Sentinel: strain, pure-white, wide-open, cup-shaped; dark-brown
  pollen
Verona: clone, fuchsia-red; selected from Pink Perfection; very
  vigorous
Heart's Desire: strain, wide-open saucers; white, cream, yellow and
  orange
New Era: greenish-white; wide-open saucers
Golden Showers: strain, wide-open saucers; butter-yellow; nodding
Bright Star: star-shaped flowers, silver-white with orange centre
Golden Sunburst: strain, star-shaped, golden-yellow, greenish back
Lightening: deep golden-yellow, green star in centre
Pink Sunburst: strain, fuchsia-red stars
Silver Sunburst: strain, ivory-white and white stars
Stardust: silver-white stars with orange centre; very strong
Thunderbolt: melon-yellow stars

EDGAR L. KLINE, of Lake Grove, Oregon, is the distributor of the
Carleton Yerex varieties. Apart from the various trumpet and Aurelian
strains the following clones are also available:

Aurabunda: a recently introduced, profusely flowering clone with
  Auratum-shaped, jasmine-yellow blooms, 5–6 feet

Bright Cloud: white, broad, recurved petals with yellow centre

Carnival Queen: strongly reflexed petals, white with apricot markings; 4–5 feet

Citrolirion: very strong clone; lemon-yellow trumpets

Eventide: pyramidal inflorescence; cream with yellow and orange centre

Goldspire: wide-open blooms, eggyolk-yellow, suffused with green on outside

Greensprite: flaring type, white with greenish centre; elegantly waved petal margins

Lady Allice: similar to *Greensprite*, but with apricot-coloured centre; 4–5 feet; late

Mme Edouard Debras: broad-petalled trumpets, sulphur-yellow; 4 feet

Moonlight Sonata: large flowers, recurved petal tips; golden-yellow framed in white; 5 feet

Pink Frills: pink trumpets from Aurelian cross, waved petal margins; 5 feet; late

Shenandoah: wide-open blooms, dual colouring, outer half cream, apricot centre; 5 feet; late

Ta Ming: strongly reflexed petals, nankeen-yellow; 5 feet; late

Whirlybird: large flaring blooms, white with bronze-yellow centre; 5–6 feet; late

White Wings: large blooms, spider-shaped, delicately apricot-tinted centre; 4–5 feet; late

The following Temple hybrids from JOHN M. SHAVER are also available:

Amethyst Temple: large trumpets of light to dark amethyst colour; 5 feet–6 feet 6 inches; July

Golden Temple and *Sun Temple:* from sulphur-yellow to orange-yellow with partly pink, purple and brownish markings on the outside

Marble Temple: white, ivory, and cream, although the trumpets are pink, wine-red, brownish, olive-green, and green on the outside; 5 feet–6 feet 6 inches; July/August

Topaz Temple: pastel yellow shades on inside, stronger colours of various shades on outside; 4 feet–6 feet 6 inches; July/August

Greatheart: an Aurelian hybrid from B. L. Palmer, flaring type; orange with cream-coloured margins; up to 30 blooms on pyramidal inflorescence; 6 feet 6 inches–8 feet; July

Shellrose hybrids: from Shaver; pale-pink to purple trumpets, although the only colour is often on the petal margins of the otherwise white perianth segment, purple on outside; 4–6 feet; July

The above-mentioned trumpet lilies and Aurelian hybrids from de Graaff, Yerex, and Shaver are also available from the Rex Bulb Farms, Newberg, Oregon.

Romaine B. Ware, of Canby, Oregon, and Wayside Gardens, Mentor, Ohio, also make the Jan de Graaff lilies available.

Oriental (Japanese) hybrids

This group includes hybrids produced from *L. auratum*, *L. speciosum*, *L. japonicum* and *L. rubellum* and also those obtained from crosses with *L. henryi*. Subdivisions are:

(a) all hybrids with trumpet-shaped flowers
(b) all hybrids with saucer-shaped flowers, e.g., *Emperor of India*
(c) all hybrids with flat-shaped flowers, e.g., Imperial strain
(d) all hybrids with reflexed flowers, e.g., Jamboree strain

The Japanese *L. auratum*, *L. speciosum*, *L. japonicum*, and *L. rubellum* are the breeding partners of this group. The extraordinary beauty of these lilies (particularly of *L. auratum*) and the many natural forms of *L. auratum* and *L. speciosum* are the reason for the large number of hybrid forms. But as with the Goldband Lily, these hybrids are not easily raised or kept in a garden; they are susceptible to virus diseases, as well as fusarium, and prefer lime-free soils and maritime climates.

L. auratum was already being crossed with various *L. speciosum* forms in 1869, barely seven years after it was first imported from Japan. The best one – its beauty was astonishing for the time – was named *L.* ×

parkmanii in honour of the American historian Francis Parkman. The coloured illustration of it in Elwes' *Monograph of the Lily* proved an inspiration and spur to lily breeders; unfortunately it now has only historical interest, as all the bulbs died soon after they were sold to England. But Roy M. Wallace, of Warburton, Victoria, Australia, was later successful in crossing the two species, namely *L. speciosum Gilray* and *L. auratum Crimson Queen*, and called the hybrid *Jillian Wallace*. Breeders clamoured for this lily with its carmine segments of 8 inches diameter marked with white tips and waved white margins. The quite flat petals, heavily spotted in red and with papillae, were a new step forward, and increased the size and beauty of lily flowers.

G. L. Slate, of Geneva, New York, was also successful with his Parkmanii cross. Dr S. L. Emsweller, of Beltsville, carried out a number of crosses between *L. speciosum* and *L. auratum*, which he back-crossed with *L. speciosum* before releasing them in 1953; they are known as

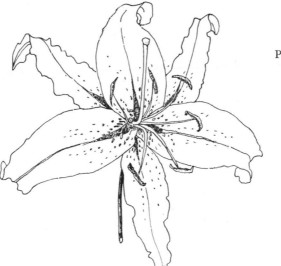

Potomac hybrid

Potomac hybrids, and have very flat, large, pure-white, white and red or deep-carmine blooms. The year 1960 saw the introduction of the white *Allegra* – a hybrid with few pink papillae produced by crossing *L.*

speciosum var. *album* with *L. auratum* var. *platyphyllum*. Raising these hybrids from seed presents great difficulty, as the seeds contain growth inhibitors which nullify any normal cross, although the problem can be solved by careful removal of the embryo, which is germinated and grown on a nutrient medium under sterile conditions.

Dr Norma E. Pfeiffer, of the Boyce Thompson Institute, Yonkers, New York, aimed to combine the delicate pink of *L. japonicum* and *L. rubellum* into hybrids with *L. auratum*. She completed a series of crosses, together with the appropriate back-crosses, where *L. auratum* was fertilized with *L. japonicum* and *L. rubellum* pollen.

Jan de Graaff's *Empress of China* flowered for the first time in 1949; in 1950 it was the turn of *Empress of Japan* and later of *Empress of India*. The first is pure-white with a few purple spots, the second is also white but bears a gold median band and deep-brown spots, while the last is pink with a crimson-coloured centre and dark-red papillae. In all cases the huge 12-inch diameter flowers are flat, saucer-shaped, and arise from back-crosses of *Jillian Wallace* with *L. auratum Crimson Queen* and *L. auratum Virginale*.

Jan de Graaff added three complementary strains to these three clones: Imperial Crimson, Imperial Silver, and Imperial Gold. The Pink Cloud, Pink Diamond, and Pink Glory strains arise from crosses with pink *L. japonicum*, and are therefore in part deeper and in part only delicately tinted with pink.

The 12-inch large, carmine and white-margined Centennial hybrids were brought onto the market by Edgar L. Kline, of Lake Grove, Oregon, and are back-crosses between *Jillian Wallace* and the Potomac hybrids with *L. auratum* and *L. speciosum*. His Pink Cameo and White Cameo hybrids resulted from crosses between *L. auratum* var. *platyphyllum* and *L. japonicum*. Their saucer-shaped flowers have either inherited the delicate pink of *L. japonicum* or the pure white of *L. japonicum* var. *album*.

Leslie Woodriff, of Harbor, Oregon, was equally successful in producing his large saucer-shaped Atomic hybrids from *L. auratum*, *L. speciosum*, *L. japonicum*, and *L. rubellum*. More important, by managing to breed *L. rubellum*'s early flowering habit into his range of white to deep-red and speckled hybrids, he made them acceptable for forcing, a point of particular commercial significance.

L. auratum and *L. speciosum* flourish in the New Zealand climate, and it is therefore not surprising that the New Zealanders work extensively with hybrids from these varieties.

The Zealandia hybrids bred by L. B. Tuffery, of Bell Block, New Plymouth, New Zealand, are an example, and have arisen from *L. auratum*, *L. speciosum*, and *L. japonicum*. They range through a wide colour spectrum from white to pink, pure-carmine and lavender.

The Melford hybrids developed by Dr J. S. Yeates, of Palmerston North, New Zealand, came from particularly good stock – *L. auratum Crimson Queen*, *L. speciosum Gilray*, and the Parkmanii hybrid *Jillian Wallace*. Some of the best hybrids out of his clones, of which over 30 are registered, are: *Pink Delight* – purple-red, saucer-shaped flowers, $8\frac{1}{2}$–10 inches in diameter, with white margins; *Pink Beauty* – even greater blooms of up to 12-inch diameter of Chinese pink with dark spots but narrower white margins; *Rising Star* – pink, saucer-shaped, somewhat erect-flowering; *Lavender Princess* – red; *Excelsior* – deep-crimson with narrow, white margins.

There was great excitement among lily breeders when Leslie Woodriff exhibited his *Black Beauty* at the North American Lily Society show in 1957. Apart from being the darkest red of all *L. speciosum* hybrids, almost a black-red in the flower centre, it measures up in all other respects, including health and ability to produce many flowers – 56 per stem! It was the only seedling selected from over 50,000 raised from seed of various types of *L. speciosum* which had been dusted with the pollen of multifarious lilies excluding, it was thought, that of *L. speciosum*. Subsequent cytological examination of chromosomes by Dr S. L. Emsweller and Joseph Uhrig determined the parentage as *L. speciosum* var. *punctatum* and *L. henryi*. At last a bridge from *L. henryi*, which had already been previously crossed with a trumpet lily (*L.* × *aurelianense*) to the Japanese group of lilies, was successfully carried out. But there is a snag – unfortunately! *Black Beauty* is not fertile, and whether self-pollinated or cross-pollinated refuses to set seed. This is unfortunate, for if it could have been used as a parent in further breeding work, fascinating and far-reaching results could foreseeably have been obtained. (NALS-LYB 1962)

But it appears that Dr S. L. Emsweller had been successful in obtaining a back-cross from *Black Beauty* with *L. speciosum* varieties. Apart from this, colchicine treatment has already helped to produce an amphidiploid with larger blooms.

The following Oriental hybrids are available in commerce:

JAN DE GRAAFF, of Gresham, Oregon

Imperial Crimson: strain, crimson with white margins

Imperial Silver: strain, red-spotted, white

Imperial Gold: strain, white with broad gold median band, dark red spots

Empress of India: clone, deep crimson-red, reflexed white margins

Empress of China: clone, pure-white with red spots

Empress of Japan: clone, white with gold median band, reflexed

Sunday Best: clone, pure-white base with purple median band shading to crimson

Nobility: strain, deep ruby-red with white markings

American Eagle: clone, pure-white, vermilion-spotted

Crimson Beauty: clone, pure-white with cherry-red band

Adventure: clone, crimson, white petal tips, wide-open

Magic Pink: strain, *L. rubellum* × *L. auratum* hybrids, delicate pink with dark-red speckles

Pink Glory: strain, *L. japonicum* cross; salmon-pink

Pink Cloud: strain, *L. auratum* var. *tricolor* × *L. japonicum* var. *platyfolium*; satin-red

Pink Diamond: strain, *L. auratum* var. *virginale* × *L. japonicum*; pink-white with white, fine golden band

Red Band: strain, white with pronounced red median band

Bonfire: clone, dark-red with small white margin

Flying Cloud: strain, pure-white

Jamboree: strain, crimson, white-margined; reflexed blooms

Enterprise: clone, selection from Jamboree strain

Everest: strain, pure-white Jamboree type

DR S. L. EMSWELLER, of Beltsville, Maryland
Potomac hybrids: *L. auratum* × *L. speciosum* hybrids, pink to red, white
   margins; flat, recurved
Allegra: clone, parentage as above, pure-white, green star

EDGAR L. KLINE, of Lake Grove, Oregon
Centennial hybrids: pink to carmine, red-spotted, white margins
Pink Cameo hybrids: delicate pink
White Cameo hybrids: pure-white

LESLIE WOODRIFF, of Harbor, Oregon
Atomic hybrids: *L. rubellum* hybrids, various shades of pink, both early
   and late-flowering
Cameo hybrids: *L. auratum* × *L. japonicum*, white and pink
Little Fairy hybrids: *L. auratum* × *L. rubellum*, pink, early May-flowering
Black Beauty: carmine with black-red centre, recurved

BLACKTHORNE GARDENS, Holbrook, Massachusetts
Crimson Dream: strain, crimson-pink to dark red, white margins

DR J. S. YEATES, of Palmerston North, New Zealand
Pink Delight: clone, saucer-shaped, purple-red with white margins, up to
   12 inches in diameter
Pink Beauty: Chinese red with dark spotting, narrow, white margins
Lavender Princess: spotted lavender-lilac
Rising Star: pink, saucer-shaped blooms
Excelsior: carmine-pink with narrow white margins

L. B. TUFFERY, of Bell Block, New Plymouth, New Zealand
Zealandia hybrids, Auratum-Speciosum hybrids

Other hybrids

Reference must be made to the Caucasian lilies extensively used by the
Russians for hybridization – *L. monadelphum, L. szovitsianum,* and *L.
kesselringianum.*

Mitchurin was successful as long ago as 1914 in producing *L. ×
fialkovaja* (Violet Lily) from *L. szovitsianum × L. × maculatum* cross.
Its up to 20 funnel-shaped, brick-orange-red blooms with carmine-lilac
tipped petals are violet-scented and of 3-inch diameter.

This lily was later used in a cross by S. N. Zwetajewa (*L. × fialkovaja×
L. concolor*) to produce *L. × zwetajewa* hybrids in 1940. They blossom
during June and have both erect and sideways-facing, cup-shaped,
scented flowers ranging from pale-yellow to dark brown-red accentu-
ated by violet-tipped petals.

J. L. Saliwski bred *L. × sestroretskaja* from *L. dauricum* and *L. davidii*
var. *willmottiae*.

Unfortunately only a few seeds from Russian-bred lilies have found
their way to the West. Despite this, and although the Russian lilies
belong to other groups, this may be the opportune place to report on them.

A number of new lily hybrids bred by V. P. Orekhov found accept-
ance in Russia and were distributed there between 1950 and 1960. He
worked, in part, with already known hybrids, but also with a number of
species – *L. × sestroretskaja*, *L × fialkovaja*, *L. × zwetajewa*, *L. ×
stroynaya* and with the species *L. amabile*, *L. davidii* var. *willmottiae*, *L.
tigrinum*, *L. dauricum*, *L. concolor*, *L. szovitsianum*, *L. monadelphum*, and
L. kesselringianum.

Careful selection of the seedlings resulted in a variety of hybrids
which were divided into seven groups:

L. × Joy of Summer – L. × Vasurus Prieks
During 1954 the hybrid lily (*L. sestroretskaja × L. zwetajewa*) was fertilized with a pollen mixture of *L. amabile*, *L. davidii* var. *willmottiae*, *L.
tigrinum*, *L. monadelphum*, and *L. stroynaya*. The subsequently selected
seedlings (14 clones were selected with particular care and later named)
grow 4–5 feet high and carry 25–30 large, saucer-shaped blooms from
the end of June onwards; large brown spots cover the pale orange to
dark apricot-red flowers.

L. × Dreaming – L. × Saptiataja
Five clones were selected from the seedlings produced when *L. ×
zwetajewa* hybrids were dusted with a pollen mixture similar to that

used in the above group. They have large, pale orange, orange-red or apricot-pink Turk's Cap blooms.

L. × Thoughtful – L. × Skumfu

Again a case of *L. × zwetajewa* hybrids being fertilized with a pollen mixture. Nine clones were selected this time, mostly for their large, red, erect and outward-facing blooms.

L. × Golden Crown – L. × Zelta Vainags

A pollen mixture from red lilies was used in 1954 to fertilize the American *L. × Golden Chalice* hybrids. The seedlings of the seven selected clones have saucer-shaped, orange-gold-yellow flowers of 5–6 inches diameter, with pink-tipped petals and red-brown spots. Stem height: 5 feet.

L. × Seastar – Juras Zvaigne

The two clones selected from a cross between *L. concolor × L. zwetajewa* proved to be superior to the parents – 10–15 erect, saucer-shaped, shiny red blooms of 5–6-inch diameter in an umbel.

L. × Gay Fellow – L. × Sautrie Bernie

Between 20–30 star-shaped, pale orange to dark red-brown blooms per stem were the result of dusting a specially selected seedling (GVS-364-4-20) with pollen from *L. davidii* var. *willmottiae*, *L. amabile*, and *L. monadelphum*.

L. × Daurskoy Hybrids – L. dauricum hybrids

Four clones: *Hawk* – saucer-shaped, dark red, 4 feet high; *Modest* – saucer-shaped, apricot-pink with yellow, 3 feet high; *Night Queen* – four to six velvety dark-red blooms up to 7 inches in diameter; *Leopoldovich* – very vigorous, 4–5 feet tall, saucer-shaped, red, 6-inch diameter blooms in umbel. All of them flower between June and July.

Various hybrids were raised in the Ukraine by V. K. Negrobov, one from *L. centigale × L. longiflorum × L. regale* and the other from *L.*

formosanum × *L. princeps* × *L regale*: both lilies carry green-sheened, cream-white trumpets. (NALS-LYB 1962, RHS-LYB 1965)

Mention must also be made of the self-fertile *L.* × *zalivskii* (*L. formosanum* var. *pricei* × *L. longiflorum*), which is hardier than *L. longiflorum*.

Reports also indicate crosses between *L. candidum* × *L. ledebourii*.

10. Exhibiting lilies

The exhibition of home-grown flowers and produce is a feature of England and America, and often engenders fierce competition among gardeners; it occupies many professional specialist judges, and allows the triumphant prize-winner to reap his reward – very often of only small financial benefit but of high prestige value. Large and small shows take place in all parts of the country, are fully reported in the press and exhibit a wide range of flowers and vegetables in and out of season; some are specialist exhibitions, and lilies are, of course, well represented. The North American Lily Society holds its lily show at a different centre every year, while the Royal Horticultural Society holds one each July in London; the two New Zealand lily organizations work on a similar system. Akersloot is the centre of the annual Dutch convention, held in July, where lily breeders and propagators meet not only to see the best lilies but also to take the opportunity of inspecting the new hybrids very often introduced on this occasion.

Lilies intended for exhibition must naturally be at their best, but this often presents great difficulties if long car, train or even plane journeys are necessary for delivery to the exhibition site. Jan de Graaff shows his lilies at most exhibitions, and always has them flown from either Oregon or Holland. Precise knowledge of how to prepare blooms for show purposes is essential, because a squashed flower, or one with pollen-dusted petals, will find favour neither with judges nor the viewing public. Such knowledge is of equal importance to the florist, who must present the best possible flowers for the best possible price.

Cutting

Cutting should be confined to taking no more than one-third to one-half of the leaved part of the stem to ensure that a sufficient number of leaves remain to maintain the bulb.

Lilies will last up to 14 days in a water-filled vase, provided they are cut just as the lowest bud is about to burst into flower. Even then, the number of buds and prevailing temperature are apt to influence the length of time a flower spike will last.

Stems intended for sale or exhibition must be cut earlier – in fact, shortly before the first bud is about to open. Early morning, while the pollen sacs are still closed, is the best time of day for cutting. It is always advisable to carry a suitable water container around the garden as cutting progresses, so that stems can be put into water as they are cut. Spikes not intended for immediate use should be stored in a cool, dark place. Constant care is necessary to keep flower spikes apart, or else individual blooms or perhaps even whole stems are likely to bruise or be smeared with pollen dust; white lilies, particularly, need special care.

Packing

The readily available, purpose-designed, long and flat containers are best for packing lilies. They are first lined with sheets of foil or greaseproof paper, but care must be taken to allow sufficient overlap along the length of the box for folding over the top of the flowers, once they are in the box, to protect them from the box lid. The paper or foil lining also preserves the moisture and provides a smooth surface, causing the minimum of friction in case the blooms should rub against it. Each stem, from the lowest flower bud downwards, is surrounded with a roll of wood shavings or newspaper, which is covered in turn with a layer of greaseproof paper to support the inflorescence and prevent the flowers from rubbing against the carton walls. Greaseproof paper balls are useful for keeping individual blooms apart. To prevent stems from sliding within the box, they should be secured to the bottom of the carton with string or rubber bands, which have previously been covered with tissue paper, to avoid bruising or cutting the stems. If one or more flowers are open, it is essential carefully to remove the anthers with tweezers, otherwise pollen is certain to spot the petals during transportation; stamens are best wrapped in tissue paper. If the carton is large enough to hold more than one flower spike, the second is usually packed in reverse direction, i.e., with its stem adjacent to the flowers of the first.

Lilies with larger than usual inflorescence are best stored in a cool place and without water for half a day before being packed. This causes almost imperceptible wilting, and eases packing. To avoid buds opening during the journey a rubber band wrapped in tissue paper, slipped along the bud, is very useful.

Transportation and show preparation

Lilies will keep perfectly for two to three days inside the package provided they have been well packed, but even then it is advisable to choose the quickest available transport.

Cartons must be opened at once on arrival at their destination, the base of the stems cut back a little, and the whole spike placed in water and stored in a cool room. It only takes one to two days for flower spikes to fully recover from their journey – after that bloom after bloom rapidly opens. Care is still necessary to prevent pollen from marring the petals, and stamens must be removed.

Sudden periods of heat or cold are apt to advance or retard flowering, and it is often impossible to synchronize the optimum flowering period of a lily with an exhibition date. Many large nurseries have facilities where cut flowers can be delayed from blooming for periods of up to one month provided they are stored at a temperature of $35 \cdot 5$–$38 \cdot 5°$F (2–$6°$c); the same process can be followed with the aid of a domestic refrigerator or a cool cellar. Lilies, cut before any of their flower buds have opened, can be stored in the same manner up to exhibition date. If flowering is to be accelerated, lilies should be stored in a warm room to 'catch up'. If, however, a naturally late-flowering lily is needed for an earlier time, the only satisfactory method is to raise it as a pot plant in a temperature-controlled greenhouse. Only experience can determine the required growing period and temperature needed to bring different varieties to perfection for a certain date; Americans have already succeeded in doing so and raise the Easter Lily with almost mathematical precision from the accumulated data of past seasons.

If lilies are to be at their best they should be arranged at least one day before the exhibition and so give time for several buds to open.

Lilies in pots need particular care during transportation. Each flower stem should be fastened with raffia to a parallel-inserted bamboo cane. Further and somewhat longer bamboo canes are used to support individual blooms, which are fastened to the supports with crepe-paper. Individual pots are then arranged in rows in a suitably sized wooden box, and packed with wood shavings; small, narrow boards are nailed horizontally across the top of the box to keep the pots firm and upright. A lattice work is erected above the box to support the vertical bamboo canes which are tied to it. Anthers are wrapped in tissue paper, and blooms carefully lined with cotton wool. Lilies in pots should be unpacked two or three days before exhibition to allow them to regain their natural form.

It need hardly be mentioned that only perfect lilies of the best possible strains should be chosen for exhibition, and that they should always be correctly and legibly labelled.

Allocation of prize points

To lend interest to exhibitions and to encourage a large number of entries, shows are divided into a number of sections or classes. These are usually: a single lily stem; a single stem of a hybrid lily; three or six stems of mixed varieties; new and unknown lilies; individual varieties. In addition, lilies are often judged on the basis of their arrangement in vases, containers or in the garden. Judges work to a fixed scale of maximum points which they award for particular characteristics; the lily awarded the highest number of points is, of course, the winner of its class. Points are allocated on the following basis:

Appearance – The more open the blooms, the better, provided they are all at their best and show no signs of wilting. Flowers, leaves and stem must be healthy and be free of botrytis and fusarium symptoms.

30 Points

Vigour – Height and strength of stem, number of blooms, appearance of leaves.   *20 Points*

Flower conformation – How the blooms are held, their spacing, the shape and length of pedicels, overall impression of inflorescence.

20 Points

Flower substance – Do well-formed petals give an appearance of strength?   *10 Points*

Flower shape – Typical of variety? Well-shaped and pleasing?

10 Points

Flower colour – Clear, pure and pleasing colours are always awarded more points than muddy and muted shades.   *10 Points*

It is interesting to note that colour, usually the public's first concern, is not rated nearly as highly by judges as conformation, health, and vigour.

11. The past and the future

The history of lilies

Sagas, fairy tales, and legends have mentioned the lily since earliest times. Archaeologists have found pictorial and sculptured evidence of *L. candidum*, native of the Mediterranean region. It is also mentioned in the Bible, to it was attributed medicinal virtues, and oil extracted from its bulb and flowers was used to heal burns and other wounds.

L. candidum and various irises were depicted in frescoes at King Minos' Palace in Crete in about 1500 BC, and are now in the Heraklion Museum. A lily bulb has been found buried with an Egyptian mummy. A wall picture of very naturally presented lilies dating back to 700 BC was found in the palace of King Assurbanipal at Nineveh.

We know that *L. candidum* grew wild on the Palestine coast, and it is therefore not surprising that it receives several mentions in the Bible. The lily was also pictorially and sculpturally depicted on ceramics in Greece and associated with the goddesses Aphrodite, Artemis, and Hera; so, too, with the Roman goddesses Diana, Venus, and Juno. Pliny pronounced the lily as the noblest of all flowers. The Romans used it for stuffing their pillows and perfuming their baths – *susinu* was their name for lily oil. The word is thought to be derived from the old Syrian *sasa*, or from the Hebrew *susan*. The girl's name 'Susan' means lily.

The white lily was probably brought over the Alps by the Romans; Abbot Wahlafried Strabo of the Benedictine Abbey of Reichenau likened it to a rose as early as 840 in his *Hortulus*. Still later, the Crusaders returned with lily bulbs from Syria and Palestine. The white lily, at one time the attribute of the Greek and Roman goddesses, is today the symbol of innocence, purity, and chastity, and the attribute of the Virgin Mary. There is no doubt that the Church took the white lily over from the pagans. The fifth- and sixth-century early Christian mosaics at Ravenna show several early examples of the white lily.

Sant'Apollinare in Classe, mosaic, sixth century

The number of pictures of the Annunciation of both the Gothic and Renaissance periods showing the white lily is countless. A 1333 picture of the Italian painter Simone Martini shows a vase of lilies in an Annunciation scene, and so, too, does a later picture by Roger van der Weyden. Sandro Botticelli, who died in 1510, shows the Madonna surrounded by eight angels, each carrying a lily. In 1436 the Dutch painter, Jan van Eyck, showed a vase of white lilies in a picture of the divine child, and in 1475 Hugo van der Goes painted a pitcher of irises, aquilegia, and *L. bulbiferum* in his *Adoration*. The German artists Stephan Lochner (*c.* 1445) and Matthias Grünewald portrayed both roses and lilies in their works, and succeeded in presenting them both true to life and botanically accurate. (72)

The lily is always used as a symbol of chastity and humility in the Christian religion, and an attribute of the Virgin Mary, St John the Baptist, St Francis of Assisi, and St Anthony of Padua.

The old herbal books dating from the Middle Ages invariably ascribed medicinal properties to plants, and Hieronymus Bock's book of 1547 was no exception. He recommended a brew of flowers and bulbs for regaining consciousness and which could also be used to alleviate inflamed livers and ease labour pains.

He also recommends that the oil extracted from the bulb be used in cases of inflammation, burns, and boils, as well as for varicose veins. He continues for another half page, and explains how to use lily roots and leaves to best effect. His most curious and interesting suggestion is that a mixture of honey and ashes of burnt lily bulbs rubbed into the scalp provides a cure for baldness.

The French Kings, the Valois and the Bourbons, are thought to have included the lily in their coat of arms, although it may only have been a stylized iris. Orders of chivalry were founded, most of them dedicated to the Virgin, but all with the lily as a heraldic symbol.

The white lily, *L. candidum*, was actually a 'prototype'. It had, and still has, beauty, singularity and mystery; it was used for medicinal purposes, as a religious symbol, and retained many of those varied facets from earliest times through the Middle Ages to the present day.

Botanical interest only came to the fore as further lilies were discovered. The Grecian *L. chalcedonicum* was known before 1573 and described before 1629 by John Parkinson, with *L. canadense*, which reached Europe from America at about the same time. In 1753, Linnaeus included it with *L. pomponium* and *L. philadelphicum* in his *Species Plantarum*.

The lilies from eastern Asia and Japan followed. E. Kaempfer wrote about *L. tigrinum* as early as 1712, although it was not imported until 1804. Thunberg, Linnaeus's successor at Uppsala, and von Siebold, a doctor from southern Germany, practising in Holland, imported three differently coloured *L. speciosum*, three varieties of *L.* × *maculatum* and *L. longiflorum*. During the nineteenth century the French missionaries David, Delavay, Farges, and Faurie investigated the flora of the Chinese provinces, and wrote about the many lilies they had collected and sent to Europe from Szechwan, Yunnan, Kwangsi and Hupeh.

Around the turn of the century, English plant collectors completed many successful and fruitful searches in the Indian states around the foot of the Himalayas, in the inhospitable mountain ranges of Burma, and in the mountainous western provinces of China. The most successful collector was the English botanist E. H. Wilson, who collected for the Arnold Arboretum in the United States. Lilies were his speciality, and his greatest discoveries were *L. regale* and *L. sargentiae* in 1904; both are described in his book *The Lilies of Eastern Asia*. This is a classic of lily literature, describing and classifying 40 lily species, their variations and forms, nearly all of which he had personally collected and seen growing in their natural surroundings. E. H. Wilson was also active in the field of lily classification, and instrumental in the discovery of many synonyms.

No less successful was Frank Kingdon Ward during his 24 journeys to the Himalayas, Burma, Assam, Tibet, and China. *L. wardii*, *L. mackliniae*, and *L. arboricola*, which grows on trees, were all first discovered by him. The number of his books nearly equals that of his journeys; they include many marvellous, lifelike descriptions of his discoveries and expeditions. Among other successful collectors who made their discoveries in China are the Englishman George Forrest (*L. stewartianum*), and the Irishman Augustine Henry (*L. henryi*).

Another lily enthusiast – Max Leichtlin of Baden-Baden – must not be forgotten. He collected many lilies in Japan, and later brought them to Europe.

The discovery of the American lilies is due to the work of Heinrich Bolander, who originally came from Hesse, and also to the efforts of the Englishmen M. Catesby, Asa Gray, Benedict Roezl, Dr A. Kellogg, Dr Charles Parry, and Carl Purdy. During more recent years Dr S. L. Emsweller, Dr Albert Vollmer, Lawrence Beane and Mrs M. G. Henry have been most active. The last 20 years have seen great progress in the acquisition of additional knowledge in the field of relationship between American lilies.

Russian work was carried out by the botanist Carl Maximowicz and the Hungarian-born J. N. Szovits, who both travelled extensively in search of lilies during the nineteenth century; they covered Manchuria and Persia as well as Russia. The wild lilies they found up to the time of the First World War were all brought into cultivation by the St Petersburg nursery of Regel and Kesselring, where *L. cernuum*, *L. callosum*, *L. concolor*, *L. kesselringianum*, and *L. ponticum* were introduced.

The future of lily-breeding

As a result of the many discoveries and introductions of lilies during the previous century, not to mention the exciting finds of the last few decades, all that is left for us is the production of new hybrids and their introduction into our gardens. The first tentative trials were made in England as long as 50 years ago. Isabella Preston succeeded with her Stenographer and Fighter hybrids, and Dr F. L. Skinner bred *L.* × *scottiae* and *L.* × *maxwill*. But the early breeders had to gain their knowledge on a trial-and-error basis, and progress was very slow in most cases. The second International Lily Conference, held in London in 1933, enabled breeders to exchange knowledge and techniques, and soon afterwards the United States inaugurated scientific research in this field. Jan de Graaff was already a leading figure in the lily world, and furthered cytological and genetic progress which led to an increased tempo in the breeding and development of new lilies in North America – a tempo which was previously thought to be impossible. Further progress is being maintained, and will not stop as long as the public's interest in lilies and gardens is maintained. The same tempo, effort, and research is paralleled in roses, where every year more and better varieties are released.

Although it is impossible to prophesy with any accuracy what the lilies of the future may hold in store for us, an attempt at forecasting the exciting prospects should not be neglected.

In the hope of obtaining fertile hybrids, we may expect a back-cross between *L. speciosum* and *Black Beauty*, and also perhaps between *Black Beauty* and *L. henryi*. Present indications point to the possibility of a fruitful *L. auratum* × *L. henryi* cross, and L. Tuffery's reports from New Zealand already seem to indicate success. The questions of whether the progeny of a cross between such very distantly related varieties will be fertile and whether they will be suitable for further breeding work are still unanswered. But if it proved possible to cross such future hybrids with *Black Beauty* (*L. speciosum* × *L. henryi*) the resulting possibilities would indeed be vast, and it is difficult to imagine the prodigious range which could ensue. *L. henryi* could substantially influence the health, vigour, and adaptability of lilies if crossed into the Speciosum-Japonicum-Rubellum complex. Achievement of this one aim alone would ensure considerable progress and lead to even wider distribution of the lily.

The cross between the rare Japanese *L. nobilissimum* into the Auratum-Speciosum complex is already a fact, and while these erect white trumpets can be expected to influence inflorescence conformation beneficially, there is a danger of weakening winter-hardiness.

Trumpet lilies offer countless opportunities, and in combination with *L. henryi*, the permutations of colour, shape and inflorescence are tremendous. Perhaps *L. henryi* may prove to be the link with the Auratum complex!

F. L. Skinner, of Dropmore, Canada, reports crosses between *L. auratum* and *L. japonicum* with *L. cernuum* and *L. davidii*, and of *L. centifolium* hybrids with *L. cernuum*, *L. davidii*, *L. amabile*, and *L.* × *maculatum*. Such hybrids, provided they prove to be fertile and can be used for breeding, will undoubtedly lead to ever more and new possibilities.

Lilies of a better and 'fast' red are expected to replace today's pink trumpets, which are apt to bleach and turn grey; it also seems feasible that more new yellow-red combinations are going to come forward among the trumpet shapes.

The successful crosses of *L. amabile* and *L. cernuum* with other Asiatic lilies have already indicated that further crosses among the many different Asiatic lilies should become a reality. The most delicate pastel-toned flowers stem from a cross between anthocyanin-containing *L. cernuum* and lilies with blooms containing carotenoids. *L. cernuum* has been instrumental in widening the range of fine pastel-toned lilies, and judging from colour photographs which have reached me from Canada, there are many more exciting things to come. Apparently new are the two-toned or multi-coloured blooms of the Cernuum range now appearing in red and lilac with lighter-coloured centres. As it has proved possible to cross *L. cernuum* into the Asiatic lilies, it may prove possible similarly to cross it with rose-pink *L. wardii*, white *L. taliense*, pink-lilac *L. lankongense*, or blackish-red *L. papilliferum*.

The diploid orange-coloured *L. tigrinum* as well as canary-yellow *L. tigrinum* var. *flaviflorum* can be crossed with various Asiatic lilies: *L. davidii*, *L.* × *umbellatum*, and *L. concolor* among them. Jan de Graaff has used many of these lilies in his crosses. Proof that the variation possibilities of these hybrids are not yet exhausted are the new hybrids from the American breeders David Stone and F. Henry Payne (*Connecticut Yankee, Nutmegger, Connecticut Maid*), and those of G. W. Darby (*Nora Darby, Sir Frederick Stern*). Further combinations can certainly be achieved among the Tiger hybrids.

Through multi-stepped crosses between Midcentury hybrids and *L. leichtlinii* var. *maximowiczii, L. tigrinum* var. *flaviflorum* and with Harlequin hybrids, Jan de Graaff achieved remarkably vigorous, large Turk's Cap-flowered plants which bloom prolifically in pyramid-shaped inflorescence.

It is still doubtful to what extent the strong-growing but small-flowered, red-lead coloured *L. callosum* can be crossed into this group.

Successful work carried out by Oliver Wyatt in England and by Dr A. M. Showalter in the United States in crossing the wild American lilies among each other has given very elegant hybrids. The future breeding potential in this field is quite considerable, and so far the surface has only been scratched.

Interesting breeding opportunities in the Martagon group appear to lie with *L. medeoloides*. Crossing *L. bulbiferum* and *L.* × *maculatum* into the Martagon group could also produce new colours and beneficially influence flower shape. Alexander Steffen produced *L.* × *martelatum* (*L. martagon* × *L.* × *maculatum*) and Olof Kumlin of Sweden has recently reported similar crosses. Further work along these lines will surely prove rewarding.

The Caucasian *L. monadelphum* and *L. szovitsianum* are extensively used by the Russians for lily-breeding and crossed with *L.* × *hollandicum* and *L. concolor*. Scented, saucer-shaped lilies with many other desirable characters can be expected from this work.

The oldest known lily hybrid is *L.* × *testaceum* (*L. candidum* × *L. chalcedonicum*). Why, therefore, should the Madonna Lily not allow itself to be crossed with *L. carniolicum* and *L. pyrenaicum* – particularly as crosses with *L. monadelphum* and *L. szovitsianum* are said to be possible? But this, again, lies in the future.

Polyploidy presents further opportunities for better lilies. Polyploid lilies possess two extremely desirable characteristics not found in diploids – more vigour, and larger blooms. Breeders do not seem to have achieved many polyploid lilies so far; they are not very difficult to produce, but, as mentioned earlier, each attempt is like a shot into the dark. Not enough shots are being fired to reach the dark targets!

The crossing of polyploid lilies with each other offers a quite new perspective, and once the number of available polyploid varieties is sufficiently high a polyploid hybrid is bound to follow – there are certainly no existing technical difficulties which could stop it. Let us also remember the tremendous progress achieved in the field of iris-breeding since the introduction of tetraploids, and the unforeseeably large number of varieties available today as a result of it. *Hemerocallis*, too, has already taken the inevitable steps towards polyploidy. There is little doubt that the breeding of polyploid lilies will widen and increase the number of variants, which in turn will necessitate raising from seed in large numbers to obtain all possible variants.

The American lily breeder F. Henry Payne wrote that the breeding of lilies is one continual, never-ending task. William C. Horsford said that it is not a mistake to make unlikely and seemingly foolish crosses; he also said that for inexplicable reasons the most unusual forms are produced from such crosses.

We have only just opened the door to the world of lily-breeding. The scientific foundation is laid, and the future will provide vast numbers of beautiful, elegant lilies in a multitude of rich colours and sumptuous shapes. All of them will bring colour and pleasure into our gardens, and in the meantime everyone can help – no one is excluded – to further this wonderful aim.

12. Choosing the right lily

Lilies for half-shade

All lilies like the sun, and most succumb if they do not get sufficient sunshine. The following lilies prefer semi-shade; the term is meant to convey a position where the plant is not exposed to full sunlight for the whole day, and will grow better if its base remains in the shade. All other lilies tolerate full sunshine.

L. amabile	*L. lankongense*	*L. washingtonianum*
L. auratum	*L. leichtlinii*	
L. bolanderi	*L. mackliniae*	Bellingham hybrids
L. brownii	*L. martagon*	Auratum-Speciosum
L. canadense	*L. michiganense*	hybrids
L. davidii	*L. pardalinum*	Martagon hybrids
L. distichum	*L. parryi*	Pink Perfection strain
L. duchartrei	*L. rubellum*	Pink Trumpet
L. grayi	*L. rubescens*	hybrids
L. hansonii	*L. speciosum*	Aurelian hybrids, par-
L. japonicum	*L. tsingtauense*	ticularly orange-
L. kelloggii	*L. wardii*	coloured varieties

Lilies for damp but well drained soils

The following lilies need to be planted in a damp soil, but the planting site must have good drainage.

L. *auratum*. var.
   platyphyllum
L. *bolanderi*
L. *canadense*
L. *columbianum*
L. *distichum*
L. *grayi*
L. *harrisianum*

L. *lankongense*
L. *nepalense*
L. *pardalinum*
L. *parryi*
L. *rubellum*
L. *speciosum*
L. *superbum*
L. *tsingtauense*

L. *wigginsii*

Auratum hybrids
Bellingham hybrids
Pink Perfection
   strain
Pink Trumpet
   hybrids

Lilies for acid soils

Most lilies grow best in neutral or slightly acid soils, but a few only continue to flourish if planted in acid, lime-free soils.

L. *auratum*
L. *canadense*
L. *catesbaei*
L. *japonicum*
L. *lankongense*

L. *occidentale*
L. *pardalinum*
L. *philadelphicum*
L. *pitkinense*
L. *rubellum*

L. *speciosum*
L. *superbum*
Bellingham hybrids
Auratum-Speciosum
   hybrids

Lilies for calcareous soils

The large majority of lilies tolerate a certain alkalinity, but those native to America must be planted in lime-free soils. Additions of leaf-mould and peat help to increase the acidity of soils. Lime-loving plants are:

L. *bulbiferum*
L. *candidum*
L. *carniolicum*
L. *chalcedonicum*

L. *henryi*
L. *longiflorum*
L. *martagon*
L. *monadelphum*

L. *pomponium*
L. *szovitsianum*
L. × *testaceum*
Martagon hybrids

Lilies for planting in leaf-mould and peat

The following lilies should be planted in pure leaf-mould to which small quantities of peat and pumice or quartz sand only have been added.

L. auratum	*L. medeoloides*	*L. wallichianum*
L. bakerianum	*L. neilgherrense*	All *Cardiocrinum*
L. japonicum	*L. nepalense*	varieties
L. leichtlini var.	*L. pitkinense*	
maximowiczii	*L. rubellum*	

Appendix

AMERICA: The North American Lily Society, Inc., North Ferrisburg,
Vermont 05473, United States
Secretary: Fred M. Abbey
Publications: Lily Year Book, Four newsletters
Annual subscription: 7½ dollars
Approximately 1,000 members

AUSTRALIA: Australian Lily Society, c/o Mr Robert F. Nelson,
5 Willow Road, Upper Fern Tree Gully, Victoria, Australia

ENGLAND: The Lily Committee of the Royal Horticultural Society,
Vincent Square, London SW1
Secretary: P. M. Synge
Publication: RHS Lily Year Book

GERMANY: Deutsche Iris- und Liliengesellschaft e.V., 725 Leonberg
bei Stuttgart, Justinus-Kerner-Strasse 11.
Secretary: Hermann Hald
Publications: Four quarterly newsletters
Annual subscription: 20 DM
Approximately 900 members

NEW ZEALAND: 1. The Auckland Lily Society, 50 Kohimaramara Road, Auckland E1, New Zealand
Secretary: Miss M. Crichton
2. New Zealand Lily Society, Box 1394, Christchurch, New Zealand

RUSSIA: V. P. Eremin, Secretary of USSR Lily Breeders, Moscow v-292, ul. Ivana Babuskkina 23 corpus 3, kv. 56

SOUTH AFRICA: South African Lily Society, c/o Miss Beryl I. Reynolds, P.O. Box 71, Pretoria, South Africa

Glossary

Acuminate Drawn out into a long point

Acute Sharp-pointed

Anther The upper part of a stamen bearing the pollen

Campanulate Bell-shaped

Capsule Seed vessel

Chromosome The element in the cell nucleus carrying the hereditary characters

Ciliate Fringed with fine hairs at the margin

Clawed Having the base of the perianth segments narrowed into the semblance of a stalk

Clone A group of plants propagated only by vegetative and asexual means, e.g. by bulb division or by scales

Cordate Heart-shaped

Cultivar A highly selected plant that originated in or is maintained in cultivation (cv)

Filament The stalk of a stamen

Glabrous Devoid of hairs

Glaucous Bluish-green or with a grey bloom

Globose Spherical

Imbricate Overlapping

Inflorescence The flower bearing part of a stem

Lanceolate Broader below the middle and tapering to a tip

Linear Long and narrow

Monocarpic Dying after flowering

Nectary furrow A furrow at the base of the perianth segments

Ovate   Egg-shaped

Papillose   Covered with minute projections

Pedicel   Stalk of a single flower

Perianth   The outer and usually conspicuous part of a flower

Petiole   Stalk of a leaf

Pistil   Female part of a flower comprising ovary style and stigma

Pollen   The male powdery material contained in an anther

Raceme   An arrangement in which the flower stalks are evenly spaced up the top of the stem

Reflexed   Bent backwards abruptly

Scabrid   Rough to the touch

Scale   The fleshy members making up a lily bulb

Segment   One of the separate parts of the perianth

Stigma   The organ at the tip of the style that receives the pollen

Stolon   A fleshy branch bearing a new plant at the end

Style   The stigma bearing part of the pistil

Tepal   A perianth segment

Umbel   An inflorescence in which the flower stalks arise evenly from the top of the stem

Undulate   Wavy

Variety   A variation of a plant occurring in the wild (var.)

Versatile   Applied to an anther that swings freely on the filament

Whorl   A ring of leaves arising at the same level on the stem

Bibliography

Craig, W. N., *Lilies and their Culture in North America*, Florists Publishing Co., Chicago, 1928

De Graaff, J., *The New Book of Lilies*, Barrows, New York, 1951

De Graaff, J., and Hyams, E., *Lilies*, Nelson, London, 1967

German Iris and Lily Society, *Jahrbücher* 1960–65; *Nachrichtenblatt* 1960–65

Gilbert, C. C., *Success without Soil*, Gilbert, San Diego, 1949

Grove, A., *Lilies*, T. C. & E. C. Jack, 1911

Howie, V., *Let's Grow Lilies*, North American Lily Society, 1964

Jefferson-Brown, M. J., *Modern Lilies*, Faber & Faber, London, 1965

Jekyll, G., *Lilies for English Gardens*, Country Life, London, 1901

Jelitto, L., and Schacht, W., *Die Freiland-Schmuckstauden*, Eugen Ulmer, Stuttgart, 1963 and 1966

Leeburn, M. E., *Garden Lilies*, Collingridge, London, 1963

Leeburn, M. E., *Lilies and their Cultivation*, Foyle, London, 1955

Macfie, D. T., *Lilies for Garden and Greenhouse*, Collingridge, London, 1939

Macneil, A. and E., *Garden Lilies*, OUP, New York, 1940

Marshall, W. E., *Consider the Lilies*, Marshall, New York, 1947

Maxwell, A. C., *Lilies in their Homes*, Collins, London, 1953

North American Lily Society, *Lily Year Books*, New York, 1948–65; *Quarterly Bulletin*, 1948–65

Preston, Isabella, *Lilies for every Garden*, Orange Judd Publishing Co., 1947

Rockwell, F. F., Grayson, E. C., and De Graaff, J., *The Complete Book of Lilies*, Doubleday, New York, 1961

Royal Horticultural Society, *Lily Year Books*, London, 1933–37, 1949–67; *The International Lily Register*, London, 1960; *Supplement to the International Lily Register*, London, 1961–64

Wallace, Dr, *Notes on Lilies*, Own publisher, 1879

Ward, F. K., *Burma's Icy Mountains*, Cape, London, 1949

Ward, F. K., *Pilgrimage for Plants*, Harrap, London, 1960

Wilson, E. H., *The Lilies of Eastern Asia*, London, 1925

Woodcock, H. B. D., and Stearn, W. T., *Lilies of the World*, Country Life, London, 1950

Index of Lilies

The figures in **bold type** refer to the illustration numbers

General Index